THOMAS
FRANCIS
MEAGHER

THOMAS FRANCIS MEAGHER

Irish Rebel, American Yankee,
Montana Pioneer

Gary R. Forney

To order additional copies of this book, contact:
Xlibris Corporation
1-888-795-4274
www.Xlibris.com
Orders@Xlibris.com
20146

CONTENTS

To the women in my life—
Cathy, Natalie Hope, and Angela Marie.

My life's story is filled with happiness because of you.

ACKNOWLEDGEMENTS

I am grateful to many friends and family members who have been so encouraging during this project—especially the "L & M Ranch Gang." Your interest in my efforts and your kind words often provided just the right motivation at just the right time. Elaine Sullivan, an e-mail friend from "down under," has been a wonderful resource and support. I must especially express my thanks to Sally and Bill Miller for their unfailing support and to Jerry Bartos, an entertaining and well-read companion who shares my sense of adventure for exploring the back roads, museums, and libraries of the last best place.

I also want to recognize the untiring kindness and assistance of Kathy Knack (librarian of the Madison County Library) and Joanne Erdall, Faye Rutherford, and Evalyn Johnson (librarian and staff of the Thompson-Hickman Library of Virginia City). Their patience in filling my many requests for inter-library book loans and with my many hours "camping" in their facilities while I rummaged through collections and files was essential.

Finally, to Hillary Block my deep appreciation for helping to make this a better story and me a better writer.

INTRODUCTION

"A book ought to be like a man or a woman,
with some individual character in it, though eccentric,
yet its own; with some blood in its veins
and speculation in its eyes."

John Mitchel

For some time I've had an interest in the American Civil War and was well aware of a unit of the Union Army commonly known as the Irish Brigade. The Irish Brigade included many men who had recently fled famine and religious and political persecution in their homeland. The Brigade consistently distinguished itself in virtually all the major engagements of the eastern theater. The man most responsible for the existence of the Irish Brigade, a man who shared the danger and tragedies of their battlefields, was Thomas Francis Meagher. While generally aware of Meagher's role in organizing the Brigade and his role as its brigadier-general, I had no comprehensive understanding of Meagher's life prior to, or following, the Civil War. Meagher's post-war life is commonly summarized by words to the effect, "he later served as Governor of the Montana Territory until his drowning in the Missouri River in 1867." It's unlikely I would have ever attempted to learn more of Thomas Francis Meagher—until I saw that statue.

On my first visit to Helena, I was attracted to a large statue of a man with upraised sword sitting upon a spirited horse, as if guarding the principal entrance to the state capitol building. The statue, I was surprised to learn, is dedicated to Thomas Francis Meagher which seemed curious given his brief term of service to Montana. What I have subsequently learned is the reason for the statue, as with many aspects of Meagher's life, is often formed by several complicated layers. I also quickly learned that some authors have painted a portrait of Meagher that is often inaccurate and monochromatic.

In the work that follows, I have attempted to present a biographical sketch of a man who was not only a participant, but also a significant personality upon the stage of world events during his lifetime. I have particularly attempted to provide a more comprehensive review of Meagher's life which I believe neglected in previous works, his time in the Montana Territory. I have made an effort to more fully develop the context of that time and circumstances, focusing on three defining issues of his tenure: the reinstatement of the territorial legislature, the temporary pardon of James Daniels, and the Indian conflict. Whereas others have tended to portray Meagher's motives related to these issues as little more than self-promotion, such premise ignores both the popular attitude of Montana's residents at that time and the depth of Meagher's character. Although I have not intended this work to serve as either a tribute to Meagher or to provide a defense for his actions, I have grown to admire him. While certainly not all of his traits or decisions were admirable, Meagher never left uncertainty as to his position. He made difficult decisions—often with significant personal sacrifice—was intensely loyal to his friends, and remained fiercely devoted to the great cause of his life—the political independence of Ireland. With the opportunity to live a life of privilege he instead chose to face death for the land of his birth and, again, in his adopted home. He evolved from a young man filled with ideas, idealism, and energy into a man who was exiled from family and native land, witnessed the horrible brutality of war, and came to face the fickle nature of celebrity. He was from a family of wealth and power, but was able to feel empathy for the poor, and he forfeited a life of assured comfort for one of uncertainty. Meagher basked in the spotlight of center stage before thousands of admiring spectators, yet may have discovered some of his happiest moments among the quiet remote majesty of Montana's mountains. Whatever else may be said of him, it must be admitted he lived his life true to his family's motto; "Boldness in dangers and trust in heaven."

In his book, *Four Years of Irish History 1845-1849*, Sir Charles Gavan Duffy would set the theme of that turbulent period as being " . . . for the most part a story of hopes disappointed, of sacrifices made in vain, of great power fatally squandered, of horrible calamity and suffering." Perhaps nothing more succinctly, and appropriately, may serve as a theme for the life of Thomas Francis Meagher than those words.

O! Eri Mo Chroidhe 'Ta M'Intinn Ort

Gary R. Forney
March 17, 2003

PART I

Life As A Rebel, Life As An Exile

CHAPTER 1

"Thus it came to pass, that the boy's first glance
at the outer world lighted on the estuary of the noble river
whose fountain-springs are situated
in the anchestral patrimony of his father's race."

Michael Cavanagh

As if setting the stage for a mythical drama, author Michael Cavanagh begins the story of Thomas Francis Meagher's life by paying tribute to his deep Irish heritage. One can almost picture an infant floating along in a wicker basket upon a river leading from the misty region of his ancestry to the city which would be his home. It is also poignantly ironic that the boy whose first sight was to be the Suir River would become the man whose last sight would be a river half a world away.

The infant Thomas Francis Meagher (commonly pronounced "Maher" or "Mahr") took his first look at the world in Waterford, Ireland, on August 3, 1823. Thomas was the first-born son of three children, and although he did not have "Junior" attached to his name, Meagher's father was also named Thomas Francis Meagher. It appears that within the family circle the young man was called Thomas Francis, but his father was simply called Thomas. The paternal family lineage is directly linked to the O'Meagher clan of Tipperary County, whose family crest proudly proclaims the motto, "In periculus audacia et firmitas in coelo (Boldness in dangers and trust in heaven)."

Thomas Meagher was a very wealthy merchant who had inherited a shipping trade from his father, who was also named Thomas Francis. His father had broken away from the family's traditional agrarian life and developed a very profitable shipping route between Waterford, Ireland, and the port of St. John's, Newfoundland, during the mid-to late 1700's, a time when many Irish were emigrating to Newfoundland. Thomas was the eldest of three sons; Henry would briefly work in the family business before his death in 1839 and Patrick became a priest in the Jesuit order.[1] Thomas was a prominent and respected man who would become the first Catholic elected to serve as the mayor of Waterford following the passage of the Roman Catholic Emancipation Act in 1829.

The mother of Thomas Francis was Alicia Quan (" . . . or, as it is called in Irish, O'Cain . . ."[2]), also from a well-established Irish family. She was a daughter of a prominent Waterford merchant associated with the firm of Wyse, Cashin, and Quan. Alicia died in February, 1827 shortly after giving birth to a second son, Harry. Upon Alicia's death an unmarried sister (identified only as "Miss Quan" by Cavanagh, she was probably Honora Quan) would assume responsibility for raising Thomas, Harry, and a first-born daughter. Not only did this woman become a devoted guardian to these children, but years later she would also provide " . . . the same devoted care over her exiled nephew's motherless boy."[3] The Meagher family made its home in an elegant residence located near the Suir River, now the site of an area known as Meagher's Quay.

Thomas Francis received an excellent formal education befitting a young man of his high social status. After spending his elementary years in Waterford, at the age of eleven he was sent to attend the prestigious Jesuit boarding school Clongowes Wood. Clongowes Wood, located near the town of Kildare, Ireland, would subsequently be the school of James Joyce. Meagher would later describe its setting: "The dear old college stood very nearly in a circle of ancient towns. There was Clane . . . Kilcock . . . Celbridge . . . Maymooth . . . Very old and ragged, with very little life stirring in them, they seemed to have gone to sleep many years ago . . . ."[4]

While Thomas Francis was not a particularly distinguished student, he certainly showed signs of intellectual curiosity. One of the young man's treasured finds in the Clongowes Wood library was a book of speeches by Richard Shiel; an attorney turned playwright and political activist. Shiel had been an ally of Daniel O'Connell and a principal spokesman for the cause of Catholic Emancipation, and was elected to Parliament in 1841. Richard Shiel was not only a fellow Irishman, he was also a native son of Waterford and Meagher became an avid reader of Shiel's speeches. Meagher would later write, "There were not more than a dozen of Shiel's speeches in the volume. All of them brilliant and exciting to excess, drove the blood burning through my veins, and filled my mind . . . with the visions which were the inspiration of whatever strong words fell from from me in later years."[5] While he seems to have been generally positive regarding his Clongowes Wood education, Meagher would later write, " . . . but as far as Ireland was concerned, they left us like blind and crippled children, in the dark."[6] The British-governed educational system did not promote the study of Irish history in school curriculums.

It was also while at Clongowes Wood that Meagher would find his voice. Thomas Francis began to exhibit a special gift—and love—for public speaking. At age 15, Meagher would become the first Medalist of the Clongowes Wood Debating Society, making him the youngest in the history of the academy to receive such distinction. It's unlikely any of his teachers, or Meagher himself, would have imagined how his voice would resonate throughout Ireland in just a few short years.

After six years at Clongowes Wood, Meagher progressed to advanced studies at Stonyhurst, another Jesuit boarding school located near Lancashire, England, where his uncle, Patrick, and Richard Shiel had also studied. Thomas Francis continued to be erratic in his academic efforts, showing excellent accomplishment in those subjects in which he had interest (particularly oratory and writing), but very average marks in other areas. One of his essays, which drew special praise, was entitled, "The American Government and the Slave Trade." By all indications he was a spirited member of the student body, and it may have been only through the influence of his uncle Patrick that Meagher managed to remain enrolled. It was while he was at Stonyhurst that his instructors made an effort to eliminate a part of his Irish heritage, "'his detested Irish brogue,' replacing thereof with the orthodox English accent."[7] While they were apparently successful in conforming his accent and manner of speech during his four years at Stonyhurst, they weren't as successful in controlling his spirit. One story, later related by Meagher, was that he had been originally cast in a lead role for the school's production of King Lear; but the faculty member directing the play was so unnerved by Meagher's heavy accent that he steadily reduced the assignment until Meagher was finally left with only a one-line, walk-on role. On the opening night of the performance, Meagher exacted his revenge to the great delight of the young men in the audience—and the great dismay of his instructors—by delivering his one line "with the most powerful brogue I could muster."[8]

After completing the course of studies at Stonyhurst, and a fashionably obligatory tour of the continent, Meagher returned to Ireland in the spring of 1843. By this time a bold new publication known as *The Nation* was being widely read, Meagher's father was now serving as mayor of Waterford, and young Thomas Francis Meagher would step into the spotlight when he traveled to Lismore for a meeting of the Repeal Association. Meagher was invited to deliver a speech to the Association, to which the legendary leader of the Repeal Association, Daniel O'Connell, reportedly would enthusiastically respond, "Well done Young Ireland."[9] "Young Ireland" would be a term O'Connell would use again, but not with such grateful enthusiasm.

Daniel O'Connell, who was a family friend of the Meagher's, had become a prominent figure throughout Ireland and Great Britain, initially as a highly regarded attorney and later by founding the Catholic Association in 1823. The purpose of the Catholic Association was to achieve a complete repeal of the oppressive Penal Laws. Enacted by Great Britain in 1695 at the urging of the fiercely anti-Catholic King William, III, the Penal Laws effectively reduced most Irish Catholics to servitude, taking their lands, property, and civil rights.[10] Catholics were not permitted to hold political office, purchase land, or engage in certain professions, and the Catholic education system was outlawed. Although the Penal Laws had been mitigated by the Catholic Relief Acts of 1792 and 1793, O'Connell's powerful speeches and dogged persistence were successful in achieving what others had not, the Emancipation Act of 1829. The Emancipation Act restored civil rights and liberties to Ireland's Catholic population, including the right to hold office in the British Parliament, to which O'Connell, known thereafter as "the Liberator," was soon elected.

O'Connell next turned his attention to the political status of Ireland by founding the Repeal Association. The ambitious goal of his new organization was to have the forty-three-year-old Irish Act of Union repealed, thereby restoring to Ireland a measure of political independence from Great Britain. British Prime Minister William Pitt had successfully argued, following the failed revolution in 1798, that the existing Irish constitution must be abolished, and Great Britain assume greater control of Ireland, or else face the potential alignment of Ireland with France.[11]

O'Connell, however, was hopeful of establishing an Irish House of Commons and House of Lords which would manage the affairs of Ireland, yet have a pledge of loyalty to Great Britain within its charter. In the infancy of the Repeal Association's existence, O'Connell made clear that neither complete independence for Ireland nor the use of armed force to achieve such—as had been attempted in 1798—were objectives of the Association. O'Connell would proclaim: "They say we want separation from England, but what I want is to prevent separation taking place. There is not a man in existence more loyally attached than I am to the Queen . . . I want you to do nothing that is not open and legal, but if the people unite with me and follow my advice it is impossible not to get the repeal."[12] Clearly intended as a conciliatory point, the pledge of loyalty—and O'Connell's moderate, conservative approach—would become critical in the course of Ireland's history. In an effort to build membership and financial strength for the Repeal Association and to demonstrate popular support for his platform, O'Connell initiated a series of what became known as "monster meetings." Held during the summer of 1843, the enormous gatherings dramatically bolstered the Repeal Association and strengthened O'Connell's, already formidable, reputation. The British authorities did not regard O'Connell's proposals as moderate, however, but rather as dangerously inflammatory. As the crowds O'Connell addressed swelled into the thousands at meeting after meeting, Great Britain's concern also grew and finally resulted in a warning to him not to appear at the scheduled mass meeting at Clontarf or be liable to arrest. Faced with what would prove to be a "lose/lose" situation, O'Connell cancelled his appearance at the Clontarf meeting only to still be arrested and charged with seditious conspiracy the very next day. Moreover, his decision to back down produced concern within the rebellious young faction of the Repeal Association. While there was no public outcry in the pages of the *Nation*, seeds of distrust had been planted. "O'Connell did not embrace federalism, and there was as yet no question of a formal alliance with the opposition Whigs. But his apparent readiness to enter into discussions with these groups was profoundly disturbing . . . ."[13]

Meagher, who had attended some of the monster meetings in the previous summer, traveled to Dublin in January of 1844 to begin his professional studies at Queens Inn. It was his intention to prepare for a legal career—intentions which were very quickly set aside. The city of Dublin was alive with excitement arising from the arrest and ongoing trial of Daniel O'Connell. In anticipation of possible trouble, the English military garrison at Dublin had been increased to approximately ten thousand men as daily meetings of the Repeal Association were being held in the organization's elegant new headquarters, Conciliation Hall. Meagher shuttled between the courtroom drama and the huge, boisterous, open meetings of the Repeal Association. Among the impassioned speakers to appear before the large gatherings was Meagher's boyhood hero, Richard Shiel (who would split from O'Connell's repeal effort); but it was the fiery speech of William Smith O'Brien which Meagher witnessed that most convincingly captured the young man's attention.

William Smith O'Brien was something of a political anomaly— he was a member of the gentry and a Protestant who supported

Catholic emancipation. He had originally been elected to Parliament in 1825 as a Conservative representative for Ennis and earned a well-deserved reputation as an outspoken, even contentious, member. O'Brien had been, at best, a reluctant ally of O'Connell in Parliament, but by late 1842 was openly disassociating himself with O'Connell's political strategies. O'Brien, however, quickly stepped into the leadership vacuum in the Repeal Association. Joining the Repeal Association following O'Connell's arrest, O'Brien attracted a new surge of other Protestants to the memberships rolls of the Association and quickly rose to a position of influence. In O'Brien's first speech at Conciliation Hall, he resolutely stated, "I have come here to tell the Attorney-General that, though not ambitious of martyrdom, if he wants another victim, I present myself to him."[14]

O'Connell was ultimately successful in his legal struggle, inasmuch as his initial conviction by the lower court would later be overturned. And while he had restored strength to the Repeal Association and appeared to be unshakeable as a political force, a fissure had developed. The impassioned rhetoric of January 1844 had set into motion an avalanche of events that would sweep over Ireland and send tremors throughout the world.

CHAPTER 2

"It was like listening to the mystical, sonorous music
of the 'Revolt of Islam' recited in Shelly's shrill treble,
to hear Meagher pour out passion and pathos and humour
in tones which possessed no note in perfection but intensity."
Charles Gavan Duffy

By 1844, the newspaper *The Nation* had established itself as a powerful voice in Ireland. The paper was founded in 1842 by the talented partnership of Thomas Davis (a Protestant), John Dillon, and Charles Gavan Duffy (Catholics). *The Nation* was a boldly outspoken messenger for the cause of Irish nationalism, and Davis was a critical component in developing a secular approach to the struggle. Davis established himself as a respected and leading force in the Repeal movement, though not in total acceptance with O'Connell's strategies. Dillon and Duffy also believed a more aggressive approach was necessary to achieve Irish independence, and set a confrontational tone to the coming struggle with the first edition of *Nation*. The first issue included a poem attributed to Duffy entitled "Faugh-a-Ballagh" (Clear the Way), which included the lines: "Slaves and Dastards stand aside—Knaves and Traitors, Faugh-a-Ballagh."[15] Despite the inflammatory rhetoric of the *Nation*, the youthful Davis was mature in terms of his expectations. "Realistically he [Davis] admitted, in a private letter to a friend late in 1842, that Federalism was in fact all that Ireland stood a chance of getting out of the present political situation."[16] It is interesting to speculate upon the course of events had the voice of Davis not been prematurely silenced with his death.

Born in 1815 the son of a Unitarian minister, John Mitchel had become a regular and eloquent contributing writer to the

Nation. Upon the untimely death of Thomas Davis in September 1845, Mitchel assumed an even more prominent role in the content of the *Nation*. Mitchel, who would become a close friend of Meagher, was not only a vociferous proponent of nationalism, but also a harsh critic of the Repeal Association which he had joined in 1843. Thomas Devin Reilly also became an active part of the *Nation* at the time of Davis's death, adding his support to the voices of Dillon, Duffy, Mitchel, and other contributors in challenging the Repeal Association and advocating complete Irish polictical independence.[17] Another notable contributor, writing under the pen name "Speranza," was Jane Elgee, who would become Lady Wilde, mother of Oscar Wilde.

The ideas expressed on the pages of the *Nation* germinated in an association formed as the '82 Club; taking its name in honor of the Irish patriots of 1782. Although identified as a social club, it adopted a uniform and its membership included not only the *Nation's* authors, but William Smith O'Brien, Thomas Francis Meagher, Richard O'Gorman, Jr., and John Martin. These men held the common belief that not only was O'Connell's agenda inadequate, but that his failure to appear at the Contarf rally demonstrated his lack of resolve. Unwilling to accept the compromise of Home Rule, and acknowledging the possibility of armed conflict as the only means by which Ireland may achieve its independence, the rhetoric of the '82 Club was in sharp contrast to the Repeal Association. Finding himself and his Association under regular attack, Daniel O'Connell attempted to dismiss the radical preaching of these young men by referring to them, now in a disparaging tone, as "Young Ireland." Much to O'Connell's regret, the young radicals not only eagerly adopted this label, but also began to gather support under this banner.

It was the contention of Young Ireland's membership that the Repeal Association had not only strayed from its founding principles, but had also begun to form questionable alliances. As an example, Young Ireland pointed to O'Connell's agreement with Prime Minister John Russell to not run a Repeal candidate in opposition to a Whig party candidate in the Dungarvan district election.[18] The gap between O'Connell and Young Ireland was widened by their conflict over what was known as the colleges bill. Offered with Prime Minister Peel's support, the bill would have established colleges in Belfast, Cork, and Galway. The problem for O'Connell, and the Catholic bishops whose support he wished to maintain, was that the colleges were to free from Catholic administration or instruction in Catholic doctrine in the curriculum. Young Ireland, on the other hand, embraced the bill as consistent with their belief that the non-sectarian approach to education was a positive step toward a unified Ireland.[19] O'Connell's apparent vacillation on his political agenda may have been in no small measure due to the influence of his son John. John O'Connell was clearly maneuvering to position himself as his father's successor in the leadership of the Association, though it was still generally recognized that Daniel O'Connell held enormous popular and political power, which was expressed by John Mitchel in the *Nation*: "As to deposing O'Connell from the leadership of the Irish People, we have met with no man insane enough to propose or contemplate that. All we mean to insist upon is this—that we will be led to the goal whither we are bound; we will not go back, or stand still: we will be led, but it must be forward—forward!"[20]

By this time there were also rumblings from within the ranks of the Repeal Association. Smith O'Brien had formed a Parliamentary Committee as a wing of the Association. It was O'Brien's publicly stated intention that this committee's purpose would be to school selected young men in the aspects of political organizations and legislative duties; however, it appears obvious that O'Brien's true intentions were to find a forum for his own agenda within the Association and to build a cadre of influential and devoted supporters. Among the first of O'Brien's handpicked disciples to be part of the Parliamentary Committee was Thomas Francis Meagher. It seems his work with the Parliamentary Committee effectively coalesced in Meagher the fierce pride in his Irish heritage, a dose of youthful rebellion, and his gift of oratory, resulting in a sense of direction and purpose.

Charles Gavan Duffy would describe Meagher by stating, "To

the common eye, indeed, the new recruit was a dandified youngster . . . but this was a vulgar error."[21] And in describing Meagher's oratorical style he would write, "Meagher's oratory delighted the people, though it was studded with allusions to facts and sentiments of which they knew nothing. He used to tell, with infinite glee, how a shrewd country doctor assured him that he was like the gaudy bottles in an apothecary's window—good to attract the vulgar, but the real medicines were opaque."[22] John Mitchel would later write of his first extended meeting with Meagher in the *Irish Citizen*, " . . . we walked out together, towards my house in Upper Leeson street; What eloquence of talk was his: how fresh, and clear, and strong! What wealth of imagination, and princely generosity of feeling! To me it was the revelation of a new and great nature . . . ."[23]

After approximately a year under the tutelage of the Parliamentary Committee, Meagher was selected by O'Brien to deliver an address to a meeting of the association's membership. Entitled "The Policy of the Repeal Association," Meagher's speech on February 16, 1846, represented one of the first salvos fired against O'Connell's policies within the confines of the Association's headquarters. Although he began his address timidly, he quickly gained his confidence and grasped the attention of the crowded hall. Urging the Association to take a forceful, uncompromising position in defense of its political agenda, Meagher admonished, "But, sir, whilst we thus endeavor wisely to conciliate, let us not, to the strongest foe, nor in the most tempting emergency, weakly capitulate. A decisive attitude—an unequivocal tone—language that cannot be construed by the English press into the renunciation or the postponement of our claim—these should be the characteristics of this assembly . . . ."[24] Meagher's defiant speech not only set the stage for the impending political battle, but also immediately cast him in a leading role as spokesman for the cause of "Young Ireland." From this time forward, Meagher would become intricately, and irrevocably, linked with the cause of Irish nationalism.

Those who identified with Young Ireland became convinced

that not only was the Repeal Association going soft on the issue of repealing the Act of Union and forming alliances with the ruling Whig Party of England, but also that John O'Connell's growing influence had alienated Protestant support. In addition to those charges, there were rumors that he had also rejected suggestions of seeking aid from other nations. William Smith O'Brien fueled the controversy by refusing to serve as a member of the House of Commons committees until the Outdoor Relief Bill passed. In a startling retaliation, Parliament ordered O'Brien held in confinement for twenty-five days. Presumably angered that O'Connell did not join him in protest, O'Brien threatened to resign from the Repeal Association. Upon learning of O'Brien's intentions, Meagher, Mitchel and other representatives of the '82 Club hastily traveled to meet with him and were successful in persuading O'Brien to withhold his resignation.[25] The confinement, which earned him the nickname "hero of the cellar," had no effect on dulling O'Brien's enthusiasm and greatly added to his stature as a spokesman for the interest of Ireland. In an article written of their meeting with O'Brien by Colman O'Loghlen, one of the '82 Club representatives, he reported: "I assure you the site of the vile dungeon . . . would have been deeply humiliating to us all . . . [but] never did O'Brien bear himself more haughtily . . . than he does in that imprisonment . . . ."[26]

By mid-July of 1846, the growing political tensions resulted in a meeting of the Repeal Association where O'Connell presented his "peace resolutions." In what may have been yet another conciliatory effort toward the Whigs, O'Connell urged the Association to adopt a platform which renounced the use of force to advance the cause of political independence.[27] In an obvious demonstration of O'Connell's strength, his resolutions were adopted by the Association's delegates with only one dissenting vote— Thomas Francis Meagher. Meagher's vote would portend the gathering storm that was on the horizon.

The theoretical fracture between the Young Ireland group and O'Connell's Repeal Association, the two groups labeled by Robert Athearn as the "physical force" (Young Ireland) versus the "moral force" (Repeal Association) became a startling reality at the Association's next meeting.[28] The conference was held in Dublin's Conciliation Hall on Monday and Tuesday, July 27 and 28. It was on the second day of the Association's conference, which was thereafter known as the "Secession Meeting," that Meagher rose to speak and, in so doing, rose to international prominence with a speech which earned him the sobriquet "Meagher of The Sword."

Meagher proposed in his address to the assembly that while it wasn't his intent to disparage the previous work of O'Connell, he could not accept that armed revolution against Great Britain should be altogether removed as a possibility, " . . . at all times, under all circumstances." "There are times when arms alone will suffice, and when political ameliorations call for 'a drop of blood,' and for many thousand drops of blood . . . ."[29] In his thrilling address, Meagher reminded the audience, using the American Revolution as his example, that armed force could be the only recourse in some struggles. Meagher immortalized himself to future generations of Irish with words that electrified the huge gathering: "Abhor the sword—stigmatise the sword? No, my lord, for, at its blow, a giant nation started from the waters of the Atlantic, and by its redeeming magic, and in the quivering of its crimson light, the crippled colony sprang into the attitude of a proud Republic—prosperous, limitless, and invincible!"[30]

John O'Connell, serving as Chairman of the meeting in the absence of his father, quickly leapt to his feet and interrupted Meagher's speech, loudly proclaiming, "The sentiments Mr. Meagher avowed were opposed to those of the founder of the Association, and therefore the Association must cease to exist, or Mr. Meagher must cease to be a member of it."[31] Smith O'Brien, who had remained a quiet observer of the proceedings up to this point, then took the floor and removed any doubt as to his allegiance by responding, "I am afraid that the alternative which has been presented to us by Mr. John O'Connell is of such a nature as necessarily to compel the termination of this discussion . . . ."[32] At this point the meeting dissolved into chaos with the men of Young Ireland, followed by many new converts, leaving the Hall

whose name now bore sad irony to the events of the previous few
hours.

Some futile attempts were made in the aftermath of the July
meeting to seek resolution between the Young Irelanders and the
Repeal Association, including one by Daniel O'Connell, which he
withdrew at the request of his son John.[33] What the July meeting
did accomplish was to set into motion the coalescence of a new
group which would have a lasting legacy. With a core of Young
Irelanders, and several defectors from the Repeal Association, an
organization (briefly labeled the Irish Party) known as the Irish
Confederation was formed in Dublin on January 13, 1847, " . . .
for the purpose of protecting our national interests, and obtaining
the Legislative independence of Ireland, by the force of opinion,
by the combination of all classes of Irishmen, and by the exercise
of all the political, social, and moral influences within our reach."[34]

Approximately forty men were initially elected to serve as the
governing Council of the Irish Confederation and among them
were: William Smith O'Brien; John Mitchel; Charles Gavan Duffy;
John B. Dillon; Richard O'Gorman, Jr.; Terence McManus; Thomas
Devin Reilly; Patrick O'Donohue; and Thomas Francis Meagher.
Meagher would also soon become the President of Waterford's
Gratten Club, an affiliate of the Confederation and a group " . . .
principally composed of educated, well-to-do young men, who
could afford to arm themselves with the most effective weapons
attainable."[35] While the Confederation would draw its membership
from a diverse socio-economic range, noticeably lacking among
the membership of the new organization was any significant support
from the Catholic clergy, a point which would later become a crucial
factor. The priests, especially those older and in leadership positions,
would remain aligned with the Repeal Association in loyalty to
O'Connell's legacy of Catholic emancipation.

While the Irish Confederation clearly maintained the radical
legacy of Young Ireland, it also sought to extend its influence via
elected offices. Meagher became one of the Confederation's tireless
stump speakers, traveling about Ireland promoting the cause of
the association, helping to form local clubs, becoming a powerful

voice for Irish nationalism—and marked for British retribution. Although the British government and landlords were the common targets of Meagher's speeches, he didn't hesitate to challenge the Irish people themselves as compliant accomplices. In a speech delivered in Belfast, Meagher pointedly reproached his audience: "And you—you who are eight million strong—you who boast that this island is the finest that the sun looks down upon . . . you will make no effort—you will whine and beg and skulk, in sores and rags, upon this favored land—you will congregate in drowsy councils and, when the very earth is loosening beneath your feet, respectfully suggest new clauses and amendments to some blundering bill . . . you will be beggared by the millions—you will perish by the thousand—and the finest island that the sun looks down upon, amid the jeers and hootings of the world, will blacken into a plague spot, a wilderness, a sepulcher."[36]

Meagher also ran for election to Parliament in his hometown of Waterford, facing off against Patrick Costelloe (the Repeal candidate) and Sir Henry Winston Barron (the Whig candidate). Following a vigorous campaign, the young Meagher was unable to win either his father's endorsement (who supported Costelloe) or the election. The unintended effect of Meagher's participation, however, was to split the vote between himself and Costelloe, giving Sir Barron the seat in Parliament The principal issue of political difference between the older and younger Meagher was that of the traditional practice of "place-begging;" political favoritism toward job seekers. It is appropriate to note that while he failed to gain his father's political support, Meagher was never estranged from his father; in fact, his father's financial and personal support were unwavering. And Thomas Francis, a little older and perhaps a little less idealistic, would later come to embrace the fine art of place-begging.

Despite some impressive efforts, and the establishment of Confederation clubs throughout Ireland as well as in England and Scotland, the Confederation candidates were not successful in the 1848 elections. In virtually every district, the influence of "old Ireland" prevailed at the polling places; but the catastrophic effects of the potato famine (" . . . a famine created not by the blight, but by the landlords"[37]) and events in France would keep the fires kindled by the Confederation burning brightly. Several members of Young Ireland entertained at this time the captain of a ship which had been sent from the United States with a cargo of corn for the starving Irish. During the evening, Meagher toasted the captain with the pledge, "Should the time come when Ireland will have to make the choice, depend upon it, Sir, she will prefer to be grateful to the Samaritan rather than be loyal to the Levite."[38]

In May 1847 Lord George William Clarendon became the lord-lieutenant of Dublin and wrote to Prime Minister Russell that, "A great social revolution is now going on in Ireland, the accumulated evils of misgovernment and mismanagement are now coming to a crisis."[39] This great upheaval was resulting not so much from rhetoric, but hunger. A common misconception of the Irish Famine years, often called "an Gorta Mo'r" (the Great Hunger), is that there was simply little or nothing available for sustenance when, in fact, there was a significant amount of grain, produce, and livestock available. Virtually all of these commodities, however, were the property of the British landowners and were being exported to England, as well as other countries, for financial profit. Consequently, potatoes—which were less desirable as an economic commodity—had become the nutritional and economic staple of Ireland's poor and middle-class, and repeated crop failures due to the potato blight had led to wretched conditions. "Between 1845 and 1851 the total population fell by about 2 million, of which half was accounted for by excess deaths and half by emigration."[40] As a traveling spokesman and organizer for the Confederation, Meagher had a first-hand familiarity with these conditions and the consequences of Ireland's political and economic impotence.

A common practice adopted by the landlords to deal with "problem" of starving tenant farmers was to pay for their passage to America or Canada rather than provide them food or pay for their accommodation at a district poor house. Typical of this sentiment was the testimony of Francis Spaight: "I found so great an advantage to getting rid of the pauper population upon my own property that I made every possible exertion to remove them . . . ."[41] The callous accounting associated with this practice is demonstrated by the agent of landlord Denis Mahon who, at the request of Mahon, calculated that, "The cost of keeping a pauper in the Roscommon Poor House averages about 7P 3s a year . . . the cost of emigration to Quebec averages 3P 12s . . . so the difference in favour of emigration is 5,769P."[42] Much to Mahon's discredit, and misfortune, he made the decision to transport approximately 500 men, women, and children to Quebec. Although conditions aboard what became known as the "Famine Ships" were commonly deplorable, the two ships carrying the majority of Mahon's former tenants, the *Viginius* and the *Naomi*, were particularly ghastly. More than 200 passengers aboard the two ships died during the voyage, and another 200 shortly after their arrival in Grosse Isle.[43] Word of this tragedy returned to Ireland and, perhaps not coincidentally, Mahon was assassinated in November, 1847. "His death ensured that there were suddenly many more absentee landlords in Ireland . . . ."[44]

In the Spring of 1848 Meagher was elected to serve as one of the Confederation's delegates to a meeting called for the purpose of considering a possible reunion between the Repeal Association and the Irish Confederation. But the meeting, held on May 4, resulted in little more than increased animosity. John O'Connell, appointed by his father to be a representative to the conference, opposed any action that would dissolve the existing structure, or share the power, of the Repeal Association. Just two weeks later, Daniel O'Connell died in Genoa during a tour of Italy and, as had been feared by Young Ireland, the mantle of leadership in the Repeal Association officially passed to John O'Connell. Mitchel would later caustically reflect on the elder O'Connell: "Poor old Dan! Wonderful, mighty, jovial and mean old man! Think of his speech for John Magee, the most powerful forensic achievement since Demosthenes—and then think of the gorgeous and gossamer theory of moral and peaceful agitation, the most astounding *organon* of public swindling since first man bethought him of obtaining money under false pretences."[45]

By the time of O'Connell's death, Mitchel had become

impatient with the failure of political maneuverings and concerned that the Irish Confederation, as well as the *Nation*, had become too cautious and conservative. Splintering off from the Confederation into a militant faction referred to as "Infant Ireland," Mitchel launched a newspaper in January 1848 known as *The United Irishman*; taking its name in honor of the revolutionary association led by the martyr Robert Emmet.[46] Mitchel, assisted by Devon Reilly and the spirited James Fintan Lalor, used this new forum to become even more direct and outspoken for the cause of Irish independence. Mitchel grew even more assertive in the belief that a direct, forceful action, rather than a political solution would be necessary to achieve the cause of Irish nationalism. The new publication's attacks against England's oppression struck a common nerve with many Irish from its very first issue. "The demand was so great that, for three days and nights the press was kept going and copies were sold by the Dublin newsvendors for five times their original price."[47]

Meagher was also continuing to fan the flames of Ireland's discontent with his oratory. In a speech before the Irish Confederation on February 4, he stated, "Sir, I know of no nation that has won its independence by an accident. Trust blindly to the future—wait for the 'tide in the affairs of men, which taken at the flood, leads on to fortune'—envelope yourselves in mist––leave everything to chance, and be assured of this, the most propitious opportunities will rise and pass away . . . this was the great error of the Repeal Association."[48]

CHAPTER 3

"We made only one mistake, but it was a serious one;
O'Brien was unwilling to commence negotiations in America
while there was still hope to gain the gentry;
and he could not invite their assistance
if this decisive step was taken."

Charles Gavan Duffy

It was during this time that a torrent of world events, particularly the recent success of the French revolution in overthrowing King Louis Philippe, gave strong impetus to the radical position held by many of those in the Irish Confederation and to the direction John Mitchel and James Lalor espoused. Another force that did not escape the notice of Young Ireland disciples was the movement established in the United States known as "Young America." The Young America proponents represented a segment of the Democratic Party that promoted the aggressive spread of democracy wherever there were oppressed peoples throughout the world. Their platform included a proposal for the United States to annex Ireland and Sicily.[49] Most prominent among the supporters of Young America were Stephen Douglas of Illinois and George N. Sanders of Kentucky. While the goals of the Young America movement obviously did not materialize, its very existence helped to stir hope among many Irish.

The Irish Confederation was called to meet on March 15, 1848, at Dublin's Music Hall. At this meeting, the Council proposed a congratulatory address to the French people and elected an emissary group representing the Confederation be sent to the new government of France. Meagher's speech during this meeting included one of his most direct attacks against the English

Government: "When the world is in arms—when the silence which, for two-and-thirty years, has reigned upon the plain of Waterloo, at last is broken—then be prepared to grasp your freedom with an armed hand, and hold it with the same . . . if the union is to be maintained against the will of the people, if Ireland is to be governed through the instrumentality of dragoons, then up with the barricades, and invoke the God of Battles."[50] Those elected to serve as delegates of the Irish Confederation to France included William Smith O'Brien, Edward Hollywood, and Thomas Francis Meagher. At a subsequent meeting on March 19, Richard O'Gorman, Jr., and John Dillon were also elected to serve as Confederation emissaries. According to Duffy, it was a part of O'Brien's agenda for this visit that the group seek permission from the French to train and equip an Irish Army on the soil of their new republic, an idea enthusiastically endorsed by Meagher.[51] The exodus of thousands from Ireland to France following the 1691 Treaty of Limerick provided a strong base of men with Irish heritage who may have responded to such a call to arms.

Whether it was Meagher's speech or the Confederation's decision to send representatives to France which represented the proverbial "last straw" is uncertain, but on March 21, Meagher, William Smith O'Brien, and John Mitchel were arrested on the charge of seditious libel. As a somewhat startling aside, John O'Connell and his brother Maurice appeared at police headquarters to post bail for O'Brien and Meagher, but learned other supporters had already done so. Following his release, Mitchel defiantly stated, "They have indicted me for 'sedition,' but I tell them that I mean to commit 'high treason.'"[52] Certainly this bold statement supported the growing concerns of government officials in Dublin as well as London and gave support to those seeking enactment of the Crime and Outrage Ireland Bill. This bill gave the lord lieutenant the power to draft any number of men into a district's police force (for which the district would be taxed), permitted firearms only with special license, and made seditious offenses—which had been previously eligible for bail and carried a maximum sentence upon conviction of only a few months' imprisonment—

into felony offenses. Passed into law as the Treason-Felony Act, it made virtually every speech of the Young Ireland orators and every issue of the papers *Nation* and *The United Irishman* de facto libel for prosecution. With steady, deliberate certainty, a noose began to tighten around the neck of Young Ireland.

Inasmuch as Meagher was allowed to remain free until his trial date, he eagerly made the visit to Paris along with the other Confederation delegates. During his time in Paris, Meagher was frequently accompanied by the celebrated Irish ex-patriot John Patrick Leonard. Leonard would later profile the young rebel with these words: "On one subject he was always serious—on everything touching that country for which he was going to sacrifice all that were dear to him . . . I remember on alluding to the famine of the previous year that his voice trembled with emotion and passion, 'You were happy,' he said to me, 'not to have witnessed those harrowing sights; they would have maddened you, as they maddened us all.'"[53]

Almost immediately following his return from France, Meagher proudly displayed a flag in Waterford which served as a symbol of the Irish Confederation, and which would later—with modifications—be adopted as the national flag of Ireland. "It is not known who designed the Irish flag, but Meagher was always fond of banners and symbols and it is more than likely he designed it, modeling it on the tricolor of the French Republic."[54] As Meagher enthusiastically introduced the banner at the Music Hall, he explained to the assembled crowd that its colors and their arrangement (white, between the colors of orange and green), he stated, " . . . signifies a lasting truce between the Orange and Green and I trust that beneath its folds the hands of the Irish Protestants and the Irish Catholics may be clasped in heroic brotherhood."[55] "Meagher's tricolour was not quite the same as the national flag. It had the orange, not the green, in the place of honour next to the flagstaff . . . and the white in the middle was bloodied with the Red Hand of Ulster, a symbol of the great war of vengeance Meagher intended to unleash on the Brits."[56]

In spite of the Confederation's great hopes, their delegation did not find support for the Irish cause in France. It seems reasonable to assume that while the new government of France may have empathized with the Young Ireland delegates, they were much more concerned with the political—and military—realities of alienating Great Britain through any show of support. Even more disconcerting, the British government's threats of retaliation had begun to escalate. Mitchel had become increasingly strident in his *United Irishman* articles toward Great Britain, and was also now attacking Smith O'Brien and the idea of any reunion with the Repeal Association. This rhetoric no doubt added volatile fuel to growing fires. The Confederation was further embarrassed on April 29 in the city of Limerick. O'Brien and Meagher were sent by the Confederation Council to meet with the Limerick Confederation Club and, much to their surprise, found Mitchel in attendance.[57] Upon learning of the meeting, local Repeal members gathered and began stoning the house in which the meeting was taking place. O'Brien went outside the house in an attempt to quell the disturbance and was hit by a stone, resulting in a cartoon parody and several "Battle of Limerick" puns in the British newspapers. Meagher rushed outside and challenged the crowd to consider who their enemy may actually be, "Yes, from this day out you must lie down and eat your words . . . Hush—beat back the passion that rushes to your heart—die—die without a groan—die without a struggle—die without a cry—for the government which starves you desires to live in peace."[58] Meagher's words weren't included in the British newspaper reports, but they surely didn't escape the notice of British authorities.

The tenuous situation continued to unravel until, on Saturday, May 13—just prior to the start of Meagher's and O'Brien's trials—when John Mitchel was again arrested, this time under the provisions of the Treason-Felony Act. The following Monday, "at least ten thousand" members of the sixteen Dublin area Confederation clubs rallied to march with the defendants to their court appearance.[59] Both O'Brien and Meagher's trials ended in hung juries, but the experience must have surely removed any doubt from their minds that the consequences of this political struggle were growing increasingly severe.

The Confederation's Council called for another Aggregate Meeting of its clubs to be held May 21, 1848. This meeting was held in the Dublin suburb of Bellview at a location provided by a local manufacturer, John Ennis. The expressed purpose of the meeting was to take such actions as necessary to see that Mitchel received a fair trial. After much wrangling, the meeting ended with only a statement of resolution which proposed that a government could not legally prosecute one accused of offenses against said government.[60] The other order of business which was agreed upon was an assignment for Meagher and Richard O'Gorman. "Meagher and O'Gorman made a personal inspection of the Dublin Clubs with a view to determine whether . . . a rescue [of Mitchel] was feasible. They sought information from all sources and they arrived at the conclusion that the people were unprepared, unorganized, unarmed, and incapable of being even roughly disciplined for such an attempt."[61]

The trial of John Mitchel took place without incident, and on May 27, the young man was found guilty and sentenced to a term of fourteen years in exile. Perhaps buoyed by a boisterous show of support at the time of his sentencing, Mitchel was hopeful of a rescue attempt, not only to provide his release from deportation but to serve as a possible flash-point for the start of a rebellion.[62] Mitchel's old comrades in the Irish Confederation did further debate the feasibility of a rescue effort—which had Meagher's qualified support—but the majority (including Duffy, who would be arrested a month later) convincingly argued that the Confederation was not sufficiently prepared for the successful of such a mission. In the pre-dawn hours of June 1, Mitchell was taken aboard a prison ship for the voyage to Bermuda, his assigned location to serve his term of exile.

The internal workings of the Confederation were now badly shaken by the events of the previous few weeks. The editors of the *Irish Tribune* appealed, "Why is not the Council of Three Hundred, which alone is required to save the country, proceeded with? We call upon Smith O'Brien—we call upon T. F. Meagher to rouse from his apathy."[63] Even despite a conciliatory appeal by John

O'Connell to reunite with his association and the promising recent development of a Protestant Repeal Association, the Council was singularly focused on its own issues. There was now deep concern over both the possibility that there were spies within their association and the cumbersome operations of the Council itself. These concerns led to a decision that reduced the size of the executive council by nearly half, to a more manageable twenty-one members.

By a vote of the existing Council, Meagher was seated on the new Council with convincing support. He received, along with Father John Kenyon, the greatest number of votes of any of the candidates.[64] During the time of this reorganization, another effort was being made by "a few of the leading Confederates" to initiate a "formal conspiracy." This proposed operation included a plan to send Meagher to America in order to "publicly solicit funds from Irish and American sympathisers."[65] Whether the effort to enlist support from the United States would have been initiated—or adopted—had O'Brien been in attendance is a matter for speculation. As expressed by Duffy, this issue was a key point of disagreement between O'Brien and some of his young supporters. Yet the fact he was elected, although absent from this critical meeting, to the reorganized Council is strong evidence there continued to be a keen awareness that O'Brien's leadership and influence was pivotal. Although Meagher was perhaps one of O'Brien's most loyal allies, he was prepared, even eager, to assume his mission to the United States. Meagher's assignment, however, was quickly changed: "It was considered in the end that his popularity could be put to better use in organising Munster."[66] But the rapid pace of events would quickly derail any realization of these formal conspiracy plans or the organization of Munster's Confederates.

While at his father's house in Waterford, Meagher was again arrested on July 11, which resulted in a near riot. "Of all the Confederates Meagher was the darling of the multitude."[67] Several hundred Club men rushed to defend Meagher and prevent his deportation to Dublin. Angry Confederates barricaded a bridge and several streets until it was only Meagher's own persistent pleas for order that avoided certain calamity. Meagher was just as quickly released on bond upon arrival in Dublin as he had been following his first arrest, and his spirit was unbroken from the experience. Less than a week following his arrest, Meagher followed through on earlier plans to appear at an open meeting of Confederate clubs at Slievenamon. Slievenamon is a prominent hill in Tipperary County celebrated in Irish mythology as home to the ancient warriors, the Fianna, providing great symbolism to the gathering. Before an estimated attendance of fifty thousand, Meagher used the setting of this landmark to issue a proclamation on the rights of Irishmen not only to independence, but also to the "fruits of the coming harvest."[68] Meagher immediately made an encore presentation of his Slievenamon address at a late night rally in Carrick, and followed that with another in Waterford.

No doubt charged by the success of Meagher's efforts, and a similar report from Smith O'Brien who had appeared at a rally in Cork, the newly established Executive Council of the Confederation decided to appoint a special committee to whom the Clubs of the Confederation would become accountable. It also appears this was another step towards developing tangible meaning to the philosophy of physical force. "The choice fell upon Dillon, Meagher, O'Gorman, McGee and . . . Devin Reilly." This group, labeled the Council of Five, clearly represented a growing sophistication of the Council's understanding to consolidate power and better organize their substantial, though disorganized, membership; but it was a classic example of too little, too late.

The intensity of circumstances would take a quantum leap on July 22, when the House of Commons suspended the right of habeas corpus in Ireland. This action was in response to growing concerns in London about misguided fanatics, but it only fueled the fires of bitterness in Ireland. The individual clubs of the Irish Confederation regarded this Act as the call to battle and awaited notice from their Council. When it became apparent that the Habeas Corpus Act was imminent, though, the leaders of the Irish Confederation fled Dublin. This leadership vacuum at such a critical juncture left the Dublin clubs uncertain and confused as to their course of action and would be the first in a series of debilitating miscues. Upon learning of the suspension of Habeas Corpus, Meagher accurately assessed the position of the Confederation by stating to his friend Patrick Smyth: "We have not gone far enough to succeed, and yet, too far to retreat."[70]

Kilkenny was the historic seat of Ireland government and also geographically strategic in its proximity to the counties of Tipperary, Wexford, and Waterford. The Council leadership, including Meagher, convened in Kilkenny on July 21st. As a result of this consultation, the Council determined they should first confirm support from other area Clubs prior to launching any attempt at an armed revolt. Based upon their experience at the time of Mitchel's arrest, and the fact there were significantly fewer armed men ready for service in Kilkenny than previously believed, this was a very prudent course of action. The Council members divided themselves into teams which were to visit key locations and assess the level of support and preparedness.[71] Smith O'Brien and Meagher traveled to Callan, where they received a strong welcome, then proceeded on to Carrick-on-Suir, which had been designated as the point of reunion for the Council teams.

By Tuesday, July 25, Smith O'Brien, Meagher, and other leaders of the Confederation Council had assembled in Carrick-on-Suir. John O'Mahony had been active in founding a Confederation Club in nearby Ballyneill, which led to the establishment of several other rural Clubs which he coordinated. This area was believed to be a well-armed Confederation stronghold from which the Council intended to launch their revolution. But when they met with the local council leadership (which did not include O'Mahony), they were very strongly dissuaded from initiating any action, despite the hundreds of Confederation men already crowding the streets of Carrick upon learning of O'Brien's presence. In response to calls from the throngs, O'Brien and Meagher spoke to the huge assembly, and "Meagher, who was very impressionable, and had been disappointed by the want of alacrity he found among the local leaders, is described as speaking in a despondent tone, which chilled his audience."[72] Faced with this disappointing turn of events, the Council leaders would separate and leave Carrick during the night, even as several thousand men from O'Mahony's rural Confederation Clubs were reportedly marching toward Carrick in response to the alarms which had been raised.[73] O'Brien encountered O'Mahony the next day and asked him to direct his men to return to their homes and await word of possible action.

Meanwhile, Meagher returned to Waterford with the intention of gathering the local Clubs in that area, only to learn that their religious counselor, Father Byrne, was not supporting the revolution despite his previous sympathy to the Confederation's efforts. Whether this was an individual decision or represented orders from his Church superiors isn't certain, but Cavanagh records that he met personally with Father Byrne at this crisis point. Cavanaugh states that Father Byrne advised him to abandon the revolt and that "he could not explain his change of opinion, but that, as matters were then, he could see nothing but ultimate disaster to the devoted men who persevered in upholding what he believed was a hopeless cause."[74] There would later be popular sentiment that it was the lack of support by the Catholic priests which led to the failure of the revolution. Although there had been some priests, especially the younger ones, who had been actively supportive of the Confederation, the "Old Church" never gave its blessing to the cause of revolution. Meagher would later attempt to address the criticism in a letter to Charles Duffy: "The priests did not betray us. As a body they were opposed to us—actively and determinedly opposed to us—from the day of the Secession . . . In not joining us, therefore—in not exhorting the people to take up arms . . . they did not act treacherously; they acted simply with strict consistency."[75]

The following days saw much anxious stirring about, but no overt action on the part of the Confederation. Clearly there was some division of support by this time within the Council, and the delays and poor communication had eroded the enthusiasm of popular support as well. This hiatus was not lost opportunity for the British, however, who wisely used the time to reinforce some of their garrisons. A few of the young rebels also took advantage of the quiet in the eye of the storm to leave Ireland. Among those who would escape to the United States were Richard O'Gorman, Jr.; Devin Reilly; John Dillon; Edward Hollywood; and Michael Doheny. John O'Mahony would briefly remain in Ireland before escaping first to France, then to join the other rebels in the United States.[76]

Author Robert Athearn expressed the view that the tide of circumstances had begun to quickly outpace the desires and control of the formal leadership of the Confederation: "Down the turbulent stream of events rode the unhappy leaders, unable to leave the vessel of revolution . . . and unable to guide its course."[77] It appears more likely, however, that the Confederation's Council, while certainly not in control of British actions, was very clearly in control of its membership. What does appear to have occurred to the Confederation's leadership is that they suddenly found themselves facing some grim realities for which they were unprepared. Even though the most modest of estimates indicated there were thousands of Confederation loyalists who were awaiting the Council's call to action, the Council leadership was confronting a potentially devastating combination of circumstances. At the very least these included: a lack of adequate armaments (most club members were armed only with pikes), no experienced leadership in military operations, divided support from within the local councils, and a loss of potential men at arms due to the lack of support from the clergy.

Another contributing factor, which should not be overlooked, is that the cumulative effect of repeated years of famine on the health and stamina of the Irish people was of major significance, and it was an issue that O'Brien was steadfastly unwilling to alleviate by force. Despite the urgings of other Council members, O'Brien would not tolerate provisioning and feeding their men through the looting of shops and storehouses of food which were the property of British and Irish gentry. It was O'Brien's unwavering conviction that, for the "revolution" of the Irish Confederation to be successful, these groups were necessary allies, and any incursion of their property would irrevocably alienate any hope of their widespread support.

Patrick O'Donohoe would attribute the failure of the Rebellion to "the interposition of the Catholic clergy" who denounced the Confederation, and both he and Duffy would be critical of O'Brien's "conscientious behaviour respecting the rights of property."[78] Meagher, reflecting on the situation at Carrick on July 25, would later write, "It was the Revolution, if we had accepted it. Why it was not accepted, I fear, I cannot with sufficient accuracy explain."[79] Yet he would later offer an explanation for the failure in a letter to Duffy: " . . . there can be no reasonable doubt that the main cause was owing to the absence of preliminary organization among the people selected by the leaders to inaugurate the insurrection, and to the utter lack of military knowledge amongst the leaders themselves."[80]

The tumultuous course of events came to a fever pitch on July 29, when Lord-Lieutenant Clarendon issued summons, and rewards, for the arrest of several members of the Irish Confederation, including O'Brien and Meagher. Although O'Brien must have certainly recognized there was little chance of success, it was probably a matter of honor that caused him to lead a hastily assembled force which included Terrance McManus, James Stephens, and approximately 300 supporters from Enniscorthy. Comprised mainly of farmers and miners, this "army" was equipped only with pikes or farming and mining tools, and those few who had guns only carried one or two rounds of ammunition. In what was the first, and only, armed conflict of the Young Ireland Rising, O'Brien's troops were met in the village of Ballingarry by a much smaller, though marginally better organized, police unit. The police, seeing themselves greatly outnumbered, hurriedly rushed to take refuge in the home of "the widow MacCormack." Although it would perhaps have been regarded as comical if the stakes had not been so seriously high, the "Battle of Ballingarry" resulted in a modest exchange of gunfire and stone throwing for a few hours, resulting in one Confederate killed and another wounded. The ill-conceived operation quickly collapsed into a retreat of the rebel troops once reinforcements to the police force finally arrived, and the events were contemptuously christened as "The Cabbage-Garden Revolution" by the British press.[81]

CHAPTER 4

" . . . as the door . . . was shut upon us
I saw that the face which had never quivered in any danger . . .
was bathed in tears. His country should have witnessed
that scene, to know the depth of his love for Ireland,
and what it cost him to be true to her."
Thomas Francis Meagher writing of W. Smith O'Brien

Government efforts to arrest the rebel leaders sharply intensified following the "Battle of Ballingarry" and finally came to fruition on August 5 with the arrest of O'Brien. Duffy reported that a Mr. Redington had brokered a letter of agreement with the lord-lieutenant which would guarantee the life of Meagher and his associates if they would plead guilty to the charge of high treason and if the weapons in all "disturbed districts" were surrendered. This offer was quickly and emphatically rejected by Meagher.[82] In the darkness of night on August 12, upon the road between Clonoulty and Holycross, police officers found and arrested Meagher, M.R. Leyne, and Patrick O'Donoghue. Reportedly, the three men were making no attempt at avoiding capture and surrendered themselves without resistance.[83] The final rebel arrested was Terence McManus, who was taken from an American ship (the *N.D. Chase*) in the Cove of Cork on August 30.[84] The charges against Leyne were dismissed, but the remaining four men were charged with treason and were held in Dublin's Kilmainham Goal until September 18. The Young Irelanders would have been well aware that the famed Irish revolutionary Robert Emmet had been imprisoned, and executed, at Kilmainham, which must have caused some sleepless nights among them. By all accounts, however, Meagher remained in good spirit throughout this time.

The "conspirators" were transferred for trial to the city of Clonmel, which is located east of Waterford and also sits beside the Suir river. No doubt the British authorities were anxious to remove the prisoners from their large base of supporters in Dublin. The men were tried by a special commission, which began its proceedings on September 28 against William Smith O'Brien. After a nine-day trial, O'Brien was found guilty and sentenced to punishment by death. Meagher wrote in his "Personal Recollections" journal, "The day he was sentenced to death in the Court-house of Clonmel, and he was brought back in that hideous prison-van to the gaol . . . almost every man in town shrunk back and cowered . . . as I sat with my noble young comrades . . . I could not help calling to mind the scene in Conciliation Hall and contrast the tumultuous enthusiasm with which O'Brien was then greeted with the bleak loneliness of the day he was sentenced to death. Did the contrast ever occur to himself? I never could bring myself to ask him. The question might have gone like a dagger to his heart."[85]

By the time Meagher appeared before the court on October 16, the other two defendants (McManus and O'Donoghue) had also been found guilty. It isn't certain whether Meagher's trial had been scheduled last in some deference to his father's influence or simply represented a lack of strength in the case against him. It may well have been that the prosecutor feared an opening verdict of "not guilty" in the case against Meagher would have influenced the subsequent trials. While Meagher had clearly been an outspoken leader in the Confederation, he had not participated in the incident at Ballingarry and had not actually taken force against the Government at any other time. Nevertheless, the verdict returned against Meagher was the same as his friends—guilty—albeit with the jury's recommendation of leniency in sentencing. Perhaps not unexpectedly, Meagher chose to take the opportunity offered by the chief justice to address the court at the time of his sentencing on October 23. Although widely misquoted as having offered a short, flippant response to the judges, Meagher actually spoke eloquently and boldly, declaring: "My lords, you may deem this language unbecoming in me, and perhaps it may seal my fate; but I am here to regret nothing I have ever done—to retract nothing I have ever spoken. I am here to crave with no lying lips the life I consecrate to the liberty of my country . . . the hope which beckoned me on to embark upon the perilous sea upon which I have been wrecked still consoles, animates, enraptures me. To lift this island up—to make her a benefactor to humanity, instead of the meanest beggar in the world—to restore her to her native power and her ancient constitution—this has been my ambition, and my ambition has been my crime. Judged by the law of England, I know this crime entails the penalty of death; but the history of Ireland explains this crime, and justifies it."[86] Despite the leniency recommendation of the jury, and perhaps in view of his lack of remorse in the docket, Thomas Francis Meagher, along with his compatriots, received the sentence common to those found guilty of treason against the Crown—he was to be hung by the neck until dead, beheaded, and his body quartered, with the quarters being sent to such locations as determined by the Queen and placed on public display. Truly an ignoble end to one with such noble intentions.

Following their sentencing, Meagher, O'Brien, McManus, and O'Donoghue continued to be held at Clonmel. During this time W.F. Lyons visited the Confederates and described Meagher's cell: "Imagine a little room, about the size of an ordinary pantry, lighted from the top by a large skylight, with bare whitewashed walls, neither fireplace nor stove, and a cold stone floor . . . he had converted into a genuine expression of the poetry which formed the basis of his character and genius. A warm crimson cloth lined the walls . . . Handsome French prints hung in rich profusion . . . A pretty sofa bedstead completely filled the farthest end of the cell. Round three sides of it were ranged well-stored book-shelves . . . ."[87] While at Clonmel, Meagher would remain active in his correspondence and writing, which included a poem with the lines:

"Not so the many hopes that bloom
Amid this voiceless waste and gloom,
Strewing my pathway to the tomb,
As though it were a bridal bed,
          And not the prison of the dead.
So should I triumph o'er my fate,
And teach this poor desponding State
In signs of tenderness, not hate,
Still to think of her old story,
Still to hope for future glory."[88]

Good news—and bad news—finally came to the Young Ireland patriots when they were advised on October 26 that Queen Victoria, by virtue of a newly established policy known as a "Writ of Error," had commuted their death sentences to life banishment. It was directed that their exile be served in the penal colony of Van Dieman's Land. It was almost certainly the realization that to execute the men would make them Irish martyrs and only further agitate an unsettled situation which must have motivated the Queen and her advisors far more so than any special compassion for the rebels. At any rate, the men were transferred back to Dublin on November 16 to await their deportation. While the young rebels had been spared their lives, the time of Young Ireland had come to an end. Several years later, in reflecting back upon the road they had traveled, O'Brien would write, "I have no hesitation in stating it to be my sincere conviction, that if in 1846 the Repealers had steadfastly resisted the temptations set before them, and had adhered to the vow of 1845, we should at this moment have been in the enjoyment of an Irish legislature without having gone beyond the limits of legal and constitutional agitation."

CHAPTER 5

*"Of all the Irish exiles who were sent to Tasmania . . .
none was more interesting than Thomas Francis Meagher."*
K.R. vonStieglitz

Perhaps it was a fitting irony—or insult—that the name of the British ship selected to transport the young rebels was known as the *Swift*, inasmuch as one of the most prominent Dublin clubs of the Irish Confederation was the Swift Club, led by Richard O'Gorman, Jr. As they set sail for Van Dieman's Land on July 9, 1849, aboard the British sloop-of-war, the reality of their situation must have become brutally clear in the minds of the young revolutionaries. As they drifted away from their homeland and passed by Waterford, the normally effusive Meagher wrote in unmistakably melancholy terms, "Will no one come out to hail me . . . I pass by, and my own people know nothing of it."[90] It seems very unlikely that any of the young rebels would have chosen to be standing on the scaffolds rather than on the deck of the *Swift*, but each must have been calculating the cost they were to pay for their efforts to promote freedom for Ireland. At the same time, there must have been a collective sigh of great relief from the lord-lieutenant and other British authorities in Ireland to have these irritating thorns finally removed from the Lion's paw. While there would be future incarnations of Young Ireland and the Irish Confederation, the time of mass demonstrations, fiery speeches, and scathing editorials promoting Irish nationalism had been snuffed out, at least for a few years.

Because they were formally regarded as prisoners of war, the circumstances of Meagher and his colleagues' transportation were not austere, unlike those who were convicted of civil and capital crimes. The men had separate cabins and were permitted to take personal possessions, including their books, and a crewmember was assigned to serve as their domestic. Meagher would record in his notes of the voyage that the ship's captain and crew were very amiable, but the harsh reality of his exile was obviously more apparent as each day took them farther and farther from his birthplace. In another poignant entry in his "Notes on the Voyage to Australia," Meagher would write, "When I had my freedom . . . why did I not see more of Ireland? I waited to see the old land free, and so defrauded my youth of the joys, and my memory of treasures without price."[91]

It was also during the voyage that Meagher announced his intention to thereafter prefix his family name with "O.'"[92] Whether he intended this as a tribute to his family's history, as a way for him to remain connected with his deep Irish heritage, or whether he simply thought it would in some way serve as an irritant to the British—or some portion of each—is never explained. In any event, Meagher's use of "O'" is found in some of his correspondence during his time of exile, but not afterwards.

With only a brief stop at Cape Town, where they learned that Mitchel's ship from Bermuda was long overdue, the *Swift* determinedly sailed on toward the southeastern coast of Australia and the island colony of Van Dieman's Land. The island had been discovered in 1642 by the Dutch explorer Abel Tasman, who named the island in honor of his employer. English explorers arrived by 1773, and the first British settlement was established at Sullivan's Cove in 1803. By 1822, the island was being used as a penal colony of Great Britain and would continue in that capacity until 1853. The island would be renamed Tasmania in 1856, this time in honor of its discoverer.

The long voyage of the *Swift* was largely uneventful but must have been an incredible assault on the senses as the young Irishmen witnessed sights unimagined even to such relatively well-educated and "worldly" men. When the *Swift* finally reached its destination port, the young exiles had arrived in Van Dieman's Land's capital city, Hobart, on October 29, 1849. They were formally met the next day aboard ship by the assistant-comptroller of convicts, Mr. William Nairn, who reviewed with the new arrivals the terms of their imprisonment.[93] The convict profile form of Thomas Francis Meagher includes the following information: "Height: 5'9", Complexion: fair, Hair: brown, Eyes: light blue, Trade or Occupation: law student."[94]

As had been promised at the time they were sentenced to exile, if the Young Ireland men were to show good behavior during their transport they would be offered a Ticket of Leave. A Ticket of Leave would seem to be very comparable to a release on one's own recognizance. In return, these tickets required a written pledge from the recipient not to attempt escape. Smith O'Brien did not initially accept the offer and was assigned to the penal facility on Maria Island, but the others accepted a six-month Ticket of Leave, with the understanding it could be renewed or revoked at the time of expiration. In explaining his decision to accept the terms, in contrast to O'Brien's reluctance, Meagher wrote, "I took a different view of the matter. It appeared to me that, whether we pledged our honour to the fulfillment of the conditions proposed by the Government or withheld it, an escape was out of the question . . . I thought it much more desirable to accept a small amount of liberty, fettered only by my word of honour, than surrender myself to the confinement of a prison . . ."[95] O'Brien would eventually accept his Ticket of Leave in December of 1850, after an unsuccessful escape attempt and as the conditions of his prison confinement caused his health to badly deteriorate.

Each of those who accepted a Ticket of Leave were assigned to reside in a separate "District" (comparable to a county). Meagher was assigned to Campbelltown District, an area approximately thirty to thirty-five miles long and ten to fifteen miles wide. Meagher was first assigned to Campbell Town, the capital of the District, but "when he arrived in that fair village, he looked at it with jaundiced eye, spoke rudely about it and asked to be moved to Ross."[96] Meagher's request was granted, and he quickly made his way to the little village located just a few miles south of Campbell Town.

Although it could not have represented any inducement to Meagher, one of the landmarks of Ross at that time was the "Female Factory," the women's prison for those who had been transported to Van Dieman's Land. The circumstances of the female factory provide a dramatic contrast to the experiences of Meagher and other Young Ireland rebels. The factory was described by Lieutenant-Colonel G. C. Mundy during his 1851 visit: " . . . the matron a dignified lady who looked quite capable of maintaining discipline . . . in charge of 49 women and almost as many babies . . . The better conducted and the pregnant women were kept apart from the troublesome and notorious characters who were under restraint. The townsfolk may have their washing done here at one shilling and sixpence a dozen, the money going towards the expense of the institution. Then there was a room of sempstresses, most of them employed on fine work."[97]

Soon Meagher had established himself in the little community of Ross, where he was immediately an object of public attention. "Meagher was a tall, good-looking man, still in his twenties and was soon known and liked by everyone in the township."[98] Meagher made his new home in a residence at the present-day intersection of Bond and High streets, which he described as "just a fancy little lodge, built from head to foot with bright red brick; two flower-beds, and a neat railing in front . . . four rooms inside, each fourteen feet by twelve . . . with a domestic servant of all work, and a legion of flies . . . ."[99] Although it is a detail which seems to have escaped documentation, the only reasonable explanation for Meagher's ability to live in such relative comfort, at this time and subsequently, was due to his father's continued support.

Despite the relative ease of his situation, Meagher soon became miserable with his life in the quiet rural village. Since the only requirement on his time was weekly personal appearances before the Campbelltown magistrate, Meagher was able to explore the District with maddening familiarity. For one who had become accustomed to the excitement of life in Ireland's cities and the intoxicating thrill of speaking before thousands of cheering admirers, life had become very painfully dull and predictable. "The English had been quite correct in their assumption that to silence an Irish orator is a far greater cruelty than to hang him."[100] Meagher began to vent his frustrations against his land of exile in letters to friends, stating in one that this was a " . . . raw, ill-formed colony . . . One without a decent lineage or history, and teeming with the vulgarities of English life."[101] In what may have been more a reflection of vanity than historical curiosity, he would also add a postscript to another letter, asking, "Bye-the-bye, did the Government ever publish a report of our High Treason Trials? If they have done so, I would feel deeply thankful to you to provide me a copy of the report."[102]

As one would expect, Meagher and his co-conspirators began to regularly exchange letters between their Districts. This correspondence, also predictably, led to clandestine gatherings of the young rebels. Under a most liberal self-interpretation of the terms of their Tickets of Leave, the young men would meet at a common geographic point which would permit each to technically remain in his own District, while literally being within arm's reach of one another. As time passed, so did any attempts to conceal that they were meeting, and the local constables benignly excused these indiscretions, believing no harm could come from such activity. However, even these diversions didn't provide much solace to Meagher, who continued to chafe at his situation. "I came to the conclusion, that between a prison and a 'district' there was just about the same difference as exists between a stable and a paddock. In the one you are tied up by a halter—in the other you have the swing of the tether."[103]

Although he had been the first of the rebels to be sentenced, it wasn't until April of 1850 that John Mitchel actually arrived in Van Dieman's Land. Mitchel, who had been held in British prisons and aboard various prisoner ships since the time of his trial, found himself much amused by conditions of "imprisonment" as permitted by the Ticket of Leave policy in Van Dieman's Land. He would write that, "To my utter amazement, I had a letter today from Patrick O'Donohue [sic], who has been permitted to live in the city of Hobart Town, informing me that he has established a newspaper called the Irish Exile, enclosing me a copy of the last number, and proposing that I should join him in the concern. Herein is a marvellous [sic] thing."[104] It must have also been a "marvellous thing" for Mitchel that his wife and children would soon join him, and together they would make their home in the village of Bothwell. Any previous malice between the rebels of Young Ireland appears to have faded during the long voyage from Ireland, and it wasn't long before Mitchel renewed his contacts with old friends and became an active part of the Irish expatriate community.

Through coincidence that seems like a Hollywood movie script, Meagher's restlessness and discontent would find an antidote—romance. While walking along one of Campbelltown District's rural roads in the autumn of 1850, he was passed by a carriage which suddenly lost a wheel. Meagher offered his assistance to the distressed party, thus becoming acquainted with the carriage occupants that included a Dr. Hall (who was the medical superintendent of Ross), some of his six children, and the young woman employed as their nanny, Miss Catherine Bennett. While Catherine didn't literally fall into Meagher's arms, the chance meeting did lead to a courtship between this eighteen-year-old farmer's daughter and the Irish rebel. Profiled by vonStieglitz, Catherine is described as " . . . a charming girl, self-sacrificing as they used to be in those days, and intelligent."[105] Catherine's father, Brian Bennett, was a "free settler," a status which provided Catherine the freedom to travel without restraint, and a fact which would have special implications at a later time. On February 22, 1851, in ceremonies officiated by Bishop Dr. Willson—the first Roman Catholic Bishop of Hobart—Catherine and Thomas were married, and the newlyweds began life together in a house Meagher had found on the shore of Lake Sorell.

The home at Lake Sorell provided a beautiful retreat for the young married couple and a time of uncharacteristic domestic recluse for Meagher. He became involved in gardening (though assisted to probably a great degree by a man he hired) and bought a sailboat. Meagher christened the boat *Speranzza*, in honor of the

Irish poetess, and he and Catherine (whom he called "Bennie") would frequently use the craft to explore the lake and to entertain their guests. Meagher had commissioned the boat to be built in Hobart Town and hauled across a hilly seventy-five miles to the lake by a team of oxen.[106] John Mitchel described the couple and their home during a visit he and John Martin made to the newlyweds: "A sunburnt man in a sailor's jacket stands in the stern-sheets, holding the tiller; by his side, on crimson cushions, sets a fair and graceful girl . . . nestling under the shelter of an untamable forest, stands a pretty cottage, with a verandah, and a gum-tree jetty stretching into the water . . . They have elegant little rooms, books, horses, boats—why it is almost like living."[107] Despite this idyllic setting, Meagher's restlessness re-emerged, and, consistent with the theme of caustic letters and articles he sent to friends and family, another plan began to take shape.

Certainly the successful escape of Terence McManus late in 1850 must have helped to rekindle Meagher's unrest, and although he would later claim it was his concern for Catherine's future that troubled him, it appears that the young rebel had wearied of isolation and lost the fervor of rebellion. In a letter to Charles Duffy, Meagher wrote that he would have, " . . . continued to endure my captivity in that sad island, had there been good news from Ireland, and did I still believe that the memory of our sacrifice was conducive to the growth of a new spirit—wiser, stronger, and nobler than that which compelled the country in '48, to the brink of revolution. I, therefore, came to the conclusion, that the example of our voluntary sacrifice . . . could no longer be of any avail . . . ."[108] Whether Meagher was aware of the undercurrent of support in the United States for the former Irish revolutionaries isn't certain, but such awareness would have only added temptation to the course of action which he already had in mind. In a letter which he wrote to Duffy on December 27, 1851, Meagher mentions that he has intentions to withdraw his Ticket of Leave and attempt escape. He further indicates that he expected " . . . to seek some land in which a useful and honorable career will be open to me . . ."[109]

In what was obviously a very thoughtfully choreographed plan of action, Meagher sent a letter to the police magistrate of Campbelltown District on January 3, 1852. In his note, sent to the Police Magistrate at approximately 11:00 a.m., Meagher announced his intention of resigning his Ticket of Leave effective at Noon of the next day when, "I shall no longer consider myself bound by the obligation which that parole imposes." [110] He would add to his note that, should the Magistrate seek to take him into custody, he would consider himself immediately relieved of his obligation.

Catherine, who was eight months pregnant, left their Lake Sorell cottage to wait with her family until such time as she could safely reunite with her husband. Meanwhile, realizing full well what the true intention of Meagher's renouncement foretold, the Magistrate quickly dispatched his deputies, with the exception of his sergeant, who refused to take part in deference to his respect for Meagher. Without providing any specific details, W. F. Lyons stated that the escape was supported by "P. J. Smith and the New York Irish Directory"; however, any financial aid related to his escape was later vigorously denied by Meagher.[111]

Meagher remained at the Lake Sorell cottage until approximately 7:00 p.m. when, accompanied by a neighbor, he rode off toward the coast, actually within sight of the officers who had been sent to arrest him and upon a horse he had purchased from the police magistrate. "The fleeing prisoner made for the mouth of the Tamar River where he was joined by two fishermen, who had waited there two days."[112] Meagher arrived at his rendezvous point on Monday, January 5, and was transported in the fishermen's small boat to Waterhouse Island. There he waited ten days in solitary seclusion for the arrival of the ship *Elizabeth Thompson*. The ship's captain had been solicited to take Meagher as a passenger to Pernambuco (now the city of Recife), Brazil. While Meagher was en route, a resolution was introduced in the United States Senate by Henry Foote of Mississippi that was "expressive of the sympathy of Congress for the exiled Irish patriots, Smith O'Brien and Thomas F. Meagher and their associates," and, obviously unaware of Meagher's escape, called for England to release these men and other political exiles.[113]

While there can be no question that Meagher made escape preparations while holding a Ticket of Leave, it seems a matter of interpretation as to whether this actually violated the terms of his parole. The fact that he formally gave notice to the Magistrate, albeit with a self-imposed caveat, implies Meagher at least gave a nodding attempt at compliance. Although Meagher would subsequently bear the weight of criticism, it should be noted that both McManus and Mitchel also escaped while holding a Ticket of Leave. In any event, after a brief layover in the South American port, Meagher took passage for America on the suitably named ship, *Acorn*. It was just over a month later, on May 26, 1852, when Thomas Francis Meagher would have his first glimpse of the land he had eulogized in his most famous speech as "started from the waters of the Atlantic" as the *Acorn* slowly sailed into the harbor of New York City.

PART II

Life of Celebrity—
From Immigrant to American

CHAPTER 6

"There is not a heart in the country but will thrill
at this news . . . who will not rejoice to hear that so gallant
a spirit is rescued from punishment and ignominy.
In him the Irish in America will find a chief
to unite and guide them."

Boston Pilot

Although Thomas Francis Meagher was only twenty-nine years old at the time he set foot on the shore of New York, his reputation was already deeply established among many Americans—especially Irish-Americans. The spark which had been struck by Foote's resolution of political amnesty for the Irish nationalists (and was endorsed by such prominent figures as Senator William Seward) was now burning brightly. A series of demonstrations honoring Meagher were held in several cities, and resolutions of support streamed from state legislatures. Sympathetic newspaper articles had boosted Meagher and his associates to martyrhood status with stories, somewhat enhanced, of his bold revolutionary exploits and piteous exile. Meagher's name was commemorated by several fraternal associations, such as the Meagher Clubs of New York City and Boston, and militia groups that included the Meagher Rifles in Boston and the Meagher Guard of Philadelphia, and a popular song had been written celebrating his escape from Van Dieman's Land.

This enthusiastic outpouring of support and adulation for the young Irishman was far from what most Irish experienced upon arrival to their United States. Of the more than one million Irish who would arrive in America between 1848 and 1854, it proved to be anything but a land of milk and honey. For the vast majority of Irish immigrants, the trials of passage did not insure a life any more comfortable than what they had known in Ireland. Most found that they had simply traded life as a rural peasant for life in an urban slum. In addition to the obvious differences in living situation, culture, and language, the new arrivals—including Meagher—quickly realized they had exchanged one set of challenges for another. "The issues, of course, changed from old world to new. In Ireland the demands were for land reform and some degree of political independence, not neccessarily in that order. American society forced the Irish to reconcile these 'Irish Questions' with new and mostly workingclass issues."[1]

Upon his arrival in New York, Meagher sought out friends and associates of the Irish Confederation who had preceded him in seeking a new life in the United States. Early on May 27, 1852, Meagher found his way to the law offices of Dillon & O'Gorman. [2] News of his arrival spread quickly, setting off a riotous welcome. By that evening, a crowd reportedly in excess of 7,000, which included the 69th New York State Militia (Second Irish Regiment), had gathered at the home of Mr. O'Gorman to boisterously greet Meagher.[3] Another of his early public appearances was on June 10 at the Astor House, where Meagher paid tribute to his Young Ireland companions still in Tasmania: "Nor do I forget the companions of my exile. The freedom that has been restored to me is embittered by the recollection of their captivity."[4] Meagher was soon receiving formal invitations from social organizations and government officials across the country, including Governor Lowe of Maryland (who had been a classmate at Clongowes Wood) and Governor Wright of Indiana, who forwarded a joint resolution of the Indiana legislature requesting Meagher's visit and including an invitation to address the legislators in session.[5]

While Meagher would initially decline most of the invitations he received to make public appearances, among the first he did accept was in conjunction with a July 4 celebration in New York City. Meagher was invited by Major-General Sanford and the mayor of New York City to review the First Division of the New York State Militia, which included several units of Irishmen. This appearance was followed by another on July 27 to review a general muster of all the area's Irish military organizations at Battery Park. Following an introduction by Lieutenant-Colonel Michael Doheny, Meagher delivered his first address before the general public in America and was genuinely moved by the sight of hundreds of properly armed, uniformed, and well-drilled young Irishmen. He must have found this a stirring contrast to those emaciated men in tattered clothes who sought to challenge the British army with pikes and stones in 1848. It is also reasonable to assume this display must have provided Meagher with dreams of what might have been—or what could yet be—a new chapter in the history of Ireland. With words which may have been seeds for the growth of a new association, Meagher shared his vision: "I speak not of the hope which Ireland may derive from your organizations, and the propitious influence it may have in some happier season, upon her interests and ultimate condition. But this I can safely say, that whether Irishmen cast their fortunes permanently here, or, answering to some wise and inspiring summons, shall return to the land whence they have been forced to fly, the use of arms will improve their character, will strengthen and exalt it, freeing it from many of the irregularities which enfeeble it and degrade it."[6]

Certainly Meagher's arrival in the United States gave new impetus to the cause of Irish nationalism among Irish-Americans; as early as July, 1852, a group of those who had been members of the Irish Confederation in Ireland had organized the "American Confederates." Yet, for his part, Meagher seemed genuinely resolved at this point to remain apart from politics and "if possible, out of trouble."[7] Assuredly a prudent attitude for one who did not have the protection of citizenship from any country and who had faced a death sentence and been held a prisoner for much of the previous four years. Meagher would waste no time, however, in setting his course. On August 9, 1852, he would appear, alone and without fanfare, to take the oath of Declaration of Intention to become a citizen of the United States. Although he initially protested the text of the oath ("I do not consider myself Queen Victoria's subject, whereas I have been declared an outlaw by the British

Government"), he would be reassured by the presiding judge regarding the intention of the Declaration and would resolutely announce that "I, Thomas Francis Meagher, do declare on oath, that it is bona fide my Intention to become a Citizen of the United States, and to renounce for ever all allegience and fidelity to any foreign Prince, Potentate, State or Sovereignty whatever, and particularly to the Queen of the United Kingdom of Great Britain and Ireland of whom I am now a subject."[8] It is interesting to speculate on whether Meagher's motivation in seeking American citizenship represented his belief that he would never be permitted to return to Ireland (which would suggest he may have resigned himself to the possibility Ireland would not be independent of Great Britain in his lifetime), or if he believed his only opportunity to safely return to his homeland would be as an American citizen.

Understandably eager to capitalize on his new-found celebrity, and anxious to find a source of income without reliance on his family, Meagher decided to undertake a lecture tour during the late autumn and winter of 1852. Then, as now, public speaking represented a good source of income for those with the "star power" to draw a crowd, and public lectures were a common form of public entertainment throughout the United States. This manner of employment certainly meshed well with Meagher's already well-honed oratory skills and provided the spotlight and stage for public adoration he so thoroughly enjoyed. It also seems to have been well suited to his spirit of restlessness and his extroverted personality to be seeing new places, meeting new people, and moving within the circles of the rich and powerful. While Meagher relished the advantages of celebrity status, it appears he was a reluctant "messiah" to the Irish people in America. Again, whether this was motivated by his perceptions of social class or his personal agenda to earn his return to Ireland isn't certain. Most likely, it was some combination of these—and perhaps other—factors which influenced Meagher's decisions.

Just prior to beginning his lecture series, Meagher received word in early November that Catherine had given birth to their son and that she intended to travel to the United States by the next spring. The boy, Henry Emmet Fitzgerald Meagher, had been born in February, but died (June 8, 1852) before Meagher even received notice of his birth.[9] Catherine made arrangements for the infant's burial in the village of Richmond, Tasmania, at the St. John's Church cemetery, then made preparations to join her husband.

Launched in late November 1852, Meagher's inaugural lecture tour was generally very well received, playing to large and enthusiastic audiences at nearly every venue. His first presentation was on the topic "Australia" and was held at the Metropolitan Hall in New York City. Reviewing his lecture, the *New York Herald* reported, "So early as five o'clock the hall was besieged; and at six o'clock the crowd became so dense and so threatening, that the committee found it necessary to open the doors . . . There were fully 4,500 persons in the building."[10] In addition to New York, the cities included among his northeast tour appearances were: Providence, Rhode Island; Concord, New Hampshire; and Boston, Salem, and Fall River in Massachusetts. During a whirlwind December tour, Meagher would make appearances in Albany, Schenectady, Utica, Auburn, Rochester, and Buffalo in New York, as well as Boston, Philadelphia, St. Louis, Cleveland, and Cincinnati.

Unquestionably there were many who came to his lectures more interested in seeing Meagher than actually listening to him, but most editorial reviews praised his eloquence, if not always agreeing with his sentiments. Meagher was apparently neither as animated nor the firebrand style speaker that some expected him to be. "His [Meagher's] gestures are rare, but quick and decisive, and he wisely avoids the attempt, which would inevitably prove fruitless, to repeat his words from memory."[11] Although this inaugural tour brought strong reviews, certainly the praise wasn't universal. The history of Young Ireland's strained relationship with the Church and Meagher's refusal to lecture on behalf of Catholic-sponsored charities, led to attacks by clerics and the Catholic press.[12] Meagher showed uncharacteristic restraint in not publicly responding to the charges made in the press and would even make an attempt to heal the wounded feelings.

Meagher concluded his first lecture tour in time to be in Washington, D.C., for the presidential inauguration on March 4. Meagher's celebrity was acknowledged there by some of the most politically powerful men of the day. Most prominent among those with whom Meagher met during his stay were President-Elect Pierce, ex-President Fillmore, and Senators Jefferson Davis, Stephen Douglas, and William Seward. It would seem that politicians of that time, just as they do now, found that spending time with popular public figures translated into press coverage. Meagher naively accepted this show of adulation as genuine, however, and would later find himself disappointed and confused when his requests for support from some of these men were ignored. Meagher must have also found encouragement for a potential strengthening of United States-Ireland relations from Pierce's inaugural address. In his remarks, Pierce gave words of support to the cause of Young America, stating, "The oppressed throughout the world . . . have turned their eyes hitherward . . . the policy of my Administration will not be controlled by any timid forebodings of evil from expansion."[13]

Following the social whirl of the inauguration, Meagher made another lecture tour, this time into several Southern states. His appearances on this tour included Charleston and Columbia in South Carolina; Augusta, Georgia; Mobile, Alabama; and New Orleans. Once again, he found large and enthusiastic audiences at each of his lectures, and the press reviews were very positive throughout his circuit. No doubt influenced by the outpouring of popular sentiment, Meagher's impressions of the South continued to be very positive, an impression which was to be even further enhanced over time. Of course, Meagher's reputation and the cause which he had espoused were easily appreciated by many people in the Southern states, many of whom were beginning to feel as if they were also in the yoke of an unresponsive government. It was during one of his New Orleans lectures that Meagher attempted to heal the rift between himself and the Catholic press with tactfully chosen words. During an address entitled "Ireland in '48," "the speaker [Meagher] told his audience that the clergy had not betrayed the revolutionists, even if that group had failed to sanction their plans and endeavors."[14] But in a letter to William Smith O'Brien, he would later—more candidly—write, "I spoke favorably of Kossuth [hero of the independence movement in Hungary] and the European movements for liberty and that was the whole of it. For this I was denounced from the pulpits, and through the bigoted Catholic press, and in highways and bye-ways. But I never replied to any of their scurrilities. The consequence is that the storm has blown over—and peace reigns between the Young Rebel and the Church."[15]

One who did find fault with Meagher's April 7 presentation in New Orleans was a visitor to the city, Henry Watkins Allen. Allen would write to a friend, "Last evening I procured a ticket . . . to hear the celebrated Thomas Francis Meagher, the great Irish Lecturer . . . I must confess I was somewhat disappointed . . . I thought his lecture much injured by his abuse of Great Britain— no doubt he feels deeply indignant at the wrongs inflicted on him, but it is still in bad taste to make one's own grievances the burden of the story."[16] Of course, it's probable that Mr. Allen had never witnessed the effects of the Irish Famine, or had the pleasure of the view from Clomnel goal. On the other hand, an opposing opinion would be offered by *The Daily Orleanian*, which reported, "Last night Mr. Meagher closed his brilliant series of lectures . . . the hall was, as usual, thronged, and the audience profoundly sensitive."[17]

By mid-May, Meagher had returned to New York City to await the arrival of his wife and father. Catherine, who was able to exercise her right of unrestricted travel, had journeyed from Tasmania to the Meagher family home in Waterford in early 1853. She had been escorted on her long voyage by Bishop Willson. Upon arriving in Waterford, Catherine found herself to be in a position of celebrity, and she was greeted by a crowd in excess of 20,000 enthusiastic and curious Irish citizens. After a brief rest in Waterford, Catherine arrived in New York in August, this time accompanied by her father-in-law. Meagher would spend much of the summer and autumn of 1853 sightseeing with Catherine and his father, traveling to Niagara Falls and making an extended stay in the Catskill Mountains of New York.

Another happy reunion also occurred during this time with the arrival of another son of Young Ireland, John Mitchel. Mitchel and his family had escaped Tasmania with significant assistance from Patrick Smyth, the man who had also aided Meagher.[18] After a brief stay in San Francisco, Mitchel and his family booked passage to New York where they arrived on November 29, 1853. Mitchel's mother had preceded their arrival and, together, they would make their home in Brooklyn. Mitchel and Meagher quickly renewed their friendship and shared the stage during another round of frenzied welcoming celebrations by the Irish-Americans of New York.

In early December of 1853, Meagher eagerly accepted an offer of free passage from the California Steamship Company to travel from New York to San Francisco. Meagher, as countless others had been previously, was taken with the dream of finding his fortune in California. He quickly scheduled a lecture tour to include several of California's flourishing cities. Just prior to Meagher's own departure, his father returned to Ireland with Catherine, who had become pregnant during her time in the United States. Why his wife would leave at this time, especially in view of her circumstances, is difficult to understand. There are some reports that she returned due to "ill health," although it seems unlikely that the level of health care in Ireland would be significantly better than that in New York, or that a winter cruise across the Atlantic would in any way be recuperative. Whether there developed some tacit understanding that their marriage worked best at a distance, or whether there was a desire the child should be born in Ireland was apparently never explained. It is possible there may have also been some uncertainty as to Meagher's future place of residence. In announcing his departure, the *Irish American* reported that Meagher was bidding adieu to New York and that California was "where he intends to reside permanently."[19]

Meagher began his west coast lecture tour in San Francisco with a series of presentations in the city's Music Hall. In his opening address on January 24, Meagher set forth the agenda for his appearances: "It is my intention, then, to give a few lectures on the lives, times, and characters of the Irish orators—Grattan, Curran, O'Connell, Shiel, and Sheridan . . . I come to speak of those whose memories are the inalienable inheritance of my poor country . . . .".[20] His California performances were generally well attended, and he was treated kindly in reviews by the local press. Meagher's subsequent stops included Sacramento, Marysville, Nevada City, and Grass Valley before returning for encore performances in San Francisco. Despite what he might have intended as a long-term stay, Meagher made the decision to conclude his California excursion and arrived back in New York City on February 28, 1854, without finding his pot of gold in California.

During this period, Meagher had been publicly goaded through articles and speeches by James Houghton, a Quaker merchant in Dublin. Houghton was determined to force Meagher to express his position on the issue of slavery. Although Meagher had stated an opposition to slavery in the paper he had written at Stonyhurst, it appears his more recent contact with the Southern aristocracy may have revealed the complexities of the situation. Nevertheless, whether he was truly undecided on the issue or unwilling to declare himself at that time—or simply unwilling to respond to such prodding—Meagher tersely replied, "Mr. Meagher . . . begs to state that he does not recognize in Mr. Houghton, nor any other person, nor the public generally, any right or title whatsoever to require from him an expression of opinion respecting the question of African slavery in America."[21]

Upon his arrival in New York, Meagher was presented with the sad, and very unexpected, news that Patrick O'Donoghue had died in late January. O'Donoghue had followed the other Young Ireland exiles from Van Dieman's Land to America, arriving in the summer of 1853 in time to attend a birthday celebration in Meagher's honor that was held in Boston. Perhaps because he had the misfortune to follow McManus, Meagher, and Mitchel, O'Donoghue's brief time of freedom in America seems to have been a bittersweet experience. As the least renowned, and least celebrated, of the Young Ireland exiles, the wounds of his sacrifice may have never healed.

With only a brief pause in New York, Meagher left for another lecture tour of the southern states. While on this tour he received more bad news—Catherine had died at the Meagher home in Waterford on May 9, 1854. Prior to her death, Catherine had given birth to another boy who had survived and was christened Thomas Francis Meagher II. Catherine Bennett Meagher was buried in the Meagher family vault at Faithlegg cemetery east of Waterford.[22] Her obituary notice would recount that Catherine had become a beloved resident of Waterford since here arrival from Van Dieman's Land. "We knew her then only as the wife of the gifted and exiled Meagher—as one who shared his lonely exile and who created around him the sweet endearments of home in the wilderness to which the 'British Law' consigned him. She has since lived among us. We have witnessed the gentle innocence and sweetness of her character, that endeared her to all who had the happiness of knowing her . . . ."[23] The notice also suggests that Catherine intended to return to America, "[she] was compelled to fly from the fierce temper of an American climate, to renew her strength in a home where he dares not meet her; and just, again as she was about joining that husband whom she so ardently loved; death interferes . . . ."[24]

Before leaving on his California tour, Meagher had agreed to a partnership with John Mitchel to establish a weekly newspaper to be known as *The Citizen*; but, as with his marriage to Catherine, Meagher showed little commitment to this endeavor. "My friend had entered eagerly into the project, but in fact, he was at that moment starting on a tour to California; and neither then or at any subsequent time had I much service from his dashing pen."[25] One has the impression that Mitchel may have accepted his friend's lack of commitment with a shrug of his shoulders and knowing smile; we can only speculate as to what may have been Catherine's feelings.

CHAPTER 7

*"For Meagher was like America. He was young,
enthusiastic, filled with optimism, and willing to struggle
for ends that seemed barely possible. He was restless,
high-strung, and eager for adventure and change."*

Robert Athearn

Before the end of 1854, Meagher's name was splashed again in the headlines of many newspapers in connection with two incidents, very different in their nature, each of which gives an interesting glimpse into his character. In July, Meagher's earlier expressed intention to "stay out of trouble" came to an end with his confrontation of James McMasters. There had been previous columns in the unfriendly press which were disparaging of the circumstances regarding Meagher's escape from Tasmania. These reports essentially challenged whether Meagher had broken his pledge of honor with respect to the terms of his Ticket of Leave.[26] McMasters had recently written an article in the Catholic *Freeman's Journal* which renewed the question of the veracity of the accounts surrounding Meagher's escape. It seems reasonable to assume that these reports may have also opened wounds of remorse caused by Catherine's recent death. On July 18, the two men encountered one another on the street and, following a verbal exchange, Meagher began to beat McMasters with a cowhide riding croup. McMasters, who carried a loaded cane and a revolver, was able to get off one shot (which resulted in powder burns to Meagher's face) before police arrived and arrested both men. The *Irish American* in reporting the incident made the point to mention, with some apparent satisfaction, that Meagher's riding croup was made of *Irish* cowhide.[27]

74 GARY R. FORNEY

By the time the McMasters incident had begun to fade from newspaper stories, Meagher was again thrust into the spotlight, this time in much more positive terms. On November 10, Meagher was among the passengers on a Great Western Railroad train near Detroit, Michigan, which collided with a freight train, resulting in numerous injuries and several fatalities. Meagher, at great personal risk, was cited for repeatedly assisting to extract fellow passengers from amidst the twisted wreckage and fire.[28] Once more, Meagher found himself proclaimed a hero of the public.

Although he was still drawing respectable attendance at his lectures, Meagher had begun to realize he was no longer front-page news and, by this time, stories of the "rebellion" must have been a bit played-out. Meagher recognized that his life as a celebrity was in eclipse and sought a more stable means of financial support. "It's full time for me to be kindly let down from my 'distinguished stranger' position, and be admitted among the several crowd as 'one of ourselves.'"[29] Meagher's answer to his dilemma was to return to the avenue he had begun to travel years earlier in Dublin, the legal profession. Under the tutelage of Judge Robert Emmet, he resumed his legal studies and was admitted to the New York Bar by a special order of the New York Supreme Court in September 1855. This special action of the court was due to the fact Meagher had not completed the minimum residency requirement of five years for Unitied States citizenship. He would subsequently form a law partnership, the firm known as Meagher and Campbell, with Malcome Campbell.

During this same time period Meagher ended his widowhood with his marriage to Elizabeth M. J. Townsend on November 14, 1855. Elizabeth was a prominent member of New York society as the daughter of Peter Townsend (a wealthy New York merchant) and the former Caroline Parish. Born in 1830 at Southfield, Elizabeth was from a very established New York family. Her great-grandfather had manufactured the chain which was used to barricade the Hudson River at West Point during the Revolutionary War, and her grandfather was the first to manufacture steel rails for railroads.[30] Father William Corby would later describe Elizabeth, who converted to Catholicism for the marriage, as " . . . a woman of more than an ordinary degree of refinement and excellent social virtues."[31]

On January 2, 1855 Meagher wrote a lengthy letter to Elizabeth in which he would "speak to you now more fearlessly and fully than I have hitherto done." Meagher provided additional background, "you know most of it already," on his life as a "rebel," his marriage to Catherine, and his decision to escape Van Dieman's Land. "Family, old friends . . . I parted from, to be true to my convictions, my conscience, and my cause. Banished to an island in the South Pacific . . . I grew sad and sick of life. In the darkest hour of that sick life, a solitary star shone down upon me, making bright and beautiful the desolate waters . . . She was the daughter of an honest, pious, venerable, poor old man who, years before, had journeyed from Ireland to that distant land . . . I had not been four months married when I saw that she had to share the privations and indignities to which her husband himself was subject. Without her, I might have hardened . . . but that she should have to drink from the bitter cup that was given me to drink . . . this I could not bear. Hence I came to the determination of breaking loose from the trammels which bound me to that hateful soil . . . ." It is clear from the letter that Meagher had already proposed marriage, and Elizabeth accepted, but he acknowledged, "That there would be . . . objections to our union." Specifically citing that she is from "a family affluent in circumstances" and that he is a man of "no fortune—at least, nothing that I know of" who must make "my own way through the world . . . nothing to show— nothing to give you—nothing to promise you—nothing but a 'true heart.'"[32]

There were some stories that Peter Townsend was among those who had serious misgivings about the union of Elizabeth with Thomas Francis Meagher. The *New York Daily Times* even reported that Peter had rewritten his will, disinheriting Elizabeth.[33] While there may have been some grains of truth among such reports, it is worth mentioning that the *Times* editor, Henry Raymond, had been outspoken for some time in his criticism of Meagher. It is also worth noting that Thomas and Elizabeth were invited to make their home at the Townsend family residence at 129 Fifth Avenue. To what degree this marriage was an affair of love or a matter of opportunity for Meagher is probably a legitimate question. Certainly he was not unaware of the influence which the Townsend family connections could potentially have meant, but it appears there were also genuine feelings of love. A year following their marriage, Meagher would write of Elizabeth in a letter to Smith O'Brien, "She is so beautiful, so intelligent, so cultivated, so generous, so gentle and unaffected."[34]

It may be appropriate to consider that Meagher had spent the greatest portion of his life at boarding schools, in prison, or in exile. It doesn't seem unreasonable to assume that his understanding of personal relationships may have been very different from that of perhaps the majority of people, even in the Victorian era. Perhaps meeting Catherine at the nadir of his young life, and the subsequent birth of son, had indeed awakened a new feelings—and maturity. It could also be said that while he certainly wasn't without appreciation for his family, he may have been happiest—even at times of great personal danger—when in the public spotlight, rather than in the quiet solace of home and family.

The tedium of attempting to establish a legal practice quickly frustrated Meagher, and soon he was again seeking another direction towards making his fortune and keeping his name on the front page. In April 1856, Meagher made another attempt at a journalism career by establishing *The Irish News* with the significant assistance of Richard Lalor as Business Manager and featuring regular columns from Ireland penned by Patrick Smyth. Meagher eagerly jumped back into the political arena via an *Irish News* editorial in support of James Buchanan's candidacy for president, which wasn't actually a matter of great controversy among Irish-Americans given his opponent's (John Fremont) affiliation with the "Know Nothing" Party. Originally organized as "The Order of the Star Spangled Banner," the Know Nothing's were a short-lived party whose basic tenets were the fanatical support of Protestantism and an anti-immigration policy. Despite the woeful conditions that had led thousands of Ireland's sons and daughters to American, for most their reception to this land of promise—unlike that of Meagher's— had been anything but compassionate. "In truth, life in American proved very hard, a bitter struggle for the new arrivals. Work was not so easy to find, and job advertisements were soon accompanied by the phrase, 'No Irish Need Apply,' shortened to NINA."[35] Meagher was not unmindful of his countrymen's condition, and would use the *Irish News* as a forum to address issues of employment opportunities and social conditions.

Meagher would also use his newspaper to report on another lecture tour he made through the Southern states during September. As he had been during his previous travels, he was deeply impressed by what he found in the Southern lifestyle and wrote some strong pro-South articles, which included support for the institution of slavery. One issue of *The Irish News* featured a mock trial story entitled "The Great Legal Controversy" that attempted to justify slavery and in which Meagher wrote, "Slavery, like every other social institution has its dark side; and it would be well, perhaps, if we could get rid of it. But we can't in our time, and should therefore confine our effort to alleviating the evils that accompany it."[36]

Likewise, John Mitchel had also used *The Citizen* as a forum for expressing not just benign tolerance, but his unequivocal support of the Southern states and the practice of slavery. Recognizing the uncomfortable situation that his position engendered in the North, Mitchel would move his family to rural eastern Tennessee, during the spring of 1855 where he would write, "Not only does America content me, the South especially delights me . . . Amongst civilized communities, none are at this moment so secure as the Southern States of America."[37] It wasn't long, however, before Mitchel grew restless with the bucolic life. By the autumn of 1857 Mitchel had moved his family to Knoxville where he established another newspaper, the *Southern Citizen*. It wasn't long before Mitchel concluded that Knoxville didn't offer the political excitement he craved and, by late 1858, moved his family, and the *Southern Citizen*, to Washington, D.C.

Meanwhile, there was yet another social force that was developing during this time which would cast a long and intriguing shadow over Thomas Francis Meagher's personal and political life.

CHAPTER 8

"I solemnly pledge my sacred word of honor as a truthful
and honest man that I will labor with earnest zeal
for the liberation of Ireland from the yoke of England
and for the establishment of
a free and independent government on Irish soil . . . ."
Membership pledge of the Fenian Brotherhood

In 1855, three of the Irish Confederation's immigrants to America—John O'Mahony, Michael Doheny, and Michael Corcoran—founded an organization known as the "Emmet Monument Association." Ostensibly the purpose of this association was to honor the memory of the famed Irish revolutionary of 1803, Robert Emmet; in reality, the group sought to lay the groundwork for an invasion of Ireland. It was the fervent hope of the Emmet Association that Britain would lose its current war with Russia and be unprepared, if not unwilling, to contest the determined resistance of an Irish army's fight for independence; but with Britain's victory in the Crimean War, the Association disbanded, but not before creating a standing committee of thirteen members who were empowered to revive the Association at their discretion.[38] With the primary leadership of O'Mahony, the Association resurfaced in 1857, briefly using the title "Irish Revolutionary Brotherhood" before adopting a name rich with Irish tradition, the "Fenian Brotherhood." The Fenians honored the memory of a fabled group of Irish knights (Fianna) of the second century, who espoused the ideals of chivalry and national honor.[39]

The Fenian Brotherhood, like the Irish Confederation, was dedicated to the cause of Irish nationalism but, rather than conduct their affairs in the public eye and ignore the development of a

79

military unit as the Confederation had done until its final months, the Fenians learned from past mistakes. This organization conducted closed meetings and quickly established a well-armed, well-trained military force. Based at its headquarters at 6 Centre Steet in New York City, the Fenian Brotherhood's membership rapidly grew, and many local chapters (known as "Circles") sprang up throughout the United States. Additionally, James Stephens was recruited to initiate the Fenian organization in Ireland.[40] Although Meagher was not a member of the Emmet Memorial Association, he certainly must have been aware of its existence, and whether he held membership in the Fenian Brotherhood would later become a matter open to some question, if not embarrassment.

Not long after becoming an American citizen in May of 1857, Meagher found his way back into the national spotlight as legal representative in the politically-charged court case against Joseph W. Fabens. Fabens was charged with violations of the Neutrality Act of 1818 while serving as an agent (Director of Colonization) of William Walker. Walker had established himself as President of Nicaragua in 1855, and it was his thinly disguised intention to flood the country of Nicaragua with American immigrants for his personal enrichment. It was understood that ex-President Franklin Pierce was among those seeking to establish the interests of the United States within Nicaragua (at the expense of the British) as a possible Atlantic-to-Pacific canal route. During the course of the trial, in fact, that Meagher disclosed that Fabens had documentation in his possession from Pierce's secretary, Sydney Webster, which made clear the president's knowledge—and support—for Fabens's work, as well as a deed of transfer which provided property in Central America to Webster.[41] Although the case quickly closed and the charges against Fabens dismissed (most likely to avoid additional political embarrassments), the experience paid an additional dividend to Meagher. His exposure to the economic and political possibilities in these developing countries of Central America led him to make requests to President Buchanan for an appointment to a consulship in South or Central America. Meagher attempted to reassure Buchanan that he had reformed since the days of Young Ireland by writing, "Becoming an American citizen I cease to be a European revolutionist."[42] Nevertheless, it was a request that Buchanan, perhaps wisely, never accepted.

Meagher would return to the lecture circuit again in the summer of 1857 and in the early spring of 1858 with tours throughout the Midwest, including stops in Pittsburgh, Cincinnati, Illinois, Iowa, and Wisconsin.[43] His work on the Fabens case, however, seems to have reawakened his desire to play upon the international stage. In early March of 1858, with Elizabeth in Ireland visiting his family, Meagher appointed James Roche as acting editor of the *Irish News* and departed for an extended tour of Central America. Meagher proclaimed the purpose of his travels: "I visit Central America,—Costa Rica especially—for the purpose of ascertaining the true condition of affairs there, and becoming familiar with a noble region, for which there inevitably approaches an eventful future."[44]

Meagher was accompanied on his tour of Central America by a former schoolmate at Stonyhurst, Ramon Paez. Ramon was the son of a famous revolutionary and former president of Venezuela, General Antonio Paez. This important connection was most probably the reason Meagher had entry to some of the highest levels of society and political access at a time when anti-American feelings were running high. Beginning his tour in Costa Rica, Meagher shared his observations and impressions of the countries he visited in a series of articles in *Harper's New Monthly Magazine* which appeared under the title "Holidays in Costa Rica."[45] He had also hoped to further capitalize on his adventures by a series of lectures on the peoples and customs of this region once he returned to the United States, but he found that Americans were much more concerned with issues nearer to home.

Upon his return to New York in June of 1858, Meagher took a renewed, albeit brief, interest in his paper and in some of the political and social issues facing Irish-Americans. With a burst of energy, Meagher wrote about such topics as flagging employment opportunities and foreign policy (inasmuch as he was now an "expert" on Central America), and he wrote critically of the

Buchanan administration, no doubt with the realization there was nothing to be lost in doing so—certainly not a consulship. Predictably, it wasn't long before his zeal had waned for the newspaper business and, once again, it appears Meagher sensed his star was fading. His name, however, still carried influence as evidenced by the visit of James Stephens late in 1858. Stephens was in the United States to gain support for the Irish Republican Brotherhood and called upon both Meagher and John Mitchel in his travels. Stephens, who had also previously visited with William Smith O'Brien, found his reception by the former leaders of Young Ireland to be rather cool. "When [Stephens] came to New York to arrange for the formation of co-operative revolutionary organizations in Ireland and America, he sought to enlist Thomas Francis Meagher in the project; but Meagher declined his overtures—on what grounds I cannot, positively, say."[46]

In April 1859, Meagher resigned as editor of *The Irish News*, appointing Richard Lalor as his successor. Although he had not been actively involved with management of the paper—and did seem pleased to be rid of it—the resulting void seems to have pulled Meagher into a deep melancholy. In a letter to O'Brien he wrote, "I've ceased to become a participator in historic commotions. I've become an impassive spectator."[47] This case of the doldrums was further exhibited early in September during a speech to the T. F. Meagher Club of New York, where he commented, "Six years have elapsed since I first met this club. I was then a dazzling novelty . . . But the most favorite novelties must fade and come down in the market . . . So it was sir, and so it is with me."[48] Despite what must have been heartwarming protests from the audience, it's likely that both Meagher and his audience knew the comment was directly on target.

Meagher's spirits were revived with the visit of William Smith O'Brien in the spring of 1859. O'Brien visited with several of his former Young Ireland colleagues, including John Mitchel in Washington. O'Brien's lingering inability to forgive—much less forget—their differences was expressed in a letter to his wife following his visit with Mitchel, "She [Mitchel's wife, Jenny] is really a charming person and though neither you nor I agree with the political views of Mr. Mitchel there are few persons more beloved by his private friends and family than this formidable monster."[49] O'Brien would end his tour of the United States back in New York his "last days in America were spent as the guest of Peter Townsend, Esq.—Mr. Meagher's father-in-law . . . ."[50] One can't help but wish to know Mr. Townsend's private thoughts on this occasion.

In early June of 1859—about the same time that William Smith O'Brien was concluding his post-exile visit to the United States and Mitchel was leaving for France—Meagher was hired to serve as associate counsel for the legal defense of General Daniel Sickles. The basis of this highly publicized case was Sickles's murder of Phillip Barton Key—son of Francis Scott Key, composer of the poem which became the national anthem of the United States. Sickles had shot Key, who was unarmed, in broad daylight after proclaiming that Key was "the despoiler of his home."[51] The defense team successfully convinced the jury that Sickles's action was reasonable in view of the affair Key had with his wife.

Meagher's time as a player on the national and international stage would continue as a result of his "expertise" on Central America, which had caught the attention of Ambrose Thompson. Thompson was an American ship line owner who had a dream that was well suited for Meagher's talents and connections. By late 1859, Thompson had retained Meagher as his special counsel for a plan known as the Chiriqui Improvement Company. Under the banner of this company, Thompson intended to build a railway connection between the Atlantic and Pacific oceans. Meagher eagerly accepted this new assignment, navigating the negotiations through some very troubled political waters in Central America. As a result of Meagher's efforts, the government of Costa Rica awarded the Chiriqui Improvement Company a land grant in July of 1860 that allowed for a right-of-way through their country. To further promote this plan, Meagher even attempted to win public support back in the United States with another *Harper's* article entitled "The New Route Through Chiriqui."[52] This triumph, and any potential for long-term financial benefits, proved to be short-lived for Meagher and Thompson. Despite having the support of President Buchanan, the U.S. Senate would not approve the contract Thompson had negotiated with Secretary of the Navy Gideon Welles for the transoceanic railroad project. There was too much concern with the country of New Granada's (present-day Colombia) border issues with Costa Rica and, perhaps more significantly, the American-based Panama Railroad Company's insisting upon its earlier claim for the rights to a similar venture through Panama.[53]

During Meagher's journey to Costa Rica, he apparently served as a government courier. In a letter to John Fogle, written while aboard the ship *Northern Light*, he excused his abrupt departure from a chance meeting with Fogle, explaining that he was off to " . . . seize the opportunity offered me by the White House. I had already intended to go to Costa Rica a month or two later however—and these Dispatches precipitated my leaving . . . ."[54] Meagher's later attempts to be financially compensated for this service would be ignored, however.

Certainly the years after his initial arrival in New York were marked with several peaks and valleys for Meagher, who seemed to be still drifting in search of his niche. W.F. Lyons recalled this unsettled time in Meagher's life: "The pleasant, hearty, and almost silent laughter . . . will not be easily forgotten by those who shared with him the hours of sunshine . . . which existed between the stormy passages of his political career in Ireland, his penal exile in Australia, and his advent upon a new battle-field as a soldier. During that period it may be said that Meagher had no well-defined purpose in life, except the general one which was born with him, to be something great and useful in the world."[55] As Thomas Francis Meagher sailed into New York harbor aboard the ship *Ariel* from Costa Rica in late January 1861, he may well have been viewing the city, and his future, with eyes which lacked any of the starry optimism he had known in May of 1852. It's unlikely, even with his characteristically bold self-confidence, that he could have imagined his star would soon be on the rise once again—and that a great and useful calling still awaited him.

PART III

Life As A Soldier—
The Civil War

CHAPTER 9

"Ye boys of the sod, to Columbia true,
Come up, boys, and fight, for the Red, White and Blue!
Two Countries we love, and two mottoes we'll share,
And we'll join them in one, on the banner we bear:
Erin, mavourneen! Columbia, agra!
E pluribus unum! Erin, go bragh!"

Song of the Irish Legion

Although it's unlikely he would have thought so as he stood on deck the ship *Ariel* slowly cruising into New York harbor in January of 1861, Thomas Francis Meagher's absence from the United States (and his discontinued role as editor of the *Irish News*) during most of the year 1860 was undoubtedly good fortune. Given the sway of popular opinion among Irish-Americans and his own empathy for the Southern states, Meagher very possibly—in fact, probably—would have spoken out in political opposition to Abraham Lincoln. The likely consequences of such criticism would have been not only the antagonism of President Lincoln, but almost certainly also the lost continued support of William Seward, whom Lincoln would appoint as his secretary of state. Much to his good fortune, the rapid pace of events gave him little time to absorb or to publicly react to the dynamics of a nation being torn apart. For a man who had won his fame as a spokesperson for rebellion, he was apparently stunned to silence by the actual secession of the Southern states.

When the actual hostilities of the Civil War became reality with the April 12 attack on Fort Sumter, Meagher made what could have been regarded as a surprising decision by aligning himself with the Union. Considering his very pro-Southern position in the past, one could have expected Meagher to align with the Confederacy, as did his friend John Mitchel. Meagher had certainly made no secret of his sympathies for their cause of rebellion through various public statements and editorials, and there were many in the South who felt betrayed by his announcement to support the Union cause. In sentiment typical of that expressed throughout the Confederate States, *The Spectator* of Staunton, Virginia, scathingly proclaimed: "Never again shall the name Thomas Francis Meagher be united with any of our Southern institutions."[1] Meagher would not waiver once he had made his decision to support the Union, however. John Mitchel's response was to also follow his convictions— which led south. The two great forces of Young Ireland, the writer and the orator, Mitchel and Meagher, would never meet again.

The 69th Regiment, New York State Militia, under the command of Colonel Michael Corcoran (military commander of the Fenian Brotherhood) was immediately called into active service. There was, interestingly enough, a bit of a glitch in the status of the 69th. At the time the unit was called to service, Corcoran was actually facing a court-martial. The charges against Corcoran stemmed from his refusal to have the 69th march in a New York City parade in October of 1860 honoring the visit of the Prince of Wales. Meagher had enthusiastically endorsed Corcoran's decision, writing that Corcoran "refused lawfully as a citizen, courageously as a soldier, indignantly as an Irishman . . . ."[2] Regardless of whatever malfeasance may have been committed, all charges were quickly dismissed, and Corcoran was ordered to resume command on April 20, 1861.[3] By April 23, Corcoran led approximately 1,000 men of the 69th to Washington, D.C.

In the meantime, Meagher quickly leaped into the patriotic frenzy and raised a company known as the Irish Zouaves. The company included a unit which called itself the Phoenix Zouaves, an existing military group organized under the auspices of the Fenian Brotherhood of New York City. It is especially interesting to note that Meagher observed at this time the potential value to be gained by Irish-Americans in learning warfare tactics, in preparation for the day they would return to claim Ireland from

Great Britain: " . . . if only one in ten of us come back when this war is over, the military experience gained by that one will be of more service in a fight for Ireland's freedom than would that of the entire ten as they are now."[4] Assuredly, the fire of Irish nationalism was still burning brightly in the heart of the Young Rebel.

After their arrival in Washington, a few days following the 69th, Meagher and the Zouaves, formally known as Company K, were directed to serve with Colonel Corcoran. The combined units were assigned to the brigade command of General William T. Sherman. The taciturn Sherman was not generally popular with the free-spirited men of the Irish Brigade, and Meagher sparked what would be an animosity with far-reaching consequences when he referred to Sherman as "a rude, envenomed martinet."[5] The units of Corcoran were assigned on May 21 to a position just outside the city, near Aqueduct Bridge, astride the road leading to Fairfax Court House. There the regiment constructed a base which they named "Fort Corcoran" in honor of their commanding officer. The units remained at this position until July 17 when the orders came to begin an advance toward the Virginia crossroads settlement of Manasass Junction, near a stream known as Bull Run. By this time, Meagher had been promoted from captain to the rank of major and was serving as an aide to Colonel Corcoran.

The advance of the Union Army toward Manassas was dreadfully slow, more attributable to the inexperience of the troops than to any action against them by the Confederates. The 69th moved from their bivouac at Centreville at 3:30 a.m. on July 21, and, by mid-morning, formed itself in position approximately a mile and a half from the enemy lines.[6] After holding in position along the south bank of Bull Run, the Regiment was ordered into the first great battle of America's Civil War. In the matter of a few hours of harshly administered education, the Regiment would learn, along with the rest of the country, that this wasn't going to be a one-battle war—and that the bright red uniforms of the Irish Zouaves made excellent targets. The 69th was held in reserve until approximately 2:30 p.m. At that time, they were ordered to charge against the Confederate position on Henry House Hill. After repeated attempts to take the position, the 69th fell back in retreat at the command of General Sherman. In recalling the action of the day, Meagher would state: "We beat their men—their batteries [artillery] beat us."[7]

Regiment historian Conyngham wrote of the Bull Run engagement that "Meagher's company of Zouaves suffered desperately, their red dress making them a conspicuous mark for the enemy. When Meagher's horse was torn from under him by a rifled cannon ball he is said to have jumped up, waved his sword, and exclaimed, 'Boys! look at the flag—remember Ireland and Fontenoy.'"[8] Whether or not this report is dramatically embellished, it is certain that Meagher did continue to lead his unit after his horse was shot from under him and, during what was to be the final assault, Meagher was again thrown to the ground by a nearby artillery explosion, causing him to momentarily lose consciousness. Meagher was rescued from capture, if not greater harm, by a young Union cavalry soldier who had witnessed his fall and rushed to carry him from the field to a safe position.

Meagher joined in the dispirited retreat of the Union Army, during which insult was added to injury when a Confederate cavalry unit attacked just as a cluster of Yankees were in the process of crossing the small stream known as Cub Run. The Rebel party was quickly dispersed, but the artillery caisson carrying Meagher was overturned, and he was thrown into the stream. The sullen retreat continued, with a slightly dazed, and now sodden, Meagher joining the humbled remnants of the 69th Regiment at the Fort Corcoran encampment. The subsequent tally of casualties would grimly reveal the price of bravery. "The 69th lost thirty-eight men killed, fifty-nine wounded and ninety-five missing in action at Bull Run."[9] Perhaps most noticeably absent from their ranks was Colonel Corcoran, who had been taken prisoner during the retreat action and would remain a prisoner-of-war until August 1862.

Although prominently mentioned in several reports for his bravery in action, Meagher was slandered by an initial report that appeared in the *New York Daily Tribune* which claimed Meagher ran away from battle. The author of the article was William Howard

Russell, a reporter for the *London Times*—and perhaps not an entirely objective source. An apology was soon issued, and the public was assured that Meagher "bore himself with distinguished gallantry."[10] George Wilkes reported in *The Spirit of the Times* on the brave men of the Irish Brigade, and that "Most prominent among them was Meagher, the Irish orator, who frequently, during the contest of that turbulent day, waved the green banner of his regiment up and down the hottest line of fire."[11] Despite some criticism of their retreat, the 69th generally was regarded as one of the "fighting units" of the battle. General Sherman, despite any pre-battle animosities, now spoke well of the Brigade in his reports, and at least two Southern news correspondents also wrote in complimentary terms of the unit's bravery and stubborn fighting spirit. One Southern writer gave a begrudging compliment to the Regiment in his report of the action, stating, "No Southerner but feels that the Sixty-ninth maintained the old reputation of Irish valor—on the wrong side. All honor to the Sixty-ninth, even in its errors."[12]

The 69th was one of several Union regiments that had signed a three-month term of enlistment. When the unit's obligation expired on July 24, the 69th returned to New York with great fanfare. Meagher found himself honored as a war hero and in much demand as the featured speaker for events honoring the soldiers of the 69th, as well as events to raise funds for the widows and orphans of their fallen comrades. Additionally, there was almost an immediate effort launched to avenge the humiliation of Bull Run. If he had not already done so by the time of his arrival in New York, Meagher apparently determined very soon afterward to return to active service. In a letter to John F. Fogle, Meagher would write, "I fear Mrs. Fogle is inflamed against me for going out again—but the disgrace of the Bull Run affair afflicts each one personally engaged in it, in the first place, and, in the second, I have become everyday more and more deeply persuaded of the justice and righteousness of the Federal Cause."[13]

Meagher initially refused offers of appointments in the Union army, including one to serve with the rank of Colonel as an aide to the hugely popular Major-General John Fremont, by stating that "I have no ambition to increase the catalog of blunderers and imposters."[14] Among those urging him to accept a command position appears to have been his wife, Elizabeth. Author Thomas Keneally writes of an incident witnessed by Maria Daly, a friend of the Meagher's, who observed an exchange between husband and wife. "In the carriage [Meagher] exchanged a very equivocal glance with his wife [telling her that he would not accept a command] 'No, Lizzie,' said he, 'no, I certainly will not. You may look as cross as you please.'"[15] Whatever the source of motivation may have been, Meagher soon found the necessary ambition, however, and accepted an offer from the War Department to serve as the Colonel of a re-formed 69th Regiment with the accompanying authorization to raise additional regiments.

Meagher would zealously invest himself and his considerable powers of persuasion in this mission to serve the Union. In a speech before an estimated crowd of 50,000 at Jones' Woods (a park of New York City), Meagher challenged his countrymen by declaring, "I ask no Irishman to do that which I myself am not prepared to do. My heart, my arm, my life are pledged to the national cause, and to the last it it will be my highest pride, as I conceive it my holiest duty and obligation, to share in its fortunes."[16] The 69th was re-established by the end of August, with their term of service being the duration of the war. "Men flocked in crowds to the headquarters of the brigade, at No. 596 Broadway, above the Metropolitan Hotel, and were enrolled . . . for Meagher was present there day by day, attending to all the details of the organization, until the brigade was sent to Fort Schuyler."[17] When considering the context of the time, Meagher's achievement merits an even greater appreciation. Many Irish were painfully aware of their second-class status attributable, in part, to the Know-Nothing movement. The men to whom Meagher made his appeals included many who had every reason to feel disenfranchised from America's promise. Moreover, many of the recent emigrants—including the Irish—were concerned with the effect the abolition of slavery may have upon their already tenuous economic toehold. There were also those who paralleled the Southern rebellion to that of Ireland's political struggle. Consequently, most Irish were, if not opposed to the Union's cause, were at least ambivalent. Meagher's outspoken support for the Union, therefore, represents a significant episode in the great drama's early acts.

It was also during this time that Meagher paid tribute to another fallen comrade. In mid-January, Terence McManus had died in San Francisco. McManus had escaped Van Dieman's Land prior to Meagher and had made his home in California. It had been the last request of McManus that he be buried in the soil of Ireland. The San Francisco Circle of the Fenian Brotherhood, in cooperation with the New York City Circle, worked to honor the wishes of the former Young Ireland patriot. Meagher, although not a Fenian, was appointed chairman of the New York memorial committee, and he arranged for a memorial mass to be held when the remains of his friend arrived from California. The mass was celebrated on September 13 by Archbishop Hughes, who used the occasion to remark that the Church did sanction cases of attempts to overthrow a tyrannical government if three conditions were met. Archbishop Hughes stated that the conditions, as prescribed by St. Thomas Aquinas, were: "(1) The grievance must be genuine; there must be an actual oppression of the people, (2) the impulse to resist must be general among the population, and (3) the possession of the means and ability wherewith to accomplish, with a reasonable hope of success . . . if they have not the ability and the other conditions requisite it becomes a crime to undertake the task . . . in the case to which I have referred there can be no reproach. The young man . . . to whose memory and remains you pay your respects, was one who was willing to sacrifice—and may I say did sacrifice— his prospects in life, and even his life itself, for the freedom of the country which he loved so well . . . ."[18] After spending more than a month at Calvary Cemetery, the body of McManus left New York on October 19 and was finally interred in his native land, a land he had last viewed from the deck of the prison ship *Swift*.

CHAPTER 10

*"... Colonel Meagher, aided by his numerous friends and
friends of the cause, decided on forming an Irish Brigade...."*
David Conyngham

Meagher eagerly threw himself to the task of raising additional
units of Irish volunteers in New York City and soliciting his
numerous contacts in Boston to do likewise. Meagher's oratory
skills in this energized environment proved to be tailor-made for
the task. In his recruiting speeches in New York and Boston, Meager
regularly made the point to his Irish audiences that the government
of England was hopeful the South would win the war. It is very
likely Meagher employed this impassioned rhetoric to not only
fuel the enlistment rolls, but also to keep alive the dream of Irish
nationalism and Irish unity. Conyngham describes one such address:
"Meagher delivered one of his most brilliant addresses to a crowded
audience in the Academy of Music . . . The gifted speaker seemed
almost inspired as he described the many battle-fields in which
the Irish soldier had made his mark . . . and the duty Irishmen
owed to a Government which threw open its protecting arms to
receive them . . . This truly eloquent speech had good effect, and
brought many a stalwart recruit to the ranks of the Irish Brigade."[19]
Among his remarks during this speech was the statement: "As for
the cause of Ireland, and for the cause of the South, to these same
apologists of the South . . . when they ask me how it is possible
that while I contended for the independence of Ireland, I am
opposed to the independence of the South, I answer this, had
Ireland been under the enjoyment of such privileges and such
rights, and such guaranteed independence as South Carolina
enjoyed, I would not have been here tonight . . . ."[20]

The effectiveness of Meagher's recruiting efforts was grudgingly acknowledged by Mr. S. C. Hayes, a Southern sympathizer living in Philadelphia. Mr. Hayes would report to the Confederate president, Jefferson Davis, that, "After the first battle of Manassas, T. F. Meagher came to Philadelphia to drum up recruits for his Irish Brigade. He made a capital speech; I feared a telling one. I worked night and day to neutralize his speech. His treatment of the Irish girl who aided him in making his escape from Australia, and his subsequent marriage with a Yankee girl, was an admirable argument against him."[21] Hayes also suggested that there were large numbers of Irish in the North who would willingly fight for the Confederacy in response to their bitterness with the Know Nothing's policies and potential effects of abolition. Apparently Davis considered this possibility seriously enough to refer Hayes's letter to Braxton Bragg, who responded: "This paper contains suggestions which I deem valuable and practicable. The employment of some judicious person to operate on this class of people through our own press and that of the North would no doubt be attended with good results."[22]

It had been the original intention of the Brigade organizers that General James Shields, another native son of Ireland and regular army officer, would serve as the unit commander. In addition to having served with distinction in the Blackhawk War and Mexican War, Shields had the dubious honor of already being a footnote in history. Shields once challenged Abraham Lincoln (long prior to his election as president) to a duel—a matter that was resolved peacefully and to mutual good feelings. Shields was on a duty assignment in California and, as no confirmation of his appointment came forth, an order went out dated October 21, 1861, ordering the newly enlisted companies to report no later than October 25 to Fort Schuyler, New York. The order was signed by "Acting Brigadier-General" Thomas Francis Meagher.

The Brigade spent a generally pleasant time at Fort Schuyler as they went through what may best be described as a casual basic training. Many of the men were regularly visited during this time by their wives and children. The atmosphere was so relaxed that

Meagher urgently requested the War Department to assign the Brigade to a post removed from the proximity of New York City. Meagher would also spend the time attending to the hundreds of details associated with preparing the units for war, including ordering their armaments. "[Meagher] specifically requested .69 caliber smoothbores . . . although these guns were deemed obsolete by many, Meagher felt that smoothbores loaded with 'buck and ball' were the most effective weapons available for the close fighting he envisioned for his Irishmen."[23] Meagher's choice would prove to be appropriate.

On November 18, a ceremony was held to present the regiment with flags which had been prepared largely due to the efforts of Elizabeth Meagher. The ceremony was held at the residence of Archbishop Hughes and attended by many of the city's prominent citizens and hundreds of spectators, in addition to the men of the Irish Brigade. "The regimental flags were of a deep rich green, heavily fringed, having in the centre a richly embroidered Irish harp, with a sunburst above it and a wreath of shamrock beneath. The staff-mountings were silver-plated; the top being a pike-head, under which was knotted a long bannerol of saffron-colored silk, fringed with bullion, and marked with the number of the regiment."[24] Each of the regiments accepted their colors (the 63rd had actually received their flag in an earlier ceremony) with a speech from the respective regiment commander. Meagher—who was expected to serve as colonel for the 5th Regiment—made a brief acceptance response, which concluded with the charge to his regiment: "Boys, look on those flags; remember the 18th of November; think of those who presented them to you; die if necessary, but never surrender."[25] At the conclusion of the ceremonies, Acting Brigadier-General Meagher led the newly re-formed 69th Regiment of the Brigade toward Washington, proudly carrying their distinctive flags of emerald green and gold. The 69th was joined within the next few weeks by their comrades of the 63rd and 88th New York Regiments, also escorted by Meagher.

CHAPTER 11

Raim Nar Druid O Sbairn Lann
("Who Never Retreated From the Clash of Lances")
Motto of the Irish Brigade

The regiments of the Irish Brigade were assigned to a division under the command of Edwin V. Sumner, a brigadier-general in the "regular army." The Brigade was assigned an encampment area near Alexandria, on the Fairfax turnpike, and established a base known as Camp California. Chaplain William Corby, C.S.C., who joined the Brigade while at Camp California, offers a portrait of Meagher during this time: " . . . Meagher was more than an ordinary gentleman . . . He possessed high-toned sentiments and manners, and the bearing of a prince. He had a superior intellect, a liberal education, was a fine classical writer, and a born orator. He was very witty, but more inclined to humor; was fond of witty or humorous persons, and admired those who possessed such gifts. He was a great lover of his native land, and passionately opposed to its enemies . . . wherever he went he made himself known as a 'Catholic and an Irishman.'"[26]

It was customary for the army's officers to provide their own uniforms, and Meagher and his staff weren't modest in their appearance. "Gen. Meagher's staff was . . . composed of gallant young officers, who were decked out not only with the regulation gold straps, stripes and cords on their coats, trousers, and hats, but they had also great Austrian knots of gold on the shoulders, besides numerous other ornamentation in gold, which glittered in the Virginia sun enough to dazzle one."[27] The eager new regiments and their dazzling officers, along with the rest of the Army of the Potomac, spent the fall and winter in drills and preparations for what all hoped would be a decisive spring campaign.

It was also during this winter hiatus that Meagher officially received command of the Brigade. General Shields had arrived in Washington on January 5, 1862, from California and made it clear he did not want the assignment as commander of the Irish Brigade. Shields publicly deferred the appointment on the excuse of his health, but it is also reasonable to assume that he did not wish to take what would have been a loss in rank. At the same time, Shields added his support to the appointment of Meagher as commanding officer, putting to rest rumors of conflict between the two men. Shields clearly cited his personal feelings during a public speech in Washington, where he declared, "No, Meagher, they can never estrange you and me; we understand each other too well for that . . . the love of brothers will always exist between us."[28]

A report in the *Irish American* mentioned that President Lincoln had been encouraged to submit Meagher's name for the rank of brigadier-general.[29] In a meeting with Lincoln, a group of the Brigade's officers and prominent supporters—including Colonel Frank Blair (a former congressman from Missouri and brother of the Postmaster General), Colonel John W. Forney, and Senator Preston King of New York—urged that Meagher be awarded command of the Irish Brigade.[30] In the petition which was submitted on Meagher's behalf, it was pointed out that he was not only influential in attracting Union Army enlistments, but he also might have an even more significant benefit to the Union cause in the days to come: " . . . a large majority of Irishmen, who from previous political associations, still sympathized with the South, hesitated to what course they should pursue. Stimulated by the example of Thomas Francis Meagher they threw their former associations to the winds, clung to the flag of their adopted Country [and] formed Companies and Regiments of Irishmen." Continuing, the petitioners cited, "Nor is this [Meagher's] influence confined to the United States. It exists in Ireland, where millions of Irishmen look to him as their prophet and their guide . . . and if war with England would arise no man could, by his influence with the Irish race, so effectually strike a blow at the power of that Country by attacking her in Ireland, in the Canadas, in Australia, nay in England itself as Colonel Meagher."[31]

Lincoln submitted a recommendation for Meagher to serve as brigadier-general following the meeting, and the Senate confirmed this appointment on February 3, 1862. Unquestionably, Meagher lacked the level of military experience one would normally expect of an officer at that rank. It is equally obvious, however, that these were not "normal" times, and many others were also being placed into situations where it was expected they would learn their role just as the men who served under them. Certainly there could have been no question that the men of the Irish Brigade respected Meagher, and that he had already demonstrated the courage to lead men in battle. Nevertheless, Meagher continued to press for Shields's leadership (at this point and also later on), and petitioned Secretary of War Edwin Stanton to consolidate all Irish units into a division to be led by General Shields. Nothing was to come of this proposal, though Shields did serve a brief tour of active duty before finally resigning his commission in March 1863.

The much-anticipated spring action began when the Peninsula Campaign opened on March 15, 1862. Now under the command of Major General George B. McClellan, the Army of the Potomac awoke from their hibernation and began moving from their camps in and around Washington. The Irish Brigade was initially held to check any possible Confederate action toward the capital before moving south in late March via transport ships to Fort Monroe, Virginia. After enduring miserable weather conditions during the transport, the Brigade then marched along roads that had turned to deep mud to an assigned camp position near Yorktown, Virginia. The Brigade assumed the duties of unloading equipment transports and attempting to make roads passable by corduroying, but also found ways to entertain themselves. In an entry dated May 31, Conyngham wrote an interesting profile of a soldier's life while in camp: " . . . men playing football, a mule race for drummer-boys, and a horse race ('The Chickahominy Steeple-Chase') was organized—with the First Prize being 'A magnificent tiger-skin, presented by General Meagher, the spoil of his own gun in Central America.'"[32] For the benefit of those with an insatiable appetite for Civil War trivia, the race winner was "Katie Darling," ridden by Major Cavanagh. A theatre performance had also been planned for that evening, but it was quickly cancelled when cannon fire announced the curtain rise of another dramatic performance—the battle of Fair Oaks.

CHAPTER 12

Faugh a Ballagh
("*Clear the Way*")
Gaelic battle cry of the Irish Brigade

On their way to their first action under fire, the Irish Brigade had to first march several miles through swampy ground and cross the Chickahominy River during the night of May 31. The Brigade would play a critically important role in the action, by reinforcing the right flank which was under the command of General Erasmus Keyes. By 4:00 a.m. on June 1 the Brigade was in position along a railroad grade opposite the rebels. The 69th deployed to the left front, the 88th attaching to the 69th's left and linking with the 5th New Hampshire.[33]

The Confederate forces they opposed were under the command of General Kirby Smith. Smith's division had expected their attack to hit an exposed right flank of Keyes; however, the Irish Brigade and other units of Sumner's command had found their way into the critical, though unenviable, position of being between Smith's units and their intended target. "Johnston's juggernaut attack plan seemed at last to be rolling toward a repetition of his triumph at Manassas . . . but not for long. Aimed at Keyes, it struck instead a substantial body of men in muddy blue, who stood and delivered massed volleys that broke up the attack before it could gather speed."[34] Conyngham cites the bravery of Meagher in this engagement. "General Meagher and staff were indefatigable, riding from line to line, cheering on the men. The general was all the time under fire."[35] Another report by a Captain Fields of a Union artillery unit stated, "We saw General Sumner ride up to the Irish Brigade . . . he evidently made a short speech . . . We learned afterwards that he told them that they were his last hope . . . 'I want to see how Irishmen fight, and when you run I'll run too' . . . the brigade moved into the woods with the air of men who were going to stay . . . the fire was deafening, then it began to retire. The yells gave way to long continuous cheers . . . the battle of Fair Oaks was won . . . from that day the General swore by the Irish Brigade."[36]

In sharp contrast to the lighthearted account of the games and races he had previously offered, Conyngham described the gory aftermath of action on June 1 when he visited a field hospital. "It looks like a perfect butcher's shambles, with maimed and bloody men lying on all sides; some with their arms off; some with their legs off; some awaiting their turn; while the doctors, with upturned cuffs and bloody hands, are flourishing their fearful knives and saws around, and piles of raw, bloody-looking limbs are strewn around them: while some who have died on the dissecting-table, add to the ghastly picture. I stayed a few moments, looking on, but the ghastly picture affected me more than the roar and din of battle. I felt faint, and had to get stimulants to revive me."[37]

Following the battle at Fair Oaks, the Irish Brigade was appreciatively reinforced with the 29th Massachusetts Regiment on June 9. Generally from well-established, New England Protestant families, " . . . an outfit so rich in colonial stock that it would have been at home aboard the *Mayflower*,"[38] these men represented a distinct contrast to the other units of the Brigade; but they would also prove to be gritty and determined soldiers and were soon to see their first action with the Brigade. For eight consecutive nights the Brigade held picket duty before the Union front. By the 25th of June, McClellan had abandoned the idea of continuing his advance upon Richmond. Through a series of defensive retreats, McClellan was moving his troops and base of operations in a southeasterly direction toward the James River. In response, Confederate troops under the command of Thomas ("Stonewall") Jackson were moving against the right flank of McClellan's army, threatening to cut the possible line of retreat.

General Robert E. Lee had assumed command of Confederate

forces following the wounding of Joe Johnston, and Lee made the decision to press the reticent McClellan with a general advance of the Rebel army. The Irish Brigade was sent into support of General Fitz John Porter's units, who were attempting to hold the right wing of the Union forces at Gaines' Mill on June 26. The Brigade's determined resistance stemmed what had been a rout in the making and earned considerable praise from both Union and Confederate troops. Conyngham relates an incident which took place as the Brigade came to the relief of the 9th Massachusetts Infantry, commanded by Colonel Thomas Cass. "General Meagher was at the head of his Brigade: when he saw the colonel in his shirt, all covered with blood and dirt, he called out, 'Colonel Cass, is this you?' 'Hallo, General Meagher, is this the Irish Brigade? Thank God, we are saved.'"[39] The Confederate forces eventually won the ground after a fierce struggle, though, and the Union troops withdrew to stage subsequent "defensive victories" at Savage Station and White Oak Swamp on June 29 and 30, respectively.

In Meagher's official report of the engagements from June 27 to June 30 there is a notation by Meagher that he had been "temporarily placed under arrest" from approximately 4:00 p.m. on June 28 until 8:00 p.m. on the twenty-ninth.[40] No further details are provided in his report, and this author has been unable to determine what the circumstances of this arrest may have been. It does seem reasonable to assume that the infraction—or alleged infraction—must have been relatively minor inasmuch as Meagher was returned to command in such short order.

In the pre-dawn hours of Monday, July 1, following yet another night march, the Irish Brigade found themselves forming another defensive position at Malvern Hill. The Brigade was able to take some rest until late afternoon when four of the regiments were ordered to move against Confederates, while the 29th Massachusetts and 63rd New York were held to support some artillery batteries. As they went into action against the Rebels, the Brigade was met again by the remnants of the 9th Massachusetts—this time carrying the dying Colonel Cass. Once more the Irish Brigade found itself in a bitter struggle, and once more Meagher was in the thick of the furious action. "General Meagher and his staff rode along the lines, cheering and encouraging his men."[41] The Confederate forces repeatedly made desperate attempts to win the position but were finally withdrawn after fearful losses to both sides. Confederate General D. H. Hill may have best summarized the day's carnage by stating, "It was not war, it was murder."[42]

Darkness brought an end to the day's fighting, and the Union army pulled back, the Irish Brigade being among the last to leave the field. Despite the urging of several of his unit commanders, McClellan ordered the Army of the Potomac to complete its withdrawl to the relative safety of Harrison's Landing, on the banks of the James River. Now that Richmond was out of any immediate danger, General Robert E. Lee seemed equally content to call a halt to the hostilities, particularly in consideration of the awesome artillery firepower offered by the Union gunboats which were strategically anchored in position on the James.

The Irish Brigade, as well as many other Union brigades, had experienced heavy losses during the Peninsula campaign. It is estimated that McClellan's army suffered 20,000 casualties, although McClellan himself reported approximately 16,000 casualties.[43] By Meagher's own accounts, the Irish Brigade required approximately 1,000 men to replenish its troops and return to the minimum standard of 750 each for the regimental units.[44] The only actions which followed were nuisance sorties by Lee's troops designed to hold McClellan in place while Stonewall Jackson slipped back north into the Shenandoah Valley with his "foot cavalry" veterans. So, while the Brigade enjoyed a respite, Meagher, with the permission and encouragement of McClellan, returned to New York in an attempt to recruit replacements.[45]

One of the first recruiting meetings was held at the armory of the Seventh Regiment (NYSM) in New York City on July 25, 1862. "The vast room (the largest in the city, capable of holding about five thousand persons) was crowded to such a degree that large numbers, unable to bear the excessive heat, were compelled to go away. Their places, however, were as quickly supplied by new-comers . . . ."[46] Meagher was the featured speaker for the occasion, and he recounted the gallant service of the Irish Brigade in its engagements. Meagher's dramatic remarks wove comparisons between the struggle to save the Union with the struggles of Ireland and blended the names of fabled Irish martyrs with those men now fighting and dying on American soil. Perhaps one of the most moving portions of Meagher's address, occurred when he read a letter he had received from Lieutenant John H. Donovan.

Donovan had been severely wounded, and taken prisoner, at the battle of Malvern Hill. He was later released in a prisoner exchange and had recently corresponded to Meagher from Bellevue Hospital in New York City. In his letter, Lt. Donovan had written of his experience while in a Richmond hospital. "Generals Hill and Magruder visited the wounded the morning after the battle. General Hill . . . asked me the name of my regiment. I told him the name of my regiment and brigade with the greatest pride, when the general quietly passed away. I was told at Richmond, that had they known the precise whereabouts of the Irish Brigade on the field, they would have sent a whole division to take itself and General Meagher prisoners, and hang the 'exiled traitor' from the highest tree in Richmond."[47]

Meagher had been hopeful that another of his young officers, Lieutenant Temple Emmet, who served as a devoted and courageous aide to Meagher, would receive better medical attention at home, and asked the young man to accompany him to New York. Lieutenant Emmet was the grand-nephew of the legendary Irish Revolutionary, Robert Emmet. Tragically, the young officer had contracted typhoid fever during the Peninsula campaign and, despite dedicated care, died during leave at the home of his father on Long Island.

Meagher was also joined in his recruiting tour by the war hero, and his former legal client, General Dan Sickles. Despite Meagher's passionate speeches to large crowds and the enthusiastic cheers of the audiences, attempts to raise additional volunteers had little success. As Meagher would write to President Lincoln, "I have been detailed here for a few days—as you are probably aware—for the purpose of filling up the exhausted ranks of the Irish Brigade.

It is, with all my popularity and influence, to tell the truth, an up-hill work . . . though thousands upon thousands cheer me as I entreat and exhort them to rally round and stand to the last by the glorious Flag of the Union."[48] Meagher would close his letter by suggesting that the primary cause of his difficulties in recruiting men to serve was the deep animosity felt by Irish-Americans regarding the Senate's refusal to appoint General Shields to the rank of major general.[49]

While the Senate's snub of Shields may have rankled some Irish-Americans, it appears more likely that this was a cause Meagher espoused from a sense of personal loyalty. The lack of volunteers may have actually been more attributable to the imminent enlistment draft for the Union. Those men who were inclined to serve very likely knew there was opportunity to earn more money as a draft substitute, rather than as an enlisted man, inasmuch as the standard pay one received as a volunteer was less than the pay one received as a draftee.

Despite McClellan's belief that there was still value in an extended Peninsula Campaign, General-in-Chief Henry W. Halleck ordered him on August 3 to abandon the position at Harrison's Landing and return north with the Army of the Potomac. Moreover, McClellan was advised that he was now removed from command of the Union Army. The Irish Brigade, which was now under the temporary command of Lieutenant Colonel James Kelly in Meagher's absence, was transported from Newport News, via Aquia Creek, to its old campground near Alexandria. There Meagher rejoined his units, with little to show for his recruiting efforts. Before they had time to recuperate from their travels, the Brigade was quickly again on the march toward familiar—unpleasantly familiar—ground to some of the veterans of the 69th Regiment, Bull Run Creek.

For once, the Irish Brigade was spared a prominent role in battle. In what is known as Second Bull Run, the Brigade was called up only after the Union Army was already in retreat; consequently, they were essentially used only as part of the rear-guard to cover the demoralized retreat of the Union army. This brutal defeat marked the end of John Pope's very brief, and reluctant, term as commander of the Army of the Potomac and the reappointment of George McClellan. The Brigade was subsequently ordered to briefly encamp near Tenallytown but was soon on the march again toward the village of Sharpsburg, Maryland, and another little waterway known as Antietam Creek.

CHAPTER 13

" . . . after several hours of fighting the sunken road,
since known as 'Bloody Lane,' was in our hands . . . ."
Major General Jacob D. Cox

As the next campaign began, the Irish Brigade was now serving under the division command of Major General Israel Richardson. General Richardson was a respected regular army veteran whose First Division, II Corps, included units who had also earned respect on the battlefield. "His division contained veterans with solid reputations of their own. Of the three brigades, under Thomas F. Meagher, John C. Caldwell, and John R. Brooke, Meagher's was the most famous. It was celebrated as the Irish Brigade, 63rd, 69th, and 88th New York . . . ."[50] On September 14, the Irish Brigade arrived Antietam Creek at a point approximately a mile-and-a—half northeast of Sharpsburg and made an uneasy camp. Their position was the approximate center of the Union army, within a "V" formed by the Hagerstown Road on their right and Boonsboro Road on their left. In the pre-dawn glow of the seventeenth, Captain Jack Gosson encountered Meagher as he arose from an attempt to sleep on the ground, and Gosson offered to brush the General's uniform. Meagher replied, "we shall all have a brush soon."[51] At dawn on September 17, the horrible day of killing that would brush away the lives of so many young men began.

With the day's first light, action opened on the far right wing of the Union positions in an area afterwards known as the "West Wood" and rolled ominously toward the Brigade through killing fields called the "Cornfield" and the "East Wood." It was nearly 10:30 a.m. when the Irish Brigade would take its turn at memorializing with their blood and lives another physical feature of the Antietam battlefield, this one known as the "Sunken Road."

The Confederate forces under the command of General D. H. Hill had taken a position within a depression which served as a connecting pathway between the Hagerstown and Boonsboro roads. In addition to the protection offered by this natural depression, the Confederate troops had used wooden fence rails to build a breastworks atop the ravine and facing the Union position. The Brigade crossed Antietam Creek at a ford approximately one mile to the right of their bivouac position, and then proceeded up a slope to the edge of a cornfield. Passing through this field they encountered a fence at the edge of a clover field, just 300 yards from the enemy line. Meagher directed the Brigade into formation with the 69th and 29th regiments on the right and the 63rd and 88th to the left. Meagher remained near the 69th for "five or six volleys," then gave the order for all units to charge.[52] Across the clover field then a space of plowed ground fronting the Sunken Road charged the Irish Brigade, with Meagher conspicuously at the front of his command. The advance line of the Confederates quickly withdrew to join their comrades in the Sunken Road. The Brigade slowly, but steadily, advanced across the field in the face of unrelenting enemy fire, with the constant encouragement of Meagher. A thunderclap of gunfire greeted them as they reached the ridgeline, in volume the greatest yet delivered from the Sunken Road. "Boys, raise the colors and follow me!" Meagher shouted as his shattered line recoiled. The 63rd and 69th New York each lost some sixty percent of their numbers, most of them in these first minutes of combat.[53] In open ground, amidst a deadly hailstorm of minnie balls, the men of the Brigade, many forced to seek additional ammunition from their fallen comrades, relentlessly held their position. The engagement would last for nearly four hellish hours. Meagher later summarized the Brigade's time before the Sunken Road: "Advancing on the right and left obliquely from the center, the brigade poured in an effective and powerful fire upon the column, which it was their special duty to dislodge. Despite a fire of musketry, which literally cut lanes through our approaching line, the brigade advance under my personal command within 30 paces of the enemy . . . and thus the brigade . . . stood and delivered its fire, persistently and effectually maintaining every inch of the ground they occupied, until Brigadier-General Caldwell, bringing up his brigade, enabled my brigade . . . to retire to the second line of defense."[54]

McClellan's own report of the day's action also testified to the bravery of the command: "The Irish Brigade sustained its well-earned reputation. After suffering terribly in officers and men, and strewing the ground with their enemies as they drove them back, their ammunition nearly expended, and the commander, General Meagher, disabled by a fall from his horse shot under him, this Brigade was ordered to give place to General Caldwell's brigade . . . ."[55] The 29th Massachusetts, supplemented by the fresh Union troops of Caldwell, managed to complete the push which forced the Confederates to abandon their position and quickly retreat. After only a brief rest, the Irish Brigade drew more ammunition and was sent forward again to help hold the field in the event of a counter-attack—which never came. Meanwhile, Meagher had been carried from the field not only stunned from his fall, but also with a badly injured knee and "clothes perforated with bullets . . . ."[56] By the end of the day's fighting, it is estimated there were combined Union and Confederate casualties in excess of 13,000 men—the bloodiest day in history for Americans. In his official report of the day's engagement, Meagher stated that less than 500 men of the Brigade left the field. Among the heaps of fallen men before the Sunken Road lay John Kavanagh, who had been previously wounded in another battle in his homeland, the Battle of Ballingarry.[57]

Perhaps the most grievous loss at Antietam for the Union army, however, was one of lost opportunity. Despite having knowledge (from an intercepted communiqué) that Lee had divided his forces, McClellan had tentatively—some may say timidly—utilized his superior forces and thereby squandered an opportunity to thoroughly defeat the Army of Northern Virginia. General Longstreet would write following the war that, "Nearly one-fourth of the troops who went into the battle were killed or wounded. We were so badly crushed that at the close of the day ten thousand fresh troops could have come in and taken Lee's army and everything it had."[58]

Meagher had sufficiently recovered from his injuries to resume command September 18 and, after a very cautious delay, the Union army began its tentative movement south on September 20. The Irish Brigade was posted to an area near Harper's Ferry known as Bolivar Heights, where they remained encamped until early November. While at Bolivar Heights the 116th Pennsylvania and the 28th Massachusetts regiments were assigned to Meagher's command. The 116th was a mix of Irish and German heritage soldiers from the Philadelphia area, and the 28th a predominately Irish unit from Boston. The 29th Massachusetts, which had served with distinction as part of the Brigade but never truly formed a kinship, was reassigned.

Lieutenant Colonel St. Clair Mulholland of the 116th later recounted their welcome the Brigade that "was a celebrated one, renowned for hard fighting and famous fun."[59] "Towards evening . . . General Thomas Francis Meagher, came to make a courtesy visit to his new command. He came in state, splendidly mounted, and surrounded by a brilliant staff, the members of which seemed to wear a deal more gold lace than the regulations called for. Meagher was a handsome man, stately and courteous, with a wonderful flow of language and ideas. When the canteen had been passed around the conversation become animated, Meagher displaying a most gracious manner that was captivating and charming to a remarkable degree, forming a strange contrast to his mood at times when he tried to be stern and when his manner was not so affable. A pleasant evening it was and, when the General and his gorgeous staff rode away in the darkness, he left a pleasing impression behind him."[60]

The new units had an opportunity to see action with the Brigade's veterans in a skirmish known as the Battle of Charlestown on October 16 before moving, with the rest of the army, to a new encampment at Warrentown. It was while at Warrenton, on

November 7, that McClellan, who was very popular with the Irish Brigade—as well as most of the men under his command—was relieved from duty for the second, and final, time. Meagher dramatically reflected the attitude of many soldiers when, during McClellan's final review of the Army of the Potomac, "Brigadier Thomas Meagher had the color-bearers of his Irish Brigade throw their emerald banners on the ground before the general in a flamboyant gesture of devotion and protest; McClellan ordered the colors picked up before he would proceed." Meagher would later write, "Ah if the gentlemen of the White House could have seen what I saw this morning—could have heard the cheers from those 100,000 soldiers which rent the aid and deadened the artillery itself as the parting salute was fired—they would have felt that a mistake or crime has been committed by them, which the Army of the Union will never forgive."[61]

McClellan's controversial removal prompted several requests for resignations from officers within the Irish Brigade. In response, Meagher issued General Order No. 10 on November 19 in which he clearly stated he would deny any such requests. In addition to his refusal to accept resignations, Meagher, with typical eloquence, and despite what must have been some strong personal feelings for McClellan, would write that " . . . the great error of the Irish people in their struggle for an independent national existence, has been their passionate and blind adherence to an individual, instead of a principle or cause. Thus for generations their heroic efforts in the right direction has been feverish and spasmodic, when they should have been continuous, equable and consistent."[62] This statement provides a wonderful insight to Meagher. Not only would it seem that—even in the midst of America's greatest conflict—the struggle for Irish nationalism and the passion for his heritage was never far from his mind, but it suggests a self-deprecating attitude toward his own role in the Irish nationalism movement.

CHAPTER 14

*"When the Union troops . . . deployed upon the plain
in front of Marye's Heights, every man in the ranks knew
that it was not to fight. It was to die."*

St. Clair Mulholland

The late autumn of 1862 would find the strong pillars of Young Ireland, Meagher and Mitchel, just a few miles apart. Mitchel, with his youngest son, Willy, had returned to the United States in October after a brief stay in France and was living in Richmond. Mitchel had quickly immersed himself once again in stormy waters by assuming the position of editor of the *Richmond Daily Enquirer*.[63] Meanwhile, the Irish Brigade was encamped along the Rappahannock River opposite Fredericksburg, Virginia, and, once again, a delay by the Union army commander (now Ambrose Burnside) would result in another lost opportunity—and another horrific slaughter.

Virtually all the Union troops thought their position was one they would maintain, and eagerly constructed winter quarters to provide some relief against the cold. The lines Peter Welsh of the 28th Massachusetts wrote to his wife reflected the consensus of thousands of campfire strategists, " . . . there is no probability of our having a battle here at present and it is doutfull if there will be any fighting done at this point atall We have comenced to build houses here for winter quarters so that looks like stopping here for some time."[64] So relaxed were the attitudes of the men—both Union and Confederate—that it wasn't uncommon for those on picket duty to exchange conversation and barter such treasures as coffee, tobacco, and whiskey. "Contraband trading was carried on to a very great extent after dark, the men wading the river where fordable, and the Confederates visiting in return. Union coffee for Confederate tobacco constituted the principal commercial transactions."[65]

During this hiatus, Meagher brought William McCarter from the 116th to join his staff as a new clerk to assist with the never-ending flow of paperwork. Following the war, McCarter would write his recollections of his relatively brief service in the Irish Brigade which—as the letters of Welsh—provide the perspective of the "common" soldier. By virtue of his position as clerk, McCarter also had the opportunity to observe and interact with Meagher. McCarter provides this sketch of Meagher, " . . . five feet-eight or ten inches high, of rather stout build, and had a clear high-colored complexion. Except in battle, where he wore only the uniform of a private soldier, he nearly always appeared in the full dress of his rank. He spoke fluently not only English, but also Greek, Hebrew, French, German, Welsh, and the native Irish language. Meagher made unceasing efforts to have his soldiers all well provided for and made comfortable. He was one of the very few military leaders who never required or would not ask any of his command to go where he would not go himself."[66] The only thing which apparently prevented Meagher from walking on water in McCarter's opinion was that, "he had one besetting sin . . . intemperance."[67]

While the Union troops were building winter quarters, General Lee wisely utilized the lull to carefully position his forces on the hills above Fredericksburg and to have his men build substantial defensive works to secure their positions. On December 10, Union engineers began work to lay a pontoon bridge across the Rappahannock which immediately set the rumor mill into motion among the thousands of blue-clad units. Chaplain Corby recalled one especially anxious young soldier who came to him and exclaimed, "'Father, they are going to lead us over in front of those guns which we have seen them placing, unhindered, for the past three weeks.' I answered him: 'Do not trouble yourself; your generals know better than that.' But, to our great surprise, the poor soldier was right."[68] As Union troops crossed the Rappahannock into Fredericksburg on December 12, they were greeted by representatives of local embalmers distributing their business cards.

As if to further compound their apprehensive misery, at the command of Major-General Couch the troops were not permitted to light campfires during the bitter cold night in order to conceal their positions from the enemy—by this time a very questionable, if not pointless, attempt at deception. As the Brigade huddled among the shattered ruins of Fredericksburg's buildings from the Union's artillery bombardment, or laid on boards they placed upon the frozen mud, they witnessed the natural spectacle of the Aurora Borealis—which many interpreted as an ominous sign.

Early the next morning, the Brigade was called into battle formation, and General Meagher rode among his regiments, giving each a brief speech of encouragement amidst the bombardment from the Confederates. "Even while I was addressing the Sixty-ninth, which was on the right of the brigade, 3 men of the Sixty-third were knocked over, and before I had spoken the last word of encouragement the mangled remains—mere masses of blood and rags—were borne along the line."[69] This unnerving situation must have presented a challenge even to Meagher's legendary oratorical skills. Another salient event in the legend of the Brigade took place during Meagher's pre-battle exhortations. Most of the original battle flags of the regiments had been so tattered from enemy fire that they had been returned to New York, so Meagher asked that each man of the Brigade carry the color of their homeland by placing a sprig of boxwood into their caps. Tragically, many of them were destined to leave the color of their homeland upon the soil of their adopted country before the day would close.

After what must have seemed an interminable wait amidst the shelling of the Confederate artillery, the Irish were directed to attack at approximately noon against the left wing of the Confederate position at Marye's Heights. In addition to the support of artillery, the Confederate infantry had not only the natural advantage afforded by the high ground but were sheltered by a stonewall behind which they had entrenched. One of the first challenges the Brigade faced as they poured out of Fredericksburg, in addition to enemy fire, was the crossing of a deep millrace. "The entire brigade, . . . had to cross a single bridge, and, passing to the right, deploy into line of battle."[70] Meagher, on foot, led the Brigade into position across the millrace where they assembled in formation in a natural depression at the base of Marye's Heights, the only natural protection them. As was his custom, Meagher was with the 69th, who held the position of honor on the right wing. Meagher gave final instructions to Captain Donovan, who was directed to lead the charge, then was assisted from the field by an aide. Reportedly, there was a prominent bloodstain on Meagher's trouser leg which led several to assume he had been wounded. What actually occurred, though equally debilitating, was a rupture of the ulcerated knee injury he incurred at Antietam.[71]

By the time the Brigade surged into action, previous units of the Union army had already been decimated in their attempts at the same assignment. " . . . French's division charged in the order of Kimball's, Andrews's, and Palmer's brigades . . . Hancock followed them in the order of Zook's, Meagher's, and Caldwell's brigades, the two former getting nearer to the stonewall than any who had gone before, except for a few of Kimball's men, and nearer than any brigade which followed them."[72] In Conyngham's account of the battle, he mentions the difficulty of the Brigade's advance due not only to a murderous enemy fire, but also to the large number of Union dead and wounded bodies already piled on the field. "It was not a battle—it was a wholesale slaughter of human beings . . . ."[73] Private McCarter, contrary to Meagher's orders, had left staff duty to take part in the charge and described the horrifying experience before the stonewall as being, "blown back as if by the breath of hell's door suddenly opened."[74]

The valiant charge of the Irish Brigade, as had previous Union attempts, failed to take Marye's Heights, and those soldiers who were still capable of doing so fell back in retreat. Private Welsh would write: "our troops had to lay down to escap the raking fire of the batteries and we had but a poor chance at the enemy who was sheltered in his rifel pit and entrenchments i seen some hot work at south mountain and antetam in maryland but the were not to be compared to this every man that was near me in the right of the company was either killer or wounded except one."[75] Private

McCarter, who had been wounded as the Brigade was in formation prior to the charge, would receive four more wounds in the desperate struggle. As testimony to the ferocity of what the Union men encountered, McCarter related that, "Immediately after my comrade Foltz fell [as McCarter laid wounded on the hill] . . . the thought struck me to pull or work my blankets off my shoulder and to place them in front of my head. Fortunate, indeed that I thought of this. Double fortunate that I succeeded in doing it. My blankets were the receptacles of 32 other bullet which dropped out when I opened them up the next morning in [a Fredericksburg hospital]."[76]

Meagher was returning to the front, now on horseback, when he encountered the first of the retreating Brigade. He quickly re-formed the remaining men of the Brigade into a defensive line on the street parallel with the millrace, nearest the town. "Here I remained, by order of Brigadier-General Hancock, who personally communicated with me at the time, gathering in the fragments of my brigade, until finally I was ordered by him, through one of his aides, to fall back and concentrate on the street from which we had commenced our approach to the battle-field."[77] After remaining in this position for a few hours, still under fire from the Confederate batteries, Meagher sought permission from General Hancock to move them back across the Rappahannock, which he did upon the report of an aide who had been dispatched to request orders from Hancock. The Brigade had no sooner crossed the river when Meagher learned that General Hancock did not actually intend for such movement, so Meagher quickly reported directly to Burnside, who "Did not appear at all dissatisfied with the course I had taken."[78] The thin remnants of the Brigade were held in reserve until the battered remains of the Union army sullenly filed back across the Rappahannock, into the cold darkness. As the men gathered around their campfires it is reported they spontaneously began to sing the ballad, "Ireland Boys Hurrah." They were joined, first, by their Union kinsmen, and then, from across Rappahannock, the Irish of the Confederate army.[79]

Both Union and Confederate witnesses to the spectacle of

December 13, 1862, wrote of the bravery shown by those who struggled at Marye's Heights, including the men of the Irish Brigade. Confederate General George Pickett, who was destined to lead a similarly disastrous charge, would write, "Your soldier's heart almost stood still as he watched those sons of Erin fearlessly rush to their death. The brilliant assault . . . was beyond description."[80] Another witness who marveled at the Brigade's effort was none other than Howard Russell, the *London Times* reporter who had been initially critical of Meagher's conduct at Bull Run. In a dispatch which must have been sobering to even the most determined anti-Irish of England, Russell wrote: "After witnessing the gallantry and devotion exhibited by these troops, and viewing the hillside for acres strewn with their corpses, thick as autumn leaves, the spectator can remember nothing but their desperate courage. That any mortal man could have carried the position before which they were wantonly sacrificed, defended as it was, seems to me for a moment idle to believe."[81] The cost of such praise was, indeed, fearsome. In Meagher's report of the action written the next day he wrote, " . . . that out of 1,200 men I had led into action that morning about 250 alone had reported to me under arms from the field . . . ."[82]

Meagher agreed to proceed with a banquet arranged prior to the battle, which had been expected to be a joyous occasion with the presentation of new battle flags. The banquet atmosphere was reportedly happy, although subdued, until the dessert which Meagher had arranged. A platter, covered by a linen cloth, was presented to Meagher at the head table. Without comment, Meagher removed the cloth to reveal a cannonball and then left the hall. The distinguished orator obviously knew how silence could deliver a more effective message than words. "What Meagher took to the banquet was less a gaiety and more a manic heart. He had begun darkly to consider that the Irish Brigade had to this point been expressing a debt to the Union. Now—in his mind—the debt column was overtopped and the Union needed to express its debt to the Irish Brigade."[83]

Meagher launched a desperate attempt to obtain some relief

for his decimated Brigade, and himself. He submitted to a medical officer's examination and Dr. Reynolds would write, in his report of Meagher's exam, "I find he is suffering from a furunculous abscess of the left knee, which quite disables him . . . It is further my opinion that an absence of 20 days is absolutely necessary to prevent loss of life or permanent disability."[84] Meagher was immediately granted medical leave, and he returned to New York City on Christmas Day, accompanying the body of Major William Horgan of the 88th.[85] In a sad coincidence, the bright new regimental flags arrived at Fredricksburg at this time, and Meagher would also become the guardian of their return north. "On my departure . . . to New York—in compliance with the injunction of every officer and soldier of the Brigade—I brought back the Colors which had been sent to replace those old and illustrious ones . . . These beauteous and sumptuous new Colors remain in New York, until the Irish Brigade, reinforced as it should be, shall have the power to carry and defend them . . . ."[86]

Private McCarter had also been removed from the temporary hospitals of Fredericksburg to Eckington Hospital near Washington, D.C. McCarter was housed in a general ward of wounded Union soldiers for a few weeks, his right arm steadily deteriorating, until he was suddenly moved to an officer's ward of only six beds. Shortly afterwards, McCarter would observe a letter in Meagher's handwriting carried by his attending surgeon. "I at once recognized it . . . and said so to the doctor. He smiled as he replied, 'Yes, you are right, Mac, he is a good friend of yours. This letter contains his special request to me to take the best of care of you here.'"[87] Although he would never completely recover, the extra attention McCarter received in the officer's ward was responsible for saving his arm from amputation.

During his convalescence in New York, Meagher was visited by other Brigade officers who were on leave and several of the city's prominent citizens who presented him with a gold medal. Cavanagh described the medal as " . . . being two inches in diameter with one side featuring an Irish harp resting on American and Irish flags, surrounded by a wreath of laurel and shamrocks . . . above which are the words 'Irish Brigade' in emeralds, and beneath are the words 'Meagher' and 'Semper Fideles.' On the obverse is the inscription, 'Presented to Brigadier-General Thomas Francis Meagher by the officers of the Irish Brigade, in testimony of his gallant and patriotic services in the cause of the American Union and his devotion to the Brigade.'" Meagher proudly accepted the medal and responded, "I shall bequeath it to my son as the richest legacy he could receive . . . with the hope that, taught and inspired by its memories, its inscriptions and its emblems, he may endeavor to serve Ireland as I have tried to serve America."[88]

It was also while on leave that Meagher initiated an aggressive effort to obtain leave for his battered troops. Accordingly, he " . . . began a propaganda campaign aimed at the War Department, the object of which was to get his command (at least the original regiments of the 63rd, 69th, and 88th) away from Fredericksburg and back to New York. He felt that a triumphal return of the heroes would be of immense help in his drive to encourage more volunteers."[89] Meagher's efforts went so far as to include a New Year's Day visit with President Lincoln at the White House to press his request.[90] No doubt to the great embarrassment of the administration and Union Army commanders, Meagher's call was even taken up by the New York press.

Meagher, without authorization, extended his leave until the 11th of February and was required to appear before a military commission on the fourteenth to explain his absence from duty.[91] A physician's letter attesting to Meagher's continued debilitation, as well as perhaps his oratory skills served adequate, as no charges were filed against him. Meagher continued to relentlessly press his requests, which included a letter to Secretary of War Edwin Stanton, to obtain a period of leave for the Irish Brigade. In his letter to Stanton, Meagher cited that there remained but 139 officers and 1,058 enlisted men available for duty in the Irish Brigade and specifically requested that the regiments be relieved in order to " . . . have the opportunity of restoring, in some serviceable measure, their exhausted ranks."[92] Two of the Brigade's regiments, the 69th and 88th, had been so depleted in their officer ranks that they were now under the command of captains. Meagher further argued his case by pointedly reminding Secretary Stanton that regiments from Maine, Massachusetts, and Connecticut had already been granted similar leave.[93] Meagher's request finally landed on the desk of the Army of the Potomac's new commander, General Joseph Hooker. Hooker, with finality, also refused the request. While there is some feeling that the denials may have represented a new policy to more thoroughly integrate ethnic units, it is perhaps more probable that the refusal was based upon the desire to keep Meagher away from New York and Washington newspapers and politicians rather than any genuine need for the Irish Brigade to remain on active duty at that time.

Although they had been terribly battered, it appears that many of the Brigade's veterans had acquired something of a stubborn determination. Not unlike later generations of American soldiers, and despite—or perhaps because of—the misery, fear, absence from loved ones, and the terrible slaughter of friends, many of the common foot-soldiers gained an emotional strength from the ordeal. Even as many Irish on the home front were calling for an end to the war, it seems most of the men in the trenches clearly understood why they were there. Although he would not be regarded as an "educated" man, Corporal Welsch penned a thoughtful response to his wife who questioned the purpose of the struggle. "you may say what is it to me let them fight it out between themselves this i know is said by many but who are they! this is my country as much as the man that was born on the soil and so it is with every man who comes to this country and becomes a citezen . . . this is the first test of a modern free government in the act of sustaining itself against internal enemys and matured rebellion . . . if it fail then all the hopes of millions fall and the desighns and wishes of all tyrants will succeed . . . Contrast the condition of the masses of this with any other country in the world and the advantages we enjoy will stand out boldly so that the blindest can see them . . . And is this not worth fiting for i fancy i hear some one say those who fight for it are not the ones who will reap the benefit of it that may be true . . . [but] it becomes the duty of every one . . . to

perpetuate for the benefit future generations a government and a
national asylum which is superior to any the world has yet
known . . . there is yet something in this land worth fighting for."[94]

The spring of 1863 brought a renewal of spirit to the Army of
the Potomac as it prepared itself for another year of war. Despite
the initial misgivings of many towards the new commander of the
Army of the Potomac, Joseph Hooker had succeeded in restoring a
sense of confidence and enthusiasm to the troops. Meagher and
the men of the Irish Brigade certainly did their part to boost morale
by hosting a raucous St. Patrick's Day celebration for a large portion
of their comrades-in-arms from other units. "An arbor of evergreen
boughs decorated brigade headquarters, before which were tables
piled high with cakes and an enormous wooden tub, painted green,
filled with a near-lethal punch containing eight baskets of
champagne, ten gallons of rum, and twenty-two gallons of Irish
whiskey. The Irishmen turned no one away from their celebration,
which was attended by the army's ranking officers and their guests,
and no one went home hungry or sober."[95] Meagher set a
lighthearted tone to the festivities in his opening remarks by
advising that some enlisted men who had stationed themselves
beneath a temporary grandstand built for the distinguished guests
should move lest they be crushed by two tons of generals. All too
soon the laughter would be replaced by the anguish of battle, as
the men once again devotedly followed Meagher to another killing
field.

CHAPTER 15

*"Beware of rashness, but with energy and sleepless vigilance
go forward and give us victories."*
Abraham Lincoln to General Joseph Hooker

During the winter encampment along the banks of the Rappahannock, Hooker had carefully crafted a new plan of action against the Confederate forces. He would attempt to hold Lee in his Fredericksburg positions by demonstrating against the Confederate center and right flank with approximately half the available Union forces. At the same time, Hooker would lead his remaining troops up-river (along the same ill-fated route Burnside had attempted), cross the Rappahannock undetected, and fall upon the rear and left flank positions of Lee's army. Hooker's troop movements did not go unnoticed, however, and Lee brilliantly and courageously divided his army and met the Union forces just a little west of Fredericksburg at a little country crossroads known as Chancellorsville.

As Hooker and nearly 40,000 Union troops made their flanking movement, he assigned some units to serve, in effect, as military police. Their responsibility was to prevent any sympathetic local residents from attempting to notify the Confederate forces of the Union army's movements. "Those caught signaling, or suspected of signaling, were put in arrest by provost marshals. The widespread house-guarding extended along the route of the flanking column as it moved on upriver . . . The renowned Irish Brigade . . . performed similar duty near Banks' Ford."[96] Now a part of the First Division, II Corps, under the command of Major-General Winfield Hancock, the Irish Brigade crossed the Rappahannock on April 30 at a point known as U.S. Ford, approximately two miles north of Chancellorsville; but on May 1 the element of surprise once again belonged to Generals Lee and Jackson. The Union forces moving east toward Fredericksburg suddenly found themselves engaged by Confederate troops. Hooker, despite a significant numerical superiority, pulled back and aligned his units into defensive positions. The Union positions grew increasingly desperate throughout the next two days, due largely to the brilliant—and final—maneuver led by Stonewall Jackson to flank the unprotected Union right. Hancock's Division, which had the assignment of providing a retreat corridor, became an increasingly vital element in saving Hooker's command from complete destruction.

Early on May 3 the Irish Brigade was sent forward once again to the unenviable task of helping to hold the center of the Union position with another stubborn unit, the Fifth Maine Battery. These determined men held their position under a fearsome combination of Confederate artillery and infantry fire. Meagher, in what had become his characteristic style, was prominent in directing the Brigade's action until, under direct orders from Hancock, he was placed in charge of managing the Union retreat. Conyngham relates an incident which followed the withdrawal of the Union forces: "When we fell back to the woods I was leaning against a tree, General Meagher at the other side talking to me, when a bullet struck the tree over our heads. I remarked—'General, that was fired by a sharpshooter; they have range of you; we'd better leave this.' [Meagher replied]'Oh, no; it's but a chance shot.' Just as he spoke another bullet lodged behind our heads. 'They are improving, general,' I remarked. [To which Meagher replied] 'Well, yes; I think it is time to leave now.' 'I thought so long since, general.'"[97]

Hooker directed the Army of the Potomac to establish another defensive position in front of the U.S. Ford during the night of May 3. The troops held this position and remained under fire from the Confederates while Hooker, who had been stunned by the concussion of an artillery shell while standing on the porch of his Chancellorsville headquarters, vacillated on what his next move would be throughout May 4. Finally the order came and, under the cover of darkness late on the fourth, the Irish Brigade joined their comrades in the dismal march back across the Rappahannock to their encampment north of Fredericksburg, their columns depleted by thousands of blue-clad soldiers who remained on the fields surrounding Chancellorsville.

Following the battle, a dispirited Meagher renewed his request for leave in order to solicit new enlistment troops, the Brigade now numbering less than 500 men fit for service. His requests continued to be denied, however, and an angry, frustrated Meagher submitted his resignation May 8. In what was obviously a letter filled with deep emotions, Meagher wrote, "I feel it my first duty to do nothing that will wontonly imperil the lives of others, or, what would be still more grievous and irreparable, inflict sorrow and humiliation upon a race, who, having lost almost everything else, find in their character for courage and loyalty an invaluable gift, which, I, for one, will not be so vain and selfish as to endanger."[98] Perhaps Meagher took this dramatic step in the hope it would give emphasis to his request for reinforcements and force the hand of the Union command. If so, he must have been bitterly disappointed when he was notified that his resignation was accepted on May 14.

On May 19 Brigadier-General Meagher addressed his Brigade in the field for the final time. In taking leave of his brave little band of survivors, he delivered a heartfelt message: "A positive conviction of what I owed to your reputation, to the honor of our race, and to my own conscience, compelled me a few days ago to tender to the President of the United States my resignation of this command . . . I feel that I would be perpetuating a great deception were I to retain the authority and rank of a brigadier-general nominally commanding the same . . . The graves of many hundreds of brave and devoted soldiers, who went to death with all the radiance and enthusiasm of the noblest chivalry, are so many guarantees and pledges that, as long as there remains one officer or soldier of the Irish Brigade, . . . there shall be found for him, for his family . . . a devoted friend in Thomas Francis Meagher."[99]

One feels a depth of resignation that went well beyond

Meagher's formal statements. There is a sense that Meagher had lost confidence in his superior officers' ability to direct the army, and that he desperately wished to remove the Irish Brigade from harm's way—if only temporarily. Failing this, it seems Meagher had lost the heart to continue leading his men toward further destruction and, what he must have believed would be, the total decimation of his beloved brigade. Unquestionably, Meagher had a much deeper relationship with the men of the Irish Brigade than the average "professional" commander had with his troops. Certainly this relationship was linked to their common ancestry, but the perhaps the foundation was based upon the fact Meagher had invested himself so thoroughly in recruiting the officers and men of the Brigade. It could not have been lost upon Meagher's conscience that many of the men in the Irish Brigade had a greater sense of devotion to himself—and certainly a greater devotion to Ireland—than to the cause of the Union. This personal investment in the Brigade seems to have been the keystone to both his strength and weakness as a commander.

Despite his disappointment, Meagher remained devoted to the Union cause and assured his superiors he would be willing to accept another assignment if he could be of service.

CHAPTER 16

"Hurrah! Hurrah! for our dear old flag.
Hurrah for our gallant leader, too;
Though 'tis a torn and tattered rag,
We would not change it for the new.

We've borne it with the Stripes and Stars
From Fair Oaks to Frederick's bloody plain;
And see, my boys, our wounds and scars
Can tell how well we did the same.
Be sure, our chieftain, of his race,
Was ever foremost 'mid the brave,
Where death met heroes face to face,
And gathered harvests for the grave."

Song of the Irish Brigade

Thomas Francis Meagher returned to New York on May 29, 1863, hailed as a hero and, once again, in much demand for various war memorial events and fund-raising efforts for the Irish Brigade's widows and orphans. It was also upon his return that he reportedly took the oath of membership into the Fenian Brotherhood. Cavanagh records that Meagher became an initiated member during a private meeting with John O'Mahony at Meagher's country home in Orange, New Jersey, stating that "Though Mr. Meagher was himself an enrolled member of the Fenian Brotherhood . . . the society had been in existence for years before he sought admission into its ranks."[100] Cavanagh's claim is challenged, however, by none other than O'Mahoney. Author William D'Arcy cites that in 1864 O'Mahoney would carp that Meagher, as well as other former leaders of Young Ireland, "would have nothing to do" with the

Fenian movement.[101] Nevertheless, if Meagher did, in fact, join the Brotherhood, why he chose this time to formally affiliate—and the extent of his devotion to the society—is a curiosity. It seems likely this may have been a matter of some political posturing by both parties rather than genuine commitment. Certainly the addition of Meagher's name to the membership roll would have had great public relations value for the Fenians, and it may be that Meagher regarded the Fenian organization as the base for later political support. Cavanagh would also claim that Meagher was elected to serve as a delegate to the inaugural Fenian Brotherhood national convention to be held in November, but he would defer attending due to an "imperative call" from the War Department which required him to travel to Washington, although the exact nature of that imperative call isn't certain.[102] What is very certain is that he was no longer content to simply play the role of an orator, and that he remained eager for the excitement of center stage upon the battlefield.

Meagher began to press influential friends for the authority to raise another brigade, even extending his pleas to President Lincoln. In mid-June Meagher would telegraph Lincoln that "If called upon and authorized by the Government I shall proceed at once to raise three thousand (3,000) Irish soldiers in this city to act as cavalry and infantry wherever they may be ordered."[103] On June 16 Meagher received notice from President Lincoln that he was granted such permission, with an important caveat: the authority and coordination of any additional units had to be through New York's Governor Horatio Seymour. As difficult as it would have been to recruit three thousand Irish men for service at this time considering the general frustration with the war and the bitter response of many towards the enactment of the Emancipation Proclamation, Meagher's strained relationship with Governor Seymour would have made the task even more challenging. Author Michael Cavanagh suggests that the units which Lincoln authorized Meagher to form were to be specifically employed against England, inasmuch as " . . . war between the two countries was certain to result—unless England receded from her arrogant attitude."[104] It must be regarded, however, highly unlikely that Lincoln ever entertained such thoughts. On the contrary, one of Lincoln's great concerns throughout the conflict was to keep England from entering the war in support of the South. Nevertheless, by the time the violent New York draft riots erupted in July, Meagher must have realized that success in raising another force, regardless of purpose, was very unlikely, and he made a request to the War Department to be returned to active service, which was not answered. Repeated requests to friends and political acquaintances failed to bring action, and a painfully obvious sense of desperation began finding its way into his letters and speeches.

No doubt it would have greatly invigorated Meagher's spirits had he learned of a letter William West, U.S. Counsul to Dublin, sent in November to William Seward, Secretary of State, "It has long since occurred to me, that in compliment for his [Meagher's] valuable services, and those of the Irish soldiers generally, it would be fitting acknowledgment on the part of our Government, to select some desirable portion of our territories and call it New Ireland, of which no doubt General Meagher would in due time be elected Governor."[105] There is no evidence West's suggestion was ever taken very seriously, but it would portend an uncanny chain of events.

Meagher returned to the soldier's fellowship with an extended visit to the Virginia winter encampment area of General Corcoran and the survivors of his beloved Irish Brigade. Regrettably, this pleasant time with his former command came to a tragic conclusion. Upon his return from escorting Meagher to the Fairfax train station, Corcoran died as the result of a fall from his horse. The loss of this dear friend must have been especially painful to Meagher and cast a melancholy gloom among the remnants of the Irish Brigade. Once again, though, when the path seemed darkest, a light began to shine for Meagher with the notification he was being restored to active duty.

No doubt in appreciation of his rescue from what he regarded as potential obscurity, Meagher became an outspoken advocate for the Republican administration, a metamorphosis not appreciated by the Irish press. As if to evidence he would not be cowered by criticism, Meagher would go so far as to write, "As for the great bulk of the Irishmen in the country, I frankly confess to an utter disregard . . . they have suffered themselves to be bamboozled into being obstinate herds in the political field, contracting inveterate instincts, following with gross stupidity and the stoniest blindness certain worn out old path-ways . . . ."[106] This candid outspokenness fell heavily on those who had been his devoted supporters. Whether or not he knowingly did so, Meagher effectively terminated any hope of a political position in New York.

Moreover, it became increasingly apparent that returning Meagher to active duty status was a calculated move to keep him quiet, for no specific assignment of duty followed the notice of reinstatement. "The War Department seemed to regard the Irish general as a communicable disease . . . ."[107] Meagher renewed his pleas to a shrinking list of influential supporters to receive a command, but it wasn't until September 13, 1864, that he was finally notified to report to Major-General William T. Sherman in Nashville. In fact, it was the request of none other than Ulysses S. Grant which released Meagher from his purgatory of dormancy. On September 11 Grant had telegraphed Halleck with instructions to assign Meagher to Sherman's command.[108]

Immediately upon arriving in Nashville in mid-October, Meagher was invited to speak before Tennessee's House of Representatives at the request of Governor Andrew Johnson. Meagher eagerly took advantage of this splendid pulpit to espouse the Republican Party and the re-election of Abraham Lincoln (which would also have important implications for Governor Johnson). Although Meagher may have been an eager new disciple of the administration at this point, his outspoken support for the Republican Party was cause for increasing alarm among his former allies. In early November the *Irish American*—which had provided his most consistent and staunchest support in the press—turned on its former darling: "In General Meagher's fall from the high position he once held in the esteem and affection of his countrymen, we see only a subject for regret; our indignation at his unprovoked attack upon our people has long since subsided into contempt . . . ."[109]

As if the erosion of his long-time supporters wasn't enough of a concern, it was becoming obvious that Meagher's assignment to Nashville was just another meaningless step in shuffling him from one pigeonhole to another. Sherman finally ordered Meagher to report to Major-General George Thomas, though without specific duties, and Thomas immediately transferred him on to Major-General James B. Steedman. Steedman, under direction from Thomas, assigned Meagher command of the Military District of Etowah which consisted of two brigades of convalescents. With its headquarters in Chattanooga, the primary responsibility of this rag-tag command was to provide security along the Chattanooga and Knoxville rail line between Chattanooga and Loudon, Tennessee, and the Chattanooga and Atlanta rail line south. The duty was capably managed by General Meagher until mid-January 1865, at which time Meagher received orders to proceed with his misfit command to North Carolina.

The route that Meagher's division followed was through Nashville, Cincinnati, Pittsburgh, Washington, and finally arriving at Annapolis, where they were to be transported via ships to New Bern, North Carolina. The journey of the division was especially chaotic given the combined factors of icy winter weather, which forced changes in travel arrangements, and the challenge of coordinating thousands of men from hundreds of former units. The popular adage about "herding cats" would seem to apply to the tribulations of the operation. It was enough to drive one to drink—which Meagher reportedly did, with disastrous personal consequences.

Upon arriving at Annapolis on February 4, Meagher almost immediately clashed with Major Robert Scott, who had the assignment of coordinating ship transport for the Union troops moving south. Meagher wanted the transport convoy held until all units of his division had arrived and were on board; Scott, however, wanted to release each ship as it was appropriately loaded. Major Scott went to the top of the military ladder in an attempt to have things his way, contacting the chief of staff, General Henry Halleck. Halleck accepted Scott's request and, on February 5, gave him authority to release transports as he wished. Scott immediately sought out Meagher that evening in his headquarters, which was aboard the familiar surroundings of the ship *Ariel*, to inform him of Halleck's decision and reportedly (albeit by Scott) found Meagher in a drunken stupor.[110]

As fate would have it, General Grant inquired of Halleck on February 5 as to the situation regarding the transport of troops. Halleck very uncharitably, if not outright divisively, replied that the Provisional Brigade was in great disorder and that Meagher was unaware of where his troops were and was not capable of exercising command.[111] Whether Halleck's comments were an intentional vendetta or not, they had the same effect. Grant, who had previously been Meagher's benefactor, immediately responded to Halleck in no uncertain terms: "If he [Meagher] has lost his men it will afford a favorable pretext for doing what the service would have lost nothing by having done long ago—dismissing him."[112] By the time Meagher, and approximately 5,000 of his command, arrived at New Bern on February 13 the light of Thomas Francis Meagher's military career was nearly extinguished.

The troops he had led to New Bern were distributed as replacements among units already in the field which, therefore, left Meagher without a command. Rather than being reassigned, Meagher received formal notice from the secretary of war on February 24 that he was relieved from duty and should retire immediately to his place of residence.[113] Michael Cavanagh writes that Meagher submitted his resignation rather than serve under the command of General Sherman, who was in the process of cutting a swath of destruction through the South. In a public address made upon his return to New York, Meagher commented, "In moments of excitement *they* never gave way to the excesses . . . the men of the Irish Brigade, who went out from here to fight and put down the armed enemies of the Republic, and not to cast naked and breadless on the world, the women and children and aged fathers of the delinquent States."[114] These were clearly not words which could have endeared him to the hearts of such men as Ulysses S. Grant and William T. Sherman, who were committed to a policy of total, unrelenting warfare. Regardless of the exact circumstances, Meagher was in New York at the close of the war, unable, or unwilling, to be in the field at the time of triumph for the Union.

America's civil war was a—perhaps *the*—defining event in the life of the country, and this occurred on many levels. It was not only a struggle to preserve the Union or to abolish slavery, but it forever shaped the future of every man and woman of that time in ways great and small. For the men of the Irish Brigade, the war represented an opportunity to not only win honor for their race but to validate their claim to the American dream. For most of the Brigade, including Thomas Francis Meagher, the enemies they fought were prejudice, shame, and Great Britain. To have lost the Union would have represented the loss of a dream the Irish had been fighting for long before April 12, 1861. The extent of Meagher's influence is indelibly stamped upon the history of the Irish Brigade, if not the war itself. Although there have been some who deprecate his military skills or personal behavior, the men who served under his command were never hesitant to honor the memory of his leadership in the face of death. During the Grand Review of the Union army that was held in Washington, May 22, 1865, the men of the Irish Brigade units displayed green sprigs of boxwood in their caps in remembrance of their fallen countrymen and in acknowledgement of their commander's famous order. In subsequent years, at the reunion encampments, the old veterans of the Brigade would proudly wear green ribbons lettered in gold, "Meaghers Brigade."

> The day is not far distant when our equal boast shall be
> That our country's crown is glistened by Grant,
> Farragut and Lee!
> By Stonewall Jackson's front of flame, by Sherman,
> swift and keen,
> And Meagher, who led on to fame the boys
> who wore the green.
>
> Charles Graham Halpine
> Poet Laureate, Army of the Potomac

CHAPTER 17

*"Admit the Bearer, BrGenl T. F. Meagher detailed as
'GUARD OF HONOR' from 2 o'clock to 4 o'clock
on Monday April 23, 1865."*

Pass issued to Meagher

The primary agenda item for Lincoln's cabinet meeting held on the afternoon of April 14, 1865, was the plan for post-war reconstruction. Just as the momentous issues which had led to the war were so divisive, the policies of reconstruction promised to be bitterly contested. President Lincoln made it very clear, however, that it was his intention that any plan must have a theme of healing, not retribution. Lincoln acknowledged to his cabinet members that he recognized there were those men, including some in Congress, " . . . who, if their motives were good, were nevertheless impracticable, and who possessed feelings of hate and vindictiveness in which he did not sympathize and could not participate. We must extinguish our resentment if we expect harmony and union."[115] Much to the enormous shock of the country, it would only be a few hours later when a man filled with anger and vindictiveness would end the life of Lincoln and single-handedly end the dream of a peaceful and forgiving reunification. The venom of hatred would spread deeply and quickly, reaching into some of the most remote corners of the country, even to the banks of a little stream known as Grasshopper Creek, in a new territory where harmony and union would find it difficult to take root.

Thomas Francis Meagher, as did many others, found himself adrift at the close of the war. No longer needed as a soldier, and no longer interested in reviving any of his pre-war professions, he anxiously sought new possibilities. Although he had previously been unsuccessful in his petition for an appointment as an ambassador, Meagher obviously considered a career in political administration to be his calling. Upon learning that a friend, James O'Beirne, was now serving as an aide to President Johnson, Meagher sought to espouse his cause. In a letter addressed to President Johnson (via O'Beirne), Meagher—characteristically immodest—would write, "Could you ascertain if there is any Territorial Governorship vacant? Next to a Military Command, this is precisely what would suit me best. Indeed, for every reason, it might prove greatly more advantageous than the latter. It would enable me, after a little, to enter Congress; and once there, I have no fear but that I should make myself Master of the Situation—to my own credit, to the gratification of my friends, to the confusion and mortification of my enemies, and to the honour of our race."[116] Meagher would also press O'Beirne to confirm what seems to have been an unorthodox brevet appointment to the rank of major general.

By early July of 1865 there was no indication of any political appointment on the horizon, and it had become obvious to Meagher that his time of celebrity had passed. Having alienated so many friends and influential contacts with his caustic public statements and new political affiliations, he found himself at the age of forty-two at what was probably his most desperate point since his arrival in the United States. "When all the politicians who had fought their way forward to shake his hands proved to be distant when approached for sinecure, the political world knew this was not abnormal. But it perplexed and angered Meagher."[117] While he could have continued to live comfortably at the home of his father-in-law, it is easy to understand why this would not have been desirable, and for a man with Meagher's sense of pride and honor, this must have been an especially unpleasant scenario for the future. So, as did many men and women of the time, he looked for a new beginning in a land filled with new promise—the American West.

PART IV

Life in the Montana Territory:
"The Acting One"

CHAPTER 18

"Ten days after passing [what would become] *Last Chance
Gulch, the expedition made camp on a small creek
entering today's Beaverhead River.
The captains* [Lewis & Clark] *named it Willard's Creek,
in honor of Private Alexander Willard. It would be sixty years
before Willard's Creek was renamed Grasshopper Creek
and the Beaverhead country teemed with gold miners."*

Stephen Ambrose

How much he may have known about the incredible journey
of Lewis and Clark isn't certain, but by June of 1865, Thomas
Francis Meagher had become enthralled with the idea of seeking a
new life on the frontier of the American West. Once again setting
off to seek fame and fortune, he traveled first to St. Paul, Minnesota,
with the intention of joining an expedition led by James Fisk to
the Montana gold fields. As an army captain assigned to the War
Department's Emigrant Overland Escort Service, Fisk had led
emigrant caravans in 1862, 1863, and 1864 from Minnesota to
the mining camps of the Idaho territory via the trading post at
Fort Benton. Now promoting his own commercial interests, Fisk's
presentation on the wonders and majesty of the American West at
the Cooper Institute in New York City captured the imagination
and opened a new world of possibilities in the mind of Thomas
Meagher. Whether Fisk happened to mention in his presentation
that his 1864 emigrant train had been attacked by Indians and
under seige for sixteen days—with seven of his party killed—isn't
certain, but it's very possible the information would not have
deterred Meagher from this great adventure.

Meagher's arrival in St. Paul on July 23 undoubtedly rekindled pleasant memories of earlier days, when a large group of citizens and a band turned out to greet him. Almost immediately upon his arrival, he was also invited to return to the podium at the request of Father John Ireland.[1] Considering Meagher's somewhat clouded history with the Church, this must have seemed like a good omen for the beginning of his new life on the frontier. The invitation that Father Ireland extended Meagher was to address the Minnesota Irish Immigration Society. Meagher wasted no time in using this opportunity to build a favorable impression with both his countrymen and the Church, even donating the admission receipts from his lecture back to the Immigration Society.[2]

Meagher announced in an interview prior to his address that it was his intention to colonize Montana with Irish Catholics and to not only secure more priests for the new territory, but to also have a bishop appointed.[3] In his speech to the Immigration Society on August 2, Meagher put forth the radical proposition that, "The black heroes of the Union Army have not only entitled themselves to liberty but to citizenship, and the Democrat who would deny them the rights for which their wounds and glorified colors so eloquently plead is unworthy to participate in the greatness of the nation."[4] As noble, even as appropriate, as this proposal may have been, and although it was locally well accepted, it was not a generally popular position for anyone to promote at that time. Certainly it was not a solid plank for an Irish-American's political platform and was more likely to subvert any legitimate hope for a political career.

Almost immediately following his speech, Meagher received a telegram from President Andrew Johnson offering the appointment as secretary for the Montana Territory. Somewhat surprisingly for one who had so eagerly sought such a position, Meagher took two days to respond with his acceptance of this long-sought government appointment. It may have been that Meagher wanted the counsel of Elizabeth prior to acceptance, or that he took time to consider his options and calculate the probability that this position would boost him toward a higher rung on the political ladder. At any rate, Meagher remained in St. Paul for a few days following his acceptance, making preparations and travel arrangements to his new post.

The first leg of Meagher's journey west took him to Atchison, Kansas, where he arrived on August 23. Meagher spent the night in Atchison being entertained by local officials who treated him as a visiting dignitary, but later, claiming to be fatigued from his travel, he declined the offer of a serenade by the local Fenians. While it's certainly reasonable to expect Meagher would have been weary, it does raise further questions with respect to his degree of sincerity and devotion to the Fenian cause. He must have realized that he would rarely, if ever, pass through Atchison again. For him to forego an opportunity to extend his base of contact with some eager admirers, or to run the risk of offending them, doesn't seem to equate with what one would expect of a dedicated member of the Fenian Society.

From Atchison, Meagher continued his journey by stagecoach via Denver and Salt Lake City. There would be some who later assumed Meagher made his journey west by steamboat, as he would author an article, using a thinly disguised pen name, suggesting river travel rather than coach to his readers.[5] Meagher continued to be eagerly greeted by city officials and crowds at each stop and made very favorable impressions upon the local citizens during his brief layovers. His arrival in Salt Lake City was noted in the local press: "Major-General Thomas Francis Meagher arrived yesterday by eastern stage, en route for Montana, whither he goes as Secretary for that Territory. [He] will probably leave by Thursday's stage for Montana."[6] Meagher completed his grueling quest for the Montana Territory when he arrived in Bannack on September 28, 1865.

Montana Terrotorial offices (second floor)
Virginia City, Montana

Thomas Francis Meagher's home
in Virginia City, Montana

Memorial statue of Thomas Francis Meagher
at the Montana state capital building (Helena)

Thomas Francis Meagher portrait photo by A. C. Carter
(Montana Historical Society)

View of Virginia City, circa 1866.
(Montana Historical Society)

Commemorative Monument to Meagher and the Irish Brigade.
Antietam battlefield, at the Sunken Road

CHAPTER 19

Oro 'y Plata
(Gold and Silver)
Motto of the State of Montana

The area, that is now the southwestern portion of the state of Montana, was a largely untamed frontier in 1865, teeming with all descriptions of men—and a few women—who were seeking new lives and easy fortunes. Gold was first discovered along Grasshopper Creek in July of 1862, and the town of Bannack quickly materialized. Less than a year later, in May of 1863, a group of prospectors, led by Bill Fairweather, discovered what would be one of America's richest deposits of gold in an area northeast of Bannack which they named Alder Gulch. Several mining camps burst to life along the Alder Creek basin, most notably Virginia City. "It is estimated that by mid-1864 at least 10,000 people lived in 9 primary mining camps along the fourteen mile gulch . . . about 5,000 within Virginia City."[7]

Sidney Edgerton was an attorney by profession and Radical Republican in his politics who had previously served in the U.S. House of Representatives from the state of Ohio. In 1863 he was appointed by President Lincoln to serve as a federal justice for the newly created, and enormously large, Idaho Territory; encompassing all the area of present day Idaho, Montana, and most of Wyoming. Edgerton was assigned to serve the eastern district of the territory by Governor William H. Wallace. "[Edgerton] was assigned to that part of the territory now included in the state of Montana, because of the expressed prejudice of Wallace to 'imported attorneys' . . . ."[8]

Edgerton, perhaps unaware of the rapidly growing Alder Gulch district, chose the town of Bannack as the site of his judicial court and arrived there with his family on September 17, 1863. Just a few days prior to their arrival, the Edgertons had encountered the marshal of Bannack, Henry Plummer. Plummer was escorting the stage which was carrying his wife, via Salt Lake City, to visit her family in Iowa. Although Bannack was almost hopelessly isolated from the territory's capital in Lewiston, it represented a logical choice in terms of its booming population, most coming from the depleted mines of central and southern Idaho. Joining Edgerton and his immediate family in carving out a new life and establishing justice in this raw land would be his niece, Lucia Darling, and his nephew, Wilbur Fisk Sanders, with his family. Sanders was also an attorney who had briefly served with an Ohio regiment during the Civil War before " . . . his health was so broken that he was compelled to leave the service . . . ."[9] What the Edgerton and Sanders families found upon their arrival in the remote outpost was a rough and tumble lifestyle, unlike anything they had ever known.

One of the area's earliest settlers, Granville Stuart, would recall, "The rich 'diggings' of Grasshopper creek attracted many undesirable characters and I believe there were more desperadoes and lawless characters in Bannack in the winter of 1862-3 than ever infested any other mining camp of its size. Murders, robberies, and shooting scrapes were of frequent occurrence . . . There was no safety for life or property only so far as each individual could, with his trusty rifle, protect his own"[10] One of the few women living in Bannack at the time would write to her family, "I don't know how many deaths have occurred this winter but that there have not been twice as many, is entirely owing to the fact that drunken men do not shoot well."[11] One incident in which someone "shot well," and an example of the resigned indifference of many in Bannack, was recorded by J. H. Morley in his diary: "Another shooting scrape up town last night in which Cohart was killed and one man had his ankle badly shattered and another in his leg. Cohart buried this evening, all of which causes but little if any excitement."[12]

Despite the difficult circumstances of this primitive new territory, the Edgerton and Sanders families enjoyed an elegant Thanksgiving Day celebration courtesy of the Bannack sheriff. "Colonel Sanders and Judge Edgerton and their wives were guests of Henry Plummer and dined on turkeys from Salt Lake City which cost $50 each."[13] As events would soon unfold, it may be more appropriate to say that the dinner was courtesy of several victims of Plummer's intrigues, and Sanders would presently make another visit to his neighbor's home accompanied by a less socially-minded group of Bannack's citizens.

CHAPTER 20

"We the undersigned uniting ourselves in a party
for the Laudible purpos of arresting thievs & murderers
& recovering stollen propperty do pledge ourselves
upon our sacred honor each to all others & solemnly swear
that we will reveal no secrets, violate no laws of right
& never desert each other or our standard of justice
so help us God as our witness our hand
& seal this 23 of December AD 1863."

Oath of the Virginia City Vigilantes

In what has become a story of legendary proportions in the area, a determined group of citizens sought to bring some sense of order to the lawlessness which threatened their livelihood—and lives. George Ives, a herdsman and livery operator in Virginia City, had the great misfortune of being the first of the suspected road agents brought to "justice."[14] It was during the miner's court trial of Ives that five of the area's leading citizens " . . . held a meeting and decided to form a vigilance committee. These five men were [Paris S.] Pfouts, Nick Wall, Wilbur F. Sanders, Alvin V. Brookie and John Nye."[15] Pfouts may well have been the primary instigator, inasmuch as he had lived in San Francisco during a time when vigilance committees were formed to help rid that city of its criminal element. Sanders had served as the Prosecuting Attorney at the Ives trial and, immediately upon the pronouncement of a "guilty" verdict by the jury, successfully entreated the crowd to hang Ives on the spot.[16]

The inaugural group of five expanded their circle and "in about three days after the hanging of Ives, the original Vigilance Committee, that is the first twelve, were sworn in as Vigilantes . . .

the meeting was called by Paris Pfouts and Sanders."[17] The circle would quickly widen and on the night of December 23, 1863, at a meeting in John S. Lott's store in Virginia City, a document was signed by a resolute band of twenty-four men " . . . for the purpose of arresting thieves and murderers and recovering stolen property . . . ."[18] The organization which these men established included an Executive Committee to oversee and coordinate the efforts of the Vigilantes. The Executive Committee consisted of four officers and thirteen additional members who represented each of the various settlements of the Alder Gulch area according to their population: "4 persons from Virginia City, 3 from Nevada, 1 from Junction, 1from Highland, 1 from Pine Grove, 2 from Summit, and 1 from Bivins Gulch, and 8 of which shall constitute a quorum."[19] It was the responsibility of the Executive Committee to determine those judged to be guilty of crimes against the area's communities and direct appropriate action to eliminate undesirables, however, "The only punishment that shall be inflicted by this Committee is death."[20]

Through the years, there has been a great deal of speculation as to the relationship of the Vigilante Committee with the Masonic organization. There were several men living in the Alder Gulch and Bannack by 1863 who had Masonic membership from their previous areas of residence, and these men had made efforts to organize. The Grand Lodge of Nebraska had granted dispensation in April, 1863 for a lodge to organize at Bannack, but, as a result of the exodus to Alder Gulch, the lodge never developed. Subsequent attempts to organize in Nevada City and Virginia City, however, were successful. Permission was granted to organize a lodge in Nevada City, by authority of the Grand Master of Nebraska, during November and it was accepted as Lodge #10 of Nebraska in June, 1865. Two lodges were organized in Virginia City, the first was granted under the auspices of the Kansas Grand Lodge (#43) and a second chartered by the Colorado Grand Lodge as Montana Lodge #9.[21] Clearly, therefore, Masons were active during the same period as the Vigilantes were organized and several of the known Vigilantes were Masons. This dual membership is not altogether surprising considering that each organization would reasonably attract the participation of "leading citizens," however, the Vigilantes also included some men who were rather rough characters. One of the most respected early pioneers (and Mason) Cornelius Hedges later wrote: "I do not think it occurred to any one at that time that anybody was active in the work [Vigilantes] because he was or because he was not a Mason."[23] Further illustration of this point is provided by historian Merrill Burlingame, who notes that only three of the original twelve Virginia City vigilantes were Masons, that only two of the twenty-three men who signed the December 23 oath were Masons, and that "of the 168 names of persons who reportedly were Vigilantes . . . only twenty-nine have been identified as Masons."[22] Moreover, if it was intended that the Masons, per se, were going to bring law and order to the area, it begs the question of why they would have bothered to establish a separate organization. While some Masons had pivotal roles in the Vigilante movement, there is no reason to believe these organizations were one in the same. Wilbur Sanders, who had taken the Vigilante Oath with the founding core group of twelve men prior to the December 23 meeting, and was elected official prosecutor of the Vigilantes, was a devoted Mason. Sanders, who was never reticent in acknowledging his membership in the Vigilantes, would late in his life offer perhaps the definitive statement regarding the Vigilante/Mason connection: "It has been claimed . . . that the ancient free and accepted masons organized [the Vigilantes], but this is not true . . . they consulted as to the organization of a vigilance committee, never proposing, however, that the order should take hold of it in its capacity as a civic society."[24]

The Vigilantes wasted no time in widening the circle of their membership—and in dealing out their version of justice. Among the first of those who would feel the consequences of vigilante justice was none other than Henry Plummer, the sheriff of Bannack. Plummer was accused of being the leader of a gang of road agents who called themselves the "Innocents" and specialized in robbing gold shipments and newly enriched men from the mining communities. His position as sheriff certainly offered Plummer the tantalizing opportunity to know exactly which stagecoaches to target and their schedules.

Most of Bannack's citizens were staying near stoves and fireplaces on the cold winter's night of January 10, 1864, some curious as to why the community choir practice had been inexplicably cancelled. Suddenly a group of men burst into the home of Mrs. J. A. Vail (Plummer's sister-in-law), where Sheriff Plummer was resting. Authors Thomas Dimsdale and A. C. McClure both indicate that Wilbur F. Sanders was, if not the leader, certainly an integral player in the Vigilante posse which led Plummer and his deputies, Buck Stinson and Ned Ray, through the darkness to a gallows at the edge of town.[25] As Plummer made desperate pleas to save himself, Sanders is reported to have replied, "It is useless for you to beg for your life. That affair is settled and cannot be altered. You are to be hanged. You cannot feel harder about it than I do but I cannot help it, if I would."[26]

Formation of other Vigilante groups would take place throughout the territory and seemed to be a generally accepted, as least as a transitory, necessity. Soon after his arrival in the territory, Federal Judge Lyman Munson would relate a conversation with a local judge in Helena who would state: "I am content to let the Vigilantes go on, for the present; they can attend to this branch of jurisprudence cheaper, quicker and better than it can be done by the courts—besides, we have no secure jails in which to confine criminals."[27] There were some, however, who did not share this benevolent attitude. In September of 1864 James Fergus, the Recorder for Madison County, bravely addressed an open letter to the "Gentlemen of the Vigilance Com." in which he shared what was a growing sentiment: "Our roads were infested by Highwaymen, beyond the reach of our laws. Our own safety required that they be exterminated. Your committee performed that difficult and dangerous duty to the satisfaction of all good men. But I think for the safety of society, the powers you then exercised should only be resorted to in extreme cases . . . ."[28] Vigilante (and federal Revenue Collector) N. P. Langford would confess in his narrative regarding the Vigilante movement that it was commonly understood among the Vigilantes that they represented an extralegal force whose existence was intended to be short-term. "The Vigilantes knew full well that when the Federal courts should be organized, they themselves would in tuin be held accountable before the law for any unwarrented excerise of power."[29]

CHAPTER 21

"You inquire who selected the name Montana;
I cannot tell who first mentioned the name,
but the man who fought most earnestly for the name
was the Hon. James M. Ashley . . . . "

Sidney Edgerton

While the Vigilantes went about their business, Sidney Edgerton was also engaged with his own agenda and had determined that there were far greater opportunities than serving as a district justice for the Idaho Territory. Early in 1864, Edgerton made his way to Washington, D.C., to pay a call on an old friend from Ohio. James M. Ashley was a United States representative for the state of Ohio and, more importantly to Edgerton, he was serving as chairman of the House Committee on Territories. With the help of Ashley, and other former colleagues from the House, Edgerton was able to have a bill introduced to create a new federal territory. Ashley presented a bill which carved out the new territory by shaving off the eastern portion of the Idaho Territory and christening the new area "Montana." Ashley, at Edgerton's urging, was very generous in setting the boundary lines for the new territory and moved the border three degrees west of the line originally proposed by Idaho's delegation; creating the "panhandle" of northern Idaho.[30] The bill quickly received House approval in March but the legislation hit a wall when it reached the Senate. The "wall" was Senator Morton Wilkinson of Minnesota, and it was his contention that a provision should be written into the articles of the new territory that *any* male citizen be granted voting privileges. In the House version of the bill, the right to vote would be extended to any *white* male inhabitant. After a great deal of debate and, most likely, deal-

making, the Senate passed its version of the bill—known as The
Organic Act—in May, with the provision that those qualified to
vote would be "as determined by the Idaho Territorial Act," which
stipulated that only white males were eligible to vote. President
Lincoln signed the Organic Act into law on June 22, 1864.

The Organic Act provided that a territorial governor would
be appointed to a four-year term by the president of the United
States. The governor would have the power to serve as
commander-in-chief of any militia forces and as superintendent
of Indian affairs within the territory, and he could grant pardons
and respites until such time as the president would make a
final decision. The Organic Act also stipulated that the
president would appoint a territorial secretary, who would be
solely authorized to sign warrants for fiscal appropriations of
the territory, and that the territory could elect a delegate
(without voting privileges) to the United States House of
Representatives who would serve a two year term of office. All
of the provisions looked good on paper but would be painfully
tested in the real world now known as the Territory of Montana.
To probably no one's surprise, Sidney Edgerton was appointed
to be the first territorial governor of Montana by President
Lincoln on the same day the Organic Act was passed into law.

Upon his return to Bannack in July, Edgerton quickly began
the pursuit of bringing order to his new territory. He would soon
be joined by the other federally appointed, and all staunch
Republican, officers: Edward Neally (U.S. Attorney), George M.
Pinney (U.S. Marshall), Truman C. Everts (Assessor), and Nathaniel
P. Langford (Collector of Revenue). Three men were also appointed
to serve as federal judges: Chief Justice Hezekiah Lord Hosmer
(another native of Ohio who had served as secretary for Ashley's
Committee on the Territories), and Associate Justices Lorenzo P.
Williston (a Pennsylvania native who had served as a justice for the
Dakota Territory), and Lyman E. Munson (a Connecticut native
and cousin of William Seward).[31] The position of Secretary,
meanwhile, proved difficult to fill. Lincoln had offered the position
to two men, Rev. Henry P. Torsey of Maine and John Coburn of

Indiana, but both had declined prior to Johnson's appointment of Meagher.[32]

Perhaps motivated by personal convenience—or his purchase of property and mining claims in and around Bannack—Edgerton declared that Bannack would serve as the site for the inaugural legislative session, although Virginia City had already become the most heavily populated area of the territory. Edgerton also authorized a census in order to establish districts and voting representation; but he exercised considerable latitude in his work. "Governor Edgerton, in apportioning the members of the first session, had distributed the memberships for that session over the various counties or districts made up by him without strict regard to a very loose and approximate census that had been taken under his supervision."[33] Based upon his census, Edgerton would subsequently declare a territorial population of 20,000 and made arrangements for the initial legislative elections of the Montana Territory to be held in October.

At the time the first elections were held, there were essentially three political affiliations represented within the territory: Radical (or Union) Republicans, including Governor Edgerton and Mr. Sanders; Copperhead Democrats, those who were very strongly pro-Southern in their sympathies; and Union (or Northern) Democrats, representing the vast majority of the territory's citizens. Edgerton would set a turbulent course for territorial politics with his bitter attacks upon the Democratic candidates; attacks which included accusing Democrats of being equivalent to traitors, and that former soldiers of the confederacy had been "uncultivated savages."[34] Wilbur Sanders, a candidate for Territorial Delegate, joined in this muckraking, at one point commenting that: "The left wing of Price's army is skulking in the gulches of Montana, inciting treason."[35] By at least one objective measurement, the rhetoric of Edgerton and Sanders (as well as later authors) may have been greatly exaggerated. Although it is certainly possible some population shift occurred between 1864 and 1870, the federal census of 1870 for the territory would document 18,306 white, males of which only 1,584 were "natives of the Confederate states."[36]

Author Clark Spence suggests that while Southern sympathies did certainly exist in the territory, the extent to which this influenced political decisions has been misleading. Moreover, Spence contends that Republicans could have formed a powerful link with the Union Democrats had Edgerton been willing to compromise, "it is doubtful if Edgerton represented most Montanans or if he fully understood their political complextion."[37]

In what had to have been a bitter disappointment to Edgerton, the election of 1864 resulted in only a one-vote majority to the Republicans on the Territorial Council, a one-vote majority to Democrats in the Territorial House of Representatives, and the selection of Democrat Samuel McLean as the territorial delegate to Congress. Wilbur Sanders had managed to win a majority of votes in each district except for Madison County, the most populous district in the territory. Edgerton would do his best to grasp victory from defeat by withholding the certification of McLean's election until returns from those precincts he claimed were affiliated with Madison County for the purposes of the election had been received, specifically ballots from persons residing at Fort Union. After some delay, approximately 2,000 ballots—all supporting Republican candidates—were announced to have arrived from Fort Union. Much to their credit, N. E. Davis and James Tufts, both from Madison County and both of whom would have been elected on the basis of these returns, met with Edgerton and protested what they firmly believed was fraud. Edgerton relented, and the election results were certified as declared prior to the Fort Union ballots. It was later determined that at no time during 1864 was there ever more than 300 persons at Fort Union, and that it actually lay outside the territory's boundary.[38] Governor Edgerton, however, would still have the opportunity to exercise his very significant influence.

The first legislative session for the Montana Territory convened at Bannack on December 12, 1864, and Edgerton quickly set a confrontational tone to the proceedings. In his opening address he would refer to James Buchanan's presidency as "an imbecile administration" and accused the southern states of having fought the Civil War by "ignoring the rules of civilized warfare."[39] An additional controversy was created by Edgerton's demand that each of the elected legislators swear an oath of allegiance to the United States. Known as the "Iron Clad Oath," it included the statement that the legislators " . . . had never borne arms, or encouraged those who had, against the Union." Passed by Congress in 1862, and intended as a litmus test for federal office holders, it had been similarly used—with opposition—in other territories.[40] While Edgerton's insistence upon this protocol stirred bad feelings among several of the representatives, only John H. Rogers of Madison County flatly refused to take the oath. Rogers willingly acknowledged that he had served with the Missouri Militia, which was a de facto force against the United States Army, but had resigned once their commander (Sterling Price) took the militia into the service of the Confederate Army forces in Missouri.[41] Rogers suggested that he be permitted to take the oath of allegiance by simply omitting the specific portion which stated "never borne arms," while still declaring his loyalty to the United States. Edgerton would not agree to this proposed compromise, however.[42] Consequently, Rogers removed himself from the proceedings, but would be re-elected and seated in 1866.[43]

Under the leadership of Robert Lawrence of Madison County as president of the seven-member Council and George Detwiler of Jefferson County as Speaker of the House with its thirteen members, the legislature finally settled down to business. During the next ten weeks the legislature enacted several laws regarding operations of the new territory, including a bill setting term limitations for legislators, adoption of a Territorial Seal design and motto (Oro el Plata), establishment of the territorial capital at Virginia City, and, as specifically prescribed by the terms of The Organic Act, a territorial apportionment bill. Unfortunately, the apportionment bill—passed late in the session—never became law as Edgerton would veto the legislature's plan. As Wilbur F. Sanders later attempted to explain, Governor Edgerton's veto was based upon the legislature's plan to include an immediate increase in the number of legislators; an increase to twenty-six in the House of Representatives and to thirteen on the Territorial Council.[44] While this growth in the number of legislators was permitted within the terms of the Organic Act, it was Edgerton's opinion that such an increase was not appropriate at that time, and he directed the legislature to rewrite their plan. Of course, it may be reasonable to assume that Edgerton had already come to the realization that an increase in legislators would, most likely, have resulted in an increase of *Democratic* legislators. Edgerton's veto even drew sharp criticism from the solid Republican, and newspaper editor, Henry Blake: "A bill for this object [district apportionment] was passed and vetoed by Gov. Edgerton, a crank posing as a Radical Republican . . . ."[45] Even the U.S. Attorney for the territory, Edward Neally, would castigate Edgerton for his roughshod attempts to manage the political process. In the parlance of the time and place, Neally wrote, "It is barely possible that when they come to pan him out it will be difficult to find color."[46]

In reaction to Edgerton's veto, the legislators would not budge from their position, and no substitute bill was presented prior to the adjournment of the session on February 9, 1865. This impasse revealed a critical flaw in the Organic Act, as no provision had been made in the Act to deal directly with such circumstances. The fuse was now lit on the powder keg of political turmoil, leading to even more explosive conflict in the course of Montana politics.

In the months following the First Session's adjournment, Edgerton would resist calling a Second Territorial Session and held control of the territorial operations through the federally appointed (Republican) officials. In an open letter to the *Montana Post*, Sanders would place the blame for the First Session's failings squarely upon the legislators, writing that this historic Session " . . . met with a most lamentable disaster, only because it was caught in most scurvy company."[47] Into this raucous, politically strident, raw new territory arrived Thomas Francis Meagher—former Union Army General, "Northern Democrat," and Irish revolutionary.

The *Montana Post* enthusiastically greeted Meagher in its columns, citing that "General Meagher has arrived among us . . . Our new Secretary is no partizan. His banner is the stars and stripes."[48] In what was evidence of the new arrival's naiveté, or hopefulness, the *Post* further reported on the remarks Meagher made at a reception held in his honor: "At Bannack on Saturday night last [September 23] . . . General Meagher said that, in this Territory, men of different, and, even, of extreme opinions . . . had espoused the cause of the North or of the South, with great ardor. Now, however the strife was terminated, and [the time had come to] return to their old allegiance."[49] Further evidence of Meagher's naiveté—or the *Post's* hopefulness—was the additional statement that, "It is [Meagher's] intention to call together the Legislature at the earliest possible moment."[50]

It must have come as a great surprise to Meagher to learn—within hours of his arrival in Bannack—that Edgerton intended to leave Montana. Whether motivated from a sense of family obligation as he would later claim or, more likely, the realization that his dream of building a personal empire had become a nightmare, Edgerton acknowledged that he had decided to go back east for an indeterminate period, neglecting to add that he had not received permission from Secretary of State Seward for his absence. Within the formal proclamation of his appointment of Meagher as acting governor, Edgerton would only circumspectly refer to his departure by declaring: "Whereas I this day leave the Territory intending to be absent therefrom for a few months . . . ."[51] A declaration which would prove to be a gross understatement.

Before leaving the territory, Edgerton advised Meagher of a treaty session which had been arranged with some Indian tribes and that the first Territorial Legislature had chartered a town known as "The City of Virginia," commonly known as Virginia City, and designated it to serve as the new territorial capital. Meagher's mind must have been spinning as he made his way to Virginia City with, as related in popular lore, all the official documents of the Montana Territory in one of his coat pockets. The *Montana Post* reported that "General Meagher rode over from Bannack to this city, stopping on Wednesday night at Stone's Ranche."[52]

CHAPTER 22

"Virginia City is different from anything
which I had ever before seen. There isn't a tree in sight.
All have been cut down for wood, and all about the city,
the ground is cut and dug up by the mining
which is constantly going on."
Ellen Fletcher, July 1866

When Meagher arrived in Virginia City he found a community of dramatic contrasts and incredible wealth. "About $30 million of placer gold was removed from the gulch between 1863 and 1866."[53] What had begun as a sprawling mining camp had become the largest settlement of the territory and had acquired all the trappings of late 1800's civilization—some of the best and a good deal of the worst. Perhaps as an example of the different standards by which people of the territory lived, one local law provided that, "If any physician, or other person, while in a state of intoxication, shall prescribe any poisonous drug or other medicine to another person, he shall be punished by imprisonment in the county jail not more than one year, or by fine."[54] By the time of Meagher's arrival the Montana Theatre Company was operating, Baptist and Methodist churches had been established, a newspaper was being published, a school was in session, the Montana Historical Society had been formed, and Montana's first Masonic Lodge had been founded. "The pilgrim entering Virginia City early in 1865 saw a town so new that the clapboard and log buildings had not yet weathered . . . he could see the beginnings of a Chinatown plus the very evident red-light district."[55] Included among the prominent buildings were the elegant Stonewall Building, Leviathon Hall, and the Idaho Hotel amidst the bustling of new fortunes being found—and lost. Stark contrasts to the attempts of some to provide the trappings of "the states" were ever-present, however, in the daily life of this bawdy new town. "The streets . . . were choked with traffic [and] turned ordinary mud into deep, soupy mire . . . [and] were unusually filthy. Livery owners piled manure there from occasional stable cleanings. Dead animals lay for days where they had dropped . . . ."[56]

The town also had its own share of sectional bitterness as revealed in the circumstances surrounding the selection of its name. When the original charter of organization was presented for approval to the district judge (and ardent Union supporter), Dr. Gaylord Giles Bissell, the designation used was "Varina City" in honor of Jefferson Davis's wife. "It was pointed out to Judge Bissell that Varina Davis was without question wife of Jefferson Davis, but she was a Northern belle, nee Varina Howell, grand-daughter of the Governor of New Jersey. The city name, therefore, was chosen to please both sides. 'I'll be damned if I will,' the judge said and drew a line through Varina. That done he evidently experienced caution [and wrote in "Virginia"]."[57]

The local newspaper and social organizations—including the Fenian Circles of Nevada City and Virginia City—would effusively celebrate Meagher's appearance. Soon after his arrival in Virginia City, Meagher established the territorial office on the second floor of a merchant's building at the corner of Van Buren and Wallace streets.[58] Meagher would later make his home in an unpretentious log cabin located on Idaho Street, just a short walk from the territorial office. The acting governor had barely unpacked his bags at the Planter's House Hotel before he found himself being courted by both the Republican and Union Democrat representatives, and he immodestly accepted center stage in this political drama. "Meagher's vigorous character caused him to enter with full force into a complex situation and his participation added a great deal of color."[59] As evidence of his enthusiasm for this bustling new territory and the role of acting governor, he almost immediately began to solicit a permanent appointment to the position. Meagher wrote to his wife Elizabeth that he expected Edgerton to resign and that she should initiate contacts with President Johnson requesting her husband's appointment.[60] There is no evidence that Edgerton had spoken directly to Meagher regarding his intentions but, rather, it is more likely that Meagher was making an informed assumption. It is very doubtful that the disparate personalities of Edgerton and Meagher would have engendered an effective working relationship, much less one of shared confidence. Edgerton took his entire family with him for his trip East, which may have easily been interpreted as his lack of resolve to return. And certainly Meagher's belief, or actual knowledge, that Edgerton would not return goes a long way toward understanding some of the decisions he would subsequently make. But first, Meagher would have his initial experience with the original inhabitants of the Montana Territory.

Conflict between the territory's native population and the Whites had been escalating as the waves of miners and new settlers had grown. The *Montana Post* carried a regular column titled "The Indians" which posted news—more often rumors—regarding these conflicts. In the January 21, 1864 edition, the *Post* reported that: "General McDowell has issued an order that all Indians taken shall be handed over to the civil authorities. The step is ridiculous, expensive, and a premium on crime. Justice to the (marauding) Indian is most conveniently given in three ways—lead, steel, or hemp . . . ."[61] Governor Edgerton had been drawn into the conflict soon after the legislators had left Bannack. "In the spring of 1865 the Blackfeet killed ten men out of Fort Benton, sending the governor into near panic."[62] Edgerton made a desperate, and unsuccessful, attempt to raise a militia of 500 men under the leadership of territory pioneer James Stuart as lieutenant colonel.[63] Edgerton would also appoint Wilbur Sanders to the rank of colonel, a title Sanders would proudly carry for the remainder of his life. The governor quickly learned, however, that men were more interested in finding gold than fighting Indians, despite the inducements of hard liquor to steel their resolve. Judge Hosmer would characterize the futile enlistment efforts as: "A most melancholy waste of cheap whiskey . . . ."[64]

A treaty session was to be held at Fort Benton in October of 1865 with the Indian tribes who had been hunting and living on the land that is present-day northwestern Montana. Although the territorial governor carried the additional title of superintendent of Indian affairs, it was actually the responsibility of the federal Indian agent, Major Gad Upson, to negotiate a treaty signing. Upson was bound, however, to settle the treaty in accordance with federally legislated mandates; in fact, the treaty had already been prepared in Washington. The territorial governor's signature wasn't even required to be on the treaty (which Meagher didn't sign), but Meagher " . . . considered it his duty" to be present for the negotiations.[65] His desire to witness first-hand some of the outlying reaches of the territory and meet the Indians involved in the treaty session must have also been a powerful enticement. Among those who accompanied Meagher to the treaty session was Lyman E. Munson, one of the three federal judges who had been appointed to serve the territory and who wrote a detailed account of this experience. Meagher would later recount the beginning of the journey in a letter to the legendary Jesuit missionary Father Pierre Jean deSmet: "I set out one day . . . for Benton, from the new city of Helena (every collection of log huts is called a city in this ambitious country) . . . ."[66]

When Meagher and Munson arrived at Fort Benton, there were approximately 7,500 Indians, most from the two principal tribes of the Blackfeet and the Gros Ventres. In what became known as the "Blackfoot Treaty of 1865," or as the "Upson Treaty," the tribes were expected to relinquish all claims to the area south of the Missouri and Teton rivers. All land between those rivers and the Canadian boundary, and extending from the Continental Divide to a line drawn north from the mouth of the Milk River, was to be held for the tribes as their reservation. No whites would be permitted to live within the reservation boundaries, according to the treaty; however, the government would have the right to build roads through this land, and whites would have the right to travel upon said roads.[67] In addition to the reservation land, the tribes were to receive an annual annuity of $5,000 in farm supplies and livestock, and a $500 bonus was to be distributed to each principal chief for twenty years.[68] Although Upson was able to convince chiefs from both the Blackfeet and Gros Ventres to sign, it was clear there were many among the tribes who did not enthusiastically accept these terms. At the conclusion of the treaty session Munson reported that, " . . . we distributed to them about $7,500 in annuities, ostensibly one dollar for each indian."[69] Meagher recognized the inequities of the treaty's terms, stating that: "A comparative small reservation . . . is guaranteed to the original owners of this vast domain."[70] Meagher was critical of the treaty process and would later urge that local agents be authorized some discretion to modify Washington-dictated terms, convinced that the treaties being negotiated in the current manner had little chance for any lasting success. Before leaving the treaty session Meagher was reportedly offered gifts of buffalo robes and a horse from the Indians, but declined to accept them in view of how obviously critical such possessions were to their subsistence.[71]

On the evening of Meagher and Munson's first day's return travel from Fort Benton, a messenger rode into their camp with urgent news. Soon after the white authorities had left the treaty site, factions from the Blackfeet and Gros Ventres began quarrelling, and the tribes were about to begin full warfare with each other. Meagher commandeered a small cannon from an emigrant train camped nearby and immediately started back to Fort Benton.[72] After an all-night ride, Meagher and his small party arrived at the treaty site and called the principal chiefs together. According to Munson's account, Meagher delivered a simple, very direct message to the chiefs. If they did not end their fighting and leave the agency grounds by noon, " . . . I will order my men to begin firing and not stop until every indian is killed and the annuity goods restored to the government."[73] The tribes took the former general at his word and had completely dispersed by the assigned deadline without further incident.

As if to add insult to the injury already committed by force-feeding the treaty to the tribes, the United States Senate would never ratify the treaty. Major Upson would die en route to

Washington, so an associate delivered the treaty to Secretary of the Interior James Harlan. Apparently neither Harlan nor his successor Orville Browning was convinced that the Indians or whites of the Territory would actually observe the terms of the treaty, so it was never presented to the Senate for approval.[74] Whether the treaty would have changed the course of events is pure conjecture, but it wasn't long before the prophesy of Harlan and Browning was fulfilled.

Among Meagher's first efforts upon his return to Virginia City from the treaty negotiations was the solicitation of military support for the territory. He contacted Major General Frank Wheaton at Fort Laramie (Wyoming), requesting military protection both from the Indian threat and as a deterrent to road agents.[75] Meagher reiterated this request to Secretary of State Seward in early December, requesting a cavalry presence of no less than 1,000 troopers.[76] Not leaving any stone unturned, Meagher also pressed his request for military support to his former commanding officer, and the man he had once referred to as an "envenomed martinet," General William T. Sherman. Sherman was now serving as commander of the Department of the Missouri, the military authority for the Montana Territory. Perhaps unexpected of a former volunteer officer turned politician, Meagher urged in his correspondence to Sherman that an officer in the regular army be assigned control of the new military district, writing, "Of the Regular Army, by all means, for Volunteer Officers become politicians too rapidly in these new Territories."[77] It must have brought a smile to the face of the man Meagher thought humorless, as Sherman read this request.

In spite of all his pleadings, none of Meagher's requests for military support were realized and would consequently set the stage for another act in this unfolding drama of the Montana Territory.

CHAPTER 23

*"While I have met with much encouragement
and warm support from the Republicans of the Territory
in the undertaking of editing the organ of the party here,
I have nevertheless encountered no little opposition
from the Copperhead and rebel sentiment
which tinctures society in Helena and other parts of Montana."*
Robert E. Fisk, editor, *Helena Herald*

The paramount issues which had been facing Meagher in his role as acting governor since his arrival in the territory, were political organization and governing authority. An example of the contentious political environment is revealed in a letter Meagher received shortly after his return from the Blackfeet treaty session. Written by Edward Nealley, who had been entrusted to have the proceedings of the first legislative session printed, it confided, "I have duly arrived at this place [Burlington, Iowa] and shall go in a day or two to New York to attend to the publication of our laws. I wrote to our friend Col. Sanders from Denver to hurry him up in the preparation of the preface [which he had been requested to write] . . . but he is inclined to be indolent, and I hope you will urge upon him the necessity of sending it at once."[78]

On November 30, Meagher received a petition from leading Democrats which requested that new territorial elections be held and that such newly elected legislators be called into session.[79] Meagher's initial inclination however, had been to support the Republican party's argument that there was no legal authority to hold elections and, moreover, that a new crop of legislators would only create problems. Meagher characterized the contentious

situation in a letter to United States Secretary of State William
Seward: "Were Montana admitted as a state tomorrow, the Union
cause would have to encounter in Congress equivocal friends, if
not flagrant mischief-makers . . . ."[80] It was the Republican
contention that the first legislature had failed in its responsibilities;
therefore, the terms of the Organic Act were void, and the federally
appointed officers and judges now had sole authority to administer
the territory. Of course, it was also the opinion of leading
Republicans who had the ear of the acting governor that all
Democrats were southern sympathizers and traitors to the Union
cause for which he and the brave men of his Irish Brigade had
fought so valiantly. In an "open letter" dated December 15 to the
Montana Post, Meagher would write, "It is clearly my conviction
that the legislative functions of this Territory have lapsed," and
further suggest that it would require an enabling act of Congress
to restore legislative functions to the territory.[81] Meagher continued
to be advised by many to initiate a legislative session, including a
group from Helena whose representative wrote, "The Miners and
others in this vicinity are universally in favor of a meeting of the
Legislature."[82] Each passing day must have seemed to Meagher as
if he was being pressed ever tighter in this relentless political vise.
Finding what he believed was the solution would create a great
deal of excitement throughout the Montana Territory.

Whether motivated by political aspirations, or whether it was
simply that his personality was so boldly energetic that he embraced
any action rather than inaction, Meagher had began to shift in his
political sympathy. It appears to have been the Republican game
plan that, given enough time, they could gain political strength
through the influx of immigrants—most arriving from northern
states—and thereby control the legislative process at a time more
suitable to their interests. In the meantime, the Republicans were
very content to allow the federally appointed officials to administer
to the legal and legislative affairs of the territory. Meagher recognized
the political disparity between the territorial officers and the
territory's citizenry, however, and realized that the lethargic attitude
of the territory's Republicans was flagrantly self-serving. He

consequently chose to embrace the more aggressive agenda of the Democrats that called for not only a rebirth of the territorial legislature, but also a petition for statehood status for the fledgling—though immensely rich— new territory.

In what may have been a hopeful effort to reach some middle ground between the Democratic party's call for elections and a legislative session, and the Republican party's total lack of support for any new political machinations, Meagher announced that a Territorial Convention was to be held, "With the purpose of making known the wants and just pretentions of the Territory."[83] The acting governor picked March 1, 1866, as the date to convene the Convention and selected the town of Helena to host the gathering, probably in an effort to utilize a neutral site. Meagher further authorized, based upon Governor Edgerton's 1864 census figures, that the counties of Madison, Deer Lodge, and Edgerton would each be authorized to send ten delegates and that Beaverhead, Choteau, Gallatin, Jefferson, and Missoula counties should each send five delegates to Helena. Meagher wrote to President Johnson in January to explain his decision to call for the Convention. "Unwilling . . . to keep the Territory dumb and inactive . . . I have called a Convention, from which, it is probable, an application for immediate admission into the Union as a State, will emanate from the people of this Territory. I fear we are too great a distance from Washington, and communication between there and the Territory is too much subject to interruption, for us to benefit by our present relations with Congress and the National Government, to the extent that our necessities and interests, present and prospective require."[84]

The reaction to Meagher's Convention announcement was quick—and predictable according to one's political persuasion. While Meagher may have seen an opportunity for personal gain in an alignment with a forward-moving territory that had ambitions of statehood, it seems as likely that this was a genuine effort to ease political frustrations and serve the best interests of the territory. This may be confirmed as illustrated in the editorials of two politically disparate newspapers, the *Montana Radiator* and the *Montana Post*. In an editorial of the *Montana Radiator* the

Convention was interpreted as a reasonable solution inasmuch as, "The absence of a legislature . . . has made it necessary to improvise a substitute . . . ."[85] While the Virginia City paper, the *Montana Post*, lashed out against the idea of a convention—calling it a ploy of the Democratic Party—it also conceded that taking some action rather than remaining in a political quagmire was praiseworthy.[86] As a rule, the flame of optimism burned brightly within Thomas Francis Meagher and it is certainly possible that this caused him to hope for a seat in Congress should Montana be granted statehood. Meagher, himself, must have realized that there was no man in the territory at that time more likely to have been elected. It was also that flame of optimism, however, that often blinded him to the political realities. Regardless of how noble, or self-serving, Meagher's intentions may have been in his call for the Convention, his critics soon found fresh ammunition to use in assailing the acting governor.

During his first winter in Montana, Meagher was frequently called upon to return to the stage as a public speaker both in his official capacity as Acting Governor and as a celebrated orator. Among his audience during one performance was the prospector W. J. Boyer, who would later recall his impression of the evening: "One night during the winter a party of us went up from Adobetown to Nevada and heard a eulogy on Robert Emmet, delivered by general Thomas Francis Meagher. The large Adlephi hall was crowded and his wonderful eloquence was greeted with thunders of applause."[87]

CHAPTER 24

"[the Vigilantes] . . . committed an irreparable error."
Nathaniel P. Langford

James Daniels was found guilty of second-degree murder in a trial held at Judge Lyman Munson's Helena court. Daniels was convicted of killing Andrew Gartley as a result of an argument during a card game on the night of November 29, 1865. Although Gartley appeared to have been the aggressor, Daniels was found guilty at the conclusion of a six-day trial (December 19-24) and was sentenced by Munson to three years' imprisonment at hard labor and a $1,000 fine. Daniels was transferred to the jail in Virginia City to begin serving his sentence.

It was while Daniels was in Virginia City that his case came to the attention of Acting-Governor Meagher. Meagher received a petition signed by " . . . thirtytwo respectable citizens of Helena," including some who had served on the trial's jury, requesting that the governor pardon the accused man.[88] Meagher decided on February 22, in accordance with the powers granted in the Organic Act, as he interpreted them, to grant a reprieve of Daniels's sentence until President Johnson could review the case and pass final judgment. In the text of his reprieve, Meagher wrote, " . . . that the circumstances under which the aforesaid offence was committed, were most provoking on the part of the deceased . . . and, to a great extent, justifiable on the part of the said Daniels."[89] Meagher's decision to release Daniels became known to Judge Munson, who declared this action outrageously improper and that Daniels should be immediately returned to custody. In the meantime, Daniels, perhaps foolishly, made his way back to Helena where different versions of the subsequent events arrive at the same fatal conclusion.

One version relates that Daniels arrived in Helena heartily swearing vengeance on his detractors, which directly led to his demise. And, according to none other than Judge Munson, Daniels arrived " . . . in Helena about nine o'clock in the evening, he was immediately surrounded by the Vigilantes, and was hanged at ten o'clock with the pardon in his pocket." Additionally, although it isn't certain how he knew of this from his office in Helena, Munson further declared that Meagher " . . . while under the influence of an unfortunate habit, pardoned and set the prisoner at liberty."[90] Not surprisingly, Meagher took offense at Munson's attack upon both his authority as governor and his personal character.

In no less than five other versions of the Daniels situation—including one written by Sidney Edgerton's niece and another by the daughter-in-law of Wilbur Sanders—the details differ significantly from Munson's account. The consensus of these alternative stories indicates that Daniels, shortly after arriving in town and upon advice of his attorney, submitted himself to Deputy U.S. Marshal John Featherston. It also appears that none of the principals—Daniels, his attorney, or Marshal Featherston—had actually received notice of Judge Munson's pending order for rearrest since it had been directed to the marshal of Virginia City. It was "on the night succeeding the day of his arrival in Helena" that Featherston left Daniels in a store while he went on rounds to determine the mood of the town.[91] By the time Featherston returned to the store, Daniels was gone. The store clerk on duty later stated that three men had entered the store at about eleven o'clock and held a brief conversation with Daniels, and that "shortly afterward he [Daniels] left in their company."[92]

The next sighting of Daniels was the following morning, March 1, when he was found hanging from a tree commonly used by the Helena Vigilantes to dispatch justice. It was widely reported that the "pardon" which Governor Meagher had issued to Daniels was still in his coat pocket. Furthermore, a note was attached to the body threatening that this fate could also befall Meagher should he pardon any other murderers.[93] N. P. Langford sadly concluded that his Helena brethren had gone far beyond the role intended by the Virginia City vigilantes, "No excuse can be offered for the course that was pursued. This, at least, was one case where the Vigilantes exceeded the boundaries of right and justice, and became themselves the violators of law and propriety."[94] Helen Sanders, daughter of Wilbur, would write that the Vigilantes had concluded their role by February of 1864 but that, "On more than one occasion, and as late as 1865, so called Vigilantes hanged criminals, but without the sanction of the original [Virginia City organization], and that Daniels had been executed by a "mob.""[95] Her position is supported by Langford who wrote, " . . . among the later acts of some of the individuals, claiming to have excercised the authority of the Vigilantes, were executions of which [I] cannot approve. For these persons I can offer not apology. Many of these [individuals] were worse than those they executed."[9]6 Of course, it should also be pointed out that John Featherston had been an active, some would say leading, Vigilante in Alder Gulch during the 1863-64 purge of road agents. To what extent Featherston may have facilitated—if not even promoted—the abduction of Daniels by leaving him unguarded to go on rounds, is worthy of some consideration.

In a somewhat astonishing footnote to the Daniels story, Alexander Leggat would discover the actual two-page Daniels reprieve signed by Meagher in a St. Louis bookstore in 1916. Mr. Leggat, a Helena businessman and collector of Montana memorabilia, purchased the document for five dollars.

Regardless of which version of the Daniels incident one chooses to believe, the situation clearly resulted in problems for the acting governor. Meagher was criticized by those who felt he was circumventing the judiciary, by those who felt he was treating a convicted murderer too leniently, and by those who felt his pardon of Daniels was entirely politically motivated. One unquestionable fact regarding this matter was that it resulted in a sharp, and never healing, fracture between Munson and Meagher.

In the interval between the Daniels fiasco and the scheduled opening of the Territorial Convention in March, Meagher and Virginia City continued to be busy with the excitement and diversions of the territory's commercial and cultural development. Several Protestant congregations had been holding services for some time, and a group of Catholics likewise became actively involved in establishing a physical presence. A building that had been originally used as a theatre was identified as a possible site in Virginia City for a church. True to his word to help establish the Catholic Church in the new territory, "Acting Governor Meagher took a leading part in raising the money to purchase and repair the building."[97] Father Giorda, S.J., conducted the first mass a few days before Christmas in the building dedicated as "All Saints Catholic Church." "It is pleasant to recall that General Thomas Francis Meagher delivered a most eloquent address of welcome to the Catholic priest . . . ."[98]

Although he would never personally witness its incredible natural wonders, Meagher was deeply impressed by an account of another Catholic priest (Francis Kuppens) who would describe a wild and beautiful, and generally unexplored, area of the territory. The acting governor was so enthused by the stories of Father Kuppens, that he would reportedly remark that the area should be held safe from any damaging incursion and made an area of national refuge.[99] His idea would become a reality, but not until 1872, when this spectacular region of natural phenomena became Yellowstone National Park.

Meagher—who had recently become a Montana landowner— would assume the role of tourism proponent entreating a friend, Reverend George Pepper, to accompany Mrs. Meagher on her trip west. Meagher zealously urged Rev. Pepper to "become a mountaineer as I have done." Meagher also opinioned to Rev. Pepper that: "We have too great a preponderance of Yankee blood (not blood, but serum) out here—I want to see a strong infusion of the rich, red, generous, royal Celtic blood to counteract the acidity and poverty of the former."[100]

CHAPTER 25

"I have frankly to confess I was greatly in error."
Meagher to Seward, February 20, 1866.

By late January of 1866, the political pot had reached a boiling point in response to the approaching Convention. The Radical Republicans and their supporting press had closed ranks and were vehemently denouncing the need, and legality, of such a gathering. At the same time, the Democrats and moderates were equally outspoken in their praise for what they believed was an attempt to make some forward movement in what had become a political abyss. Of course, the Democrats could not have been unaware of their growing strength and the powerful public influence they would now command in a renewed legislative process. Meanwhile, as the public debate was raging, Thomas Francis Meagher was quietly making a study of the Organic Act and the Territorial Act and reaching a decision that would have far-reaching implications.

Meagher's about-face announcement in early February would have an explosive effect on the political landscape even more dramatic than the toll the miners were exacting upon the ore-rich Alder Gulch landscape. Citing as his authority Section 11 of the Organic Act (which dictated an annual session of the territorial legislature) and Section II of the Territorial Act, Meagher called for a Second Session of the territorial legislature to convene on March 5, 1866. Those men who had served in the first legislature's Territorial Council and the Territorial House of Representatives were directed to reassemble in Virginia City to take up the business of the territory and complete their duties as charged in the Organic Act. Those who thought Meagher's call for a convention had been the act of a traitor were now doubly outraged by this new atrocity.

Meagher (in accordance with the prescribed line of authority) confirmed his intentions in a letter to Secretary of State William Seward, with a mea culpa: "I have frankly to confess I was greatly in error. On more maturely considering the powers vested in me by the Organic Act, and the laws of the Territory, I came to the conclusion, that a Legislature did legally exist here, and that it was legally and constitutionally within the scope of my prerogatives to summon it into action."[101] There is no indication that Seward responded, or made any move to contradict Meagher's action.

The Republicans of Montana, however, did respond. Meagher's resolution was a call to arms for the territory's Radical Republicans who waged a "no quarter" campaign of newspaper articles and letters to their friends in Washington. Not only did they plead for Congress to intervene, but used the opportunity to make bitter accusations against Meagher. Typical of the substance of these letters was one from William Chumasero to Senator Lyman Trumbull which included the remark: "His [Meagher's] whole conduct since his arrival has been that of a drunken madman."[102] Some of these accusations were not only believed at the time, but became the stuff of legends which are still regarded as fact.

While some argue that Meagher's decision to reconvene the Territorial Legislature was an attempt to advance his own political fortunes, a more dispassionate review may find otherwise. Although he was certainly moving toward the position of the territory's political majority, it was not a wise move for anyone with political advancement in mind. Republicans remained firmly in control of the presidency and Congress, and it must have been commonly acknowledged that this hold on political power at the national level would exist for some time. Inasmuch as the positions of territorial governor and territorial secretary were political appointments of the president, Meagher's shift to support another legislative session may have actually been tantamount to political suicide. Contrary to the claims of his detractors, Meagher may have acted more genuinely on behalf of the majority of Montana's citizens than many other politicians before or since. Any lingering support he had among the territory's Republicans quickly dissipated, and the derisive expression "The Acting One" became a jaundiced—and lasting—reference to Thomas Francis Meagher in Montana history.

In the week prior to the Second Session's convening (the Convention's opening had been re-scheduled for March 26), Meagher would make an appearance in Helena. Meagher attempted to use the occasion to set a positive tone for the upcoming Session and to reach out to those harboring strong anti-Southern sentiments. Considering that he, more so than most of those in the territory, had witnessed the deaths and brutal maiming of friends and comrades before the Confederate Army, Meagher spoke remarkable words of healing and reconciliation. On the evening of February 21, he would speak in a tone which would certainly have reflected the wishes of President Lincoln: "On the battlefields which they held for four tempestuous years, the soldiers of the South had lowered their colors and sheathed their swords. The spirit in which they had surrendered, as well as the spirit with which they fought, entitled them to respect . . . But the war is over and I would not plant thorns where the olive has taken root. Here at all events, amoung the great mountains of the new world no echos should be awakened save those that proclaimed true and glorious peace, the everlasting brotherhood of those who had been foes upon the battlefield."[103] Regrettably, Meagher's words did not dull the swords of the Radical Republicans of the Montana Territory.

CHAPTER 26

" . . . the judges of Montana . . . claim the right and will
exercise the duty of not only construing, but of passing upon
the validity of any law the legislature may pass,
or even the legality of the session itself. . . . "

Judge Lymun Munson

On March 5, 1866, the delegates of the Territorial Legislature assembled in Virginia City and, as their first order of business, elected officers for the session. The Council, meeting on the second floor of the Idaho Billiard Hall, chose Anson S. Potter of Madison County to be their president. Holding their meetings on the second floor of the Stonewall House Saloon, the House of Representatives selected A. E. Mayhew of Deer Lodge County as Speaker of the House.

Acting Governor Meagher addressed the legislative groups on March 6, opening with the plea that this Session not attempt to wholly reconstruct the work of the First Session: "Let [the laws] not be disturbed, unless in such instances as demand the abatement of positive mischiefs."[104] Meagher, in what could be considered his "State of the Territory" address, outlined several areas of concerns and identified some areas where he urged the legislators to take action. His leading statement of concern was with the lack of an effective military presence. Although, Meagher told the legislators, he had recently received notice from Governor Edgerton, who " . . . informs me that the Secretary of War has promised to give at an early day . . . the military protection we have asked from them." Meagher further announced that he had requested federal officials for the appointment of a surveyor general to alleviate land disputes, and had included in his budget request for the territory, "a sum of not less than fifty

181

thousand dollars . . . for Territorial buildings . . . and fifty thousand dollars for cavalry barracks at different points . . . to accommodate a regiment of 850 strong."[105]

Among Meagher's recommendations were that the territory discontinue the use of territory and county script in order to put its finances on more solid footing and that the legislature petition Congress for a branch of the U.S. Mint to be established in the territory. Meagher also urged resolutions be adopted for federal appropriations to improve navigation of the Missouri River and the Niobara Route road in order to provide better access into the territory and expressed his concern with the privatization of travel routes, known as "chartered roads." Meagher warned against the covetous desires of those in the Idaho Territory to redraw territorial boundaries so as to reclaim area and, perhaps as additional justification for the Session, proclaimed, "I greatly doubt that any such proposition would have been thought of—had not Montana been sentenced to incapacity and paralysis . . . ."[106] Perhaps the recommendation which would subsequently have the greatest long-term impact was one which opened an old wound. Meagher made a strongly worded plea that the territorial legislature protest a current bill in the U.S. Congress known as the Mineral Rights Act, which allowed for the federal government's absolute authority over mineral rights throughout the territory and imposing fees. The *Montana Post* would characterize the legislation as "So crude, uncertain, unjust and ridiculous a document . . . the author ought to compose another, endowing a college for noodles, place it in his bosom, and then die."[107] Meagher, slightly more restrained, stated: " . . . had this bill been in operation three years ago, Montana would not be little better than a paltry mining camp . . . ."[108] The sponsor of the Mineral Rights bill in Congress was Senator John Sherman of Ohio—brother of General William T. Sherman. Meagher's deportment would, again, seem either the act of one totally unaware of political realities or one acting foremost in the interests of his constituents.

Meagher closed his remarks to the legislature by restating his reasons for initiating the call to convene and his firm belief in the validity of this Second Session. As if to add emphasis to his statements, he encouraged the legislature to address the matter of representative apportionment and further suggested that the Session should set a date for new elections in the territory and even select a date for the Third Session which he proposed " . . . would meet in October at the latest."[109]

The next day, March 7, Meagher appeared again before the Council after receiving a report from Neil Howie, the deputy United States marshal for the territory, " . . . by which it appears" Meagher reported to the Council, "the long threatened hostilities of the Blood and Piegan Indians . . . have assumed a decided shape . . . ."[110] This report was only one of similar letters sent to Meagher regarding conflicts with the Indians of the territory. As early as February 27 Meagher had been requested by the sheriff of Benton City that "a force be sent here sufficiently strong to put an end to all Indian troubles . . . ."[111] The acting governor concluded by asking the Council to accordingly develop plans to protect the territory's citizenry. The matter was referred to the Council's Committee on Indian Affairs, which would report back five days later that they had verified that " . . . branches of the said Blackfeet Indians are arrayed in bloody hostility against the border settlements of this Territory."[112] Lending support to this decision was, most likely, an urgent letter from S. B. Mathews requesting an armed escort of one hundred men as protection for his wagon train of supplies, "in view of the immediate outbreak of the hostile Indians . . . knowing the atrocities already committed at Sun River," and a letter from the acting agent for the Blackfeet who cited several occasions of Indian violence against whites.[113] The Committee's recommendation that a fund be established to defray expenses of an expedition against the hostiles was approved by the Council, who also petitioned the federal government for immediate cavalry protection. Meagher would soon report, however, that he had received a letter from General Sherman which left little doubt that "Montana will have to depend upon herself for protection . . . ."[114]

During the term of the Second Session, 138 bills were introduced (including eleven divorce laws), sixty-four of which

were passed by both houses.[115] Charles Bagg, a Democrat of
Madison County, was the most prolific legislator, introducing
twenty bills during the Session. Meagher would sign his approval
to forty-eight laws, acting thoughtfully in his use of the veto,
including a veto of the two surviving divorce bills, which he
concluded were issues more appropriate for the courts to determine.
Meagher also disapproved of a bill, which was subsequently
amended to his approval, establishing a Superintendent of Public
Instruction. Meagher had objected on the grounds that it did not
provide a sufficient salary and "moreover, . . . it does not authorize
the Superintendent of Public Instruction to exclude from Public
Schools of this Territory any sectarian tracts, or other
publications . . . nor does it empower him to prevent and suppress
sectarian instruction, in which as the world knows, teachers, of
every religious denomination are apt and prone to indulge."[116] In
what would prove to be a noble, albeit short-sighted, gesture,
Meagher also requested the legislature cease discussion of a bill
which would have provided a salary supplement, paid by the
territory, to the federally appointed territorial officers. Meagher
believed it was the responsibility of the federal government, not
the territory, to adequately provide for these appointees and that,
"if there is anything legally due the Executive office, it shall be
transferred to the Miner's Hospital at Helena."[117]

Even the typically critical *Montana Post* would grudgingly
concede in its editorials that several acts of the legislature were
laudable—though the paper remained unconvinced the Session
was legal. One of the bills that must have given the acting governor
a special satisfaction to sign was Council Bill #17 which created
Meagher County from a large, amorphous tract of the territory
known as Big Horn.

Before adjourning on April 14, the legislature also addressed
another issue Meagher had brought to their attention.
"Remonstrating against the passage by Congress of any act
providing for sale of the mineral lands of the United States," they
passed and forwarded a a joint resolution which protested the
Mineral Rights Act of John Sherman.[118] And, in defiant opposition

to their absent governor's wishes, the delegates passed Council Bill #52, which increased the size of the Legislative Assembly.

Just prior to the adjournment of the Second Session, Meagher submitted a closing message to the legislators that, in part, reiterated his decision to bring them together: "I called the Legislature of the Territory together for the reason that I found Montana in a state, politically speaking, of imbecility and stagnation. American communities are not properly and successfully developed unless their intelligence is let loose, and given a full and an authoritative position to express and illustrate itself."[119]

In the midst of the Second Session's term, Meagher was invited to serve as the featured speaker at a festive St. Patrick's Day celebration in Virginia City. Meagher used the occasion for some light-hearted remarks rather than as a political pulpit. To great laughter and cheers from the audience, he related that: "Sixteen years ago I spent the 17th day of March in the forest of Tasmania . . . which the gracious majesty of Great Britain enabled me to visit, having placed a sloop-of-war at my disposal for that delightful purpose. My Protestant fellow-countrymen will not, I am sure, understand me to claim that this day is exclusively a Catholic festival . . . I have no objection to their appropriating St. Patrick . . . for I well know that he would convert 'every mother's sowl of them' with that miraculous crozier of his, should he ever get among them."[120]

Although it had become something of a political orphan by this time, the Territorial Convention formally convened on April 9 in Helena with forty-seven delegates from seven counties (the postponement from March 26 was made to better accommodate travel arrangements and secure the blessing of the legislature). Robert Ewing, from Edgerton County, was elected to be chair of the proceedings.[121] Somewhat predictably, the Convention agenda was vague, and the delegates were uncertain as to their responsibilities; however, they did manage to focus on at least one significant task. Prior to the Convention's close on April 15, a draft for a state constitution was prepared and approved by the delegates. Although there were several printing presses now operating in the territory, it was decided to send the draft out of the area for printing.[122] Thomas Tutt, one of the Convention's delegates, was selected to personally transport the one and only copy of the constitution to St. Louis for printing and subsequent distribution within the territory and to Congress as a precursor to formal application for statehood recognition. In what must rank among Montana's most intriguing unsolved mysteries, the constitution draft was misplaced and has never been located. There is a theory that the constitution was actually held by the Convention's secretary, H. N. Maguire, whose records were destroyed by fire several years later.

As spring of 1866 turned into summer, the political climate in the Montana Territory warmed again. Radical Republicans redoubled their attacks against Meagher through newspaper editorials and in private letters to their allies in the U.S. Congress. While some focused on the continued charges that the newly revived legislative process was illegal, others made personally disparaging remarks toward Meagher, most of which were obvious exaggerations, if not outright lies. These attacks must have been especially troubling to Meagher on a personal, as well as a political, level since his wife had recently arrived in Virginia City. Republicans finally realized the fruition of their efforts on June 4, when Judge Lyman Munson, with Territorial Chief Justice Hezekiah Hosmer concurring, issued a ruling that the Second Legislative Session was illegal, and all acts passed by the Session were null and void. Meagher quickly responded to Munson's decision, citing that because Congress had approved the territorial appropriation for 1866-67, which included a budget for a legislative assembly, they had de facto recognized the legality of the Session. Furthermore, as if to add an "in your face" exclamation point, Meagher also announced that there would be an election on September 3 for representatives to the Third Legislative Session to be held in the autumn. Meanwhile, as if his critics needed any additional fodder for their denunciations, a specter of the past would appear to haunt Meagher.

CHAPTER 27

"We are the Fenian Brotherhood, skilled in the arts of war,
And we're going to fight for Ireland, the land we adore,
Many battles we have won, along with the boys in blue,
And we'll go and capture Canada, for we've nothing else to do."

Fenian soldier's song

The membership of the Fenian Brotherhood had continued to grow since the end of the Civil War, adding many Confederate Army veterans to its rolls; but the organization also found itself straining from fragmented internal pressures. At the Fenian Convention held in late 1865, the Brotherhood's founding father, John O'Mahony, was removed from his position of near-absolute power. The Brotherhood restructured the leadership into an organization with an elected president and a fifteen-member cabinet.[123] With the new leadership, and no doubt the battle-hardened confidence of recent war veterans, came an invigorated sense of dedication to free Ireland from the grasp of Great Britain. A bold plan was developed which called for an army of Fenians to invade and establish a separate Irish Republic within Canada. The resources of this British territory could then be utilized to prepare an invasion force to Ireland, or, alternatively, Canada itself could be used as a valuable bartering chip to gain Ireland's independence through negotiations. This plan seems to have been widely known and, many believe, had the tacit, if not direct, approval of those in the administration of President Johnson as well as Congress. Evidence of how prevalent was the knowledge of the Fenians' intentions, a report even appeared in the *Montana Post* which supported the Fenians' cause and stated that, "If prudence forbid an invasion of Ireland . . . they will endeavor to seize Canada—or some other country under British rule . . . ."[124]

An ambitious plan that intended to bring a three-pronged attack against Canada was actually initiated on June 1, 1866, but only one regiment managed to successfully reach their objective. Approximately 500 Fenian troops under the command of John O'Neill managed to initially take some thinly defended positions (most notably the city of Ridgeway), but they began to steadily fall back under pressure from regular British soldiers who responded to the invasion. As O'Neill and his men retreated across the Niagara River towards Buffalo in the early morning hours of June 3, they were taken into custody and arrested by U.S. military forces. Although charged with violations of the neutrality laws, the Fenians who stood trial were only modestly reprimanded.[125]

While Meagher had no involvement with the Fenian invasion, his membership in the Brotherhood seems to have been regarded as common knowledge. He had received a boisterous reception from the Nevada City and Virginia City Circles of the Fenians upon his initial arrival in Virginia City, and he had also been the featured speaker at a benefit for the Fenian Library in Nevada City held on January 6, where he spoke of his "unabated devotion to the cause of *Ireland*."[126] [author's emphasis] Although both events provided an opportunity and a natural forum for Meagher to profess his allegiance to the Brotherhood and embrace its cause, he seems to have held himself at a distance. Nevertheless, his critics used the occasion of the Fenians' invasion of Canada to challenge Meagher's loyalty and motives. While Meagher remained publicly silent on the entire matter, it's clear the cost of his membership in the Brotherhood was beyond that which could be stated in terms of greenbacks or gold dust.

From his home in Tallmadge, Ohio, Sidney Edgerton finally responded to the plaintive requests of the territory's Republicans who desperately sought his return to Montana. Edgerton attempted to justify his unexcused absence from the territory in a letter to Secretary of State Seward in which he sounds like a schoolboy explaining neglected homework. "The Legislative assembly does not meet this year as the last Legislature neglected to district the Territory . . . my children required better educational advantages than that new country affords. this [sic] was my private personal reason for leaving the Territory . . . I did not ask for leave because the Secretary, General Meagher, did not arrive till the last of September. Then to obtain such a leave would have required more than two months, making my stay another year certain . . . ."[127] Edgerton's attempt to save his job fell short. Seward formally removed Edgerton as governor on April 13; however, he did not name a permanent replacement, leaving Meagher as acting governor.

In the meantime, it appears that the daily challenges of the territory were taking their toll on the acting governor. Whether he was motivated by a sense of frustration with the political intrigues, or simply worn from the personal attacks—or some combination of both—Meagher seemed determined to retire from center stage. On July 13, 1866, Meagher wrote to President Johnson suggesting that it would be prudent to create the role of Superintendent of Indian Affairs as a separate position rather than a de facto responsibility of the territorial governor, and requesting that should such a position be created, he would wish such appointment.[128] Additionally, Meagher stated in an address made at Diamond City (in his first visit to his namesake county) that he intended to resign upon the arrival of the new territorial governor and return to life as a "private citizen." Sounding very much like an elder statesman, and perhaps venting some frustration, Meagher also professed to his audience that "The less of Federal officialism and the more of popular liberty and democratic power there prevails in the Republic at large, then the healthier, the stronger, the nobler would the American nation be."[129]

Meagher, seldom reticent in any circumstances, did not hesitate to speak his mind with regard to those who were critical of the second legislative session—Republicans or Democrats. Called upon to make a speech while visiting Blackfoot City in August, Meagher spoke for an hour and a half to an audience that filled a local theater to the point of standing room only. A reporter for the *Rocky Mountain Gazette* wrote that Meagher's "vindication of his action in calling the Legislature of last March was articularly forcible and satisfactory." In his remarks, Meagher insisted that "it was the people of the Territory and their Legislature, as well as he himself, who stood that day fully vindicated and victorious, whilst the envenomed enemies of each and all shivering in the exhaustion of their slime and poison, stood disconsolately and inconsolably at bay." Meagher went on to declare that he had no personal agenda nor expected any personal gain from the restoration of the legislature: "he was not interested to the value of a depreciated green-back . . . he had no interest whatever in clapping a turnpike across any jack-ass trail in the country—didn't calculate upon having a golden drop of comfort from any consolidated Ditch Company in quest of a charter—and it was a matter of felicitous and supreme indifference to him who was to be disenthralled from the matrimonial yoke. All he desired—all he was ambitious for— was to set free the people of Montana from the dictation and control of the faction he had found in the ascendant on his coming into the Territory . . . ." Leaving little doubt as to which political segment he was referring, Meagher concluded his address by resolving that, "when this wicked faction shall be driven back, routed and trampled on—exterpated from the Republic as that faction would now exterpate the South—Montana . . . shall be recognized as a pillar of granite, crowned with a sumptuous capital of gold, that helped to sustain the noble structure of a restored nation . . . ." Meagher's oration was reported as concluding "amidst a perfect outburst of enthusiasm" and "frequently interrupted with cheers throughout his magnificent discourse."[130]

Author Robert Athearn suggests that Meagher was politically frustrated and became motivated by " . . . some inkling that his quest of the [permanent] governorship was a hopeless one, or he may have thought it wise to ask for something less, in the hope of getting anything at all."[131] Meagher, however, still officially held the appointment of territorial secretary although he had only very briefly actually served in that capacity. Moreover, if Meagher feared retribution might cost him the position of secretary, it isn't clear what could lead him to believe he would receive any other federal appointment. It may be reasonable to assume that Meagher sought to be Superintendent of Indian Affairs to escape the routine of administrative duties and political intrigues of the territory, and position himself where he anticipated there might be more "excitement" in the coming months. Nonetheless, the timing of Meagher's letter to Johnson does represent an astonishing coincidence—it was written on the same date that Johnson appointed Green Clay Smith to serve as governor of the Montana Territory.

CHAPTER 28

*"The change from his 'Old Kentucky Home' to fresh
and vigorous Montana was beset with new environments
that certainly were strange—perhaps startling...."*

James E. Callaway

Green Clay Smith was serving a second term in Congress as a Republican representative from Kentucky when picked by President Johnson to replace Sidney Edgerton. It's reasonable to assume that Meagher's critics had been effective in making his permanent appointment as governor politically impossible for Johnson—if he even had such an interest. In turning to Smith, Johnson found an experienced legislator with impeccable qualifications. Smith had military service in both the Mexican War and with the Union Army during the Civil War, where he had risen from the rank of private to that of major general (brevetted). Smith was a model husband and father from a well-established Kentucky family (he was related to Henry Clay), a graduate of Lexington Law School, and a pallbearer for Abraham Lincoln.[132] Smith was actually on active duty during the war when " ... he was nominated for Congress as a Republican and resigned his military commission on December 1, 1863, in order to take his seat in the House."[133] Although subsequently reported that Smith had the misfortune of losing the Republican nomination for vice president to Andrew Johnson by only one-half of one vote, Smith—though a convention delegate—was actually not even nominated.[134] One may question whether Johnson's motivation to promote Smith as territorial governor was based more upon the nominee's southern heritage rather than his political affiliation, nevertheless, it was well received. Smith's appointment as governor was quickly confirmed, and he left for

Montana with his family via their home in Richmond, Kentucky, " . . . to accept the delicate duties and grave responsibilities as Chief Magistrate of an infant Territory, yet in its swaddling bands."[135]

Governor Smith and his family arrived in Virginia City aboard the Salt Lake City stage on October 3, 1866. The new governor was introduced the next evening during an outdoor assembly at "Content's Corner" (site of the territorial offices) by John Bruce, editor of the *Montana Democrat.* "Gov. Smith made a non-partisan speech that was warmly applauded by all parties, and avowed his intention thereafter to announce his political views."[136] In what must have seemed like a de`ja` vu experience to Meagher, the new arrival was warmly greeted by the Radical Republicans, who sought to bring Smith into their camp. Remaining true to the statement he had made at Diamond City, Meagher submitted his resignation as territorial secretary to the new governor, but Smith was unhesitant in his opposition to such a loss and persuaded Meagher to withdraw his letter of resignation.[137] In fact, it would seem that the combination of the two men's talents and personalities were very well suited as a team to successfully lead the diverse constituency and manage the irregular circumstances of the Montana Territory. Smith would later recall that, "I shall never forget the kindness and attention with which he [Meagher] received me . . . ."[138]

Regrettably, editor Henry Blake didn't limit himself to words of welcome to the new governor. In the *Montana Post* announcement of Smith's arrival, Blake predicted a bright new dawn for the territory's political future contrasted with the dark clouds previously hovering around Meagher, editorializing: "The universal contempt with which his predecessor 'the great Irish patriot' is greeted everywhere . . . ."[139] Understandably angered, Meagher demanded the satisfaction of a public retraction or that Blake meet him in a duel. As Blake recounted the incident, it was James K. Duke, brother-in-law of Green Clay Smith, who delivered the letter from Meagher on October 18. Blake refused to accept the challenge or to print a retraction, and instead wrote a follow-up article which jabbed again at Meagher's wounded pride under the heading "Pistols and Coffee for Two."[140] The two men did later manage, however, to resolve their differences outside the public forum and apart from a dueling field.

Prior to Smith's arrival in Montana, the territorial elections had been conducted in September and were remarkably subdued. And, with still no indication from Congress or the Administration regarding Munson's legal opinion, an opening date for the Third Legislative Session had been established as November 3, which appears to have been widely accepted throughout the territory. Even the normally virulent *Montana Post* would attempt to put to rest the question of whether continued elections and sessions of the legislature were valid. The *Post* grudgingly declared that any question of the legality of the legislature was " . . . in conflict with those of a respectable portion of the community."[141]

On November 2 a telegraph line was finally opened for service between Virginia City and Salt Lake City, and Governor Smith was given the honor of sending the first message over this line to President Johnson in Washington. A few days later, on November 6, Smith delivered his first address to the Territorial Legislature's Third Session. In his remarks, Smith generally echoed those Meagher had made in March. Smith reemphasized concerns with respect to territory finances, the need to establish permanent public buildings (especially government offices and prison facilities), and the need to improve road and river access in the territory. He also asked the legislature to renew its petition to Congress for military protection and the creation of a territory militia. One of the more noteworthy, and vindictive, decisions of the legislators in the Third Session was the expression of their feelings toward Judges Munson and Hosmer. The legislators would redraw the judicial districts and assign Munson and Hosmer to the most remote, largely uninhabited, sections of the territory and further dictated that the justices should reside within their respective districts.

At the conclusion of the Session on December 15, members of the legislature urged Smith to travel to Washington, D.C., and lobby the Congress on behalf of the territory. Smith eagerly accepted this charge and left for Washington on January 7, 1867, coincidentally the same day Representative James Ashley filed resolutions for the impeachment of President Andrew Johnson. One of Smith's final duties prior to leaving the territory was to officially reappoint Thomas F. Meagher as acting governor. Preceding the departure of Governor Smith by a few days were two other territory residents also bound for the nation's capital—Wilbur F. Sanders and Judge Lyman E. Munson.

As the generals of the imminent political battle moved toward Washington, Meagher's recollections of other battlegrounds provided entertainment for those spending the winter in Virginia City. John Knox Miller later related in his diary: "January 27, 1867: Attended the lecture of Thos. Francis Meagher given at the rooms of the House of Rep. of the Territory for the benefit of the funds & charities of the Catholic church . . . his subject was 'The Irish Brigade & the army of the Potomac.' Very ably treated by the Gen. As the general is upon his 'Hunting grounds' when treating upon the Irish, he was most elequent [sic], his discourse abounding in pathos and continually convulsing his audience with laughter & anon receiving long and continued applause for a brilliant rhetorical effort. The hall was densely packed, the audience coming near to the 'stack' order."[142]

Meagher would also have occasion to once again call the legislature into session during Smith's absence. Notice had been received that Congress would open its next session earlier than anticipated (in March). This created a complication for the territory inasmuch as the term of the territory's congressional delegate, Samuel McLean, had expired. "The territorial law provided for the general election in September, and hence Montana was to be without representation in congress between March and September."[143] Whether from a lack of efficiency, or, more likely, a lack of political motivation, no new election was conducted, and McLean remained the de facto delegate. Before this Special Session of the Territorial Legislature adjourned, the die of political fortunes had already been cast in the halls and cloakrooms of Congress.

CHAPTER 29

"All in all, the action of Congress went strongly against
the grain of a majority of Montanans."
Burlingame & Toole

By the close of the Third Session of the Legislature, Wilbur F. Sanders and the Radical Republicans were painfully aware of the fact that political control of the Montana Territory was rapidly slipping beyond their grasp. Desperate times call for desperate measures, and the Republicans recognized they must move quickly. Sanders would later write, "I was asked by Democrats and Republicans alike to go to Washington to untangle affairs . . . which I did late in 1866. There I met Green Clay Smith and Col. McLain [sic] trying to bolster up the bogus legislature, and with the aid of Munson we untangled the thing."[144] Whether his memory was affected by his age at the time the preceding was written, or whether he was intentionally using selective recall isn't certain, but it staggers the imagination to think that any Democrat from the territory would have encouraged Wilbur Sanders to undertake such a mission.

At any rate, what ensued in Washington during the early weeks of 1867 was a vigorous effort by both parties to gain congressional support. In this battle of influence, Sanders and Munson would ultimately prove to have the greatest number of allies in the offices of the Republican-dominated Capitol. A bill was presented by the House of Representatives that called for only minor adjustments in the Organic Act and retained the work of the Second and Third Legislative Sessions, but the House version was not agreeable to the Senate. After some late-night battles, a revised bill was approved by Congress on March 2 which nullified both the Second and Third Legislative Sessions of the Montana Territory: "And be it further enacted, That all acts passed at the two sessions of the so-called legislative assembly of the Territory of Montana, held in eighteen hundred and sixty-six, are hereby disapproved and declared null and void . . . ."[145] Furthermore, in what was no doubt a personal concession to Lyman Munson, the bill also amended the original Organic Act to provide that the federally appointed judges would now draw their own judicial districts and assign themselves to such districts irrespective of legislative mandates.

The decision of Congress hit the Montana Territory like a bomb. The news that this group of men back east, with no understanding of circumstances in the territory, and who had done very little to support requests for assistance, had erased the good-faith efforts of those attempting to bring order to this new land was a shocking disappointment. "This was the most unjust act ever perpetrated by the Congress of the United States on a Territory. It was only carried through on the grossest misrepresentation of the character of the population."[146] Historian Clark Spence skillfully summarized the unprecedented turn of events: "In a sense, the controversy boiled down into the old arguments of local versus federal sovereignty . . . Congress acted not on the merits of the case itself, but in terms of political expediency. The real issue was never the validity of the two legislative assemblies or their enactments, but rather whether or not these obstreperous Democartic upstarts should be allowed to control the legislatures."[147]

Meagher also reacted quickly, and decisively, by resigning as Territorial Secretary. His friend, John Owen, would record in his diary: "I see from My papers recd Yesterday that General Thos. Francis Meagher has resigned the Secretaryship of Montana Territory & that . . . the Genl. intends So report says taking up the practice of Law & locate himself permanently in Montana Territory."[148] Meanwhile, as disturbing as the war of politics may have been to the territory, there were soon rumors that a more ominous war was on the horizon.

CHAPTER 30

"Only remember—West of the Mississippi it's a little more look,
see, act. A little less rationalize, comment, talk."

F. Scott Fitzgerald

As the spring of 1867 opened in the mountains and valleys of the Montana Territory, the acting governor began to increasingly receive petitions from settlers requesting protection from anticipated Indian attacks. In its "The Indian Movement" column, the *Montana Post* passionately cried out: "For some time past it has been rumored that the Indian tribes between the mountains and the Missouri were pow-wowing together for the purpose of forming a coalition to make common cause against the whites. It is high time the sickly sentimentalism about humane treatment and concillatory measures should be consigned to novel writers, and if the Indians continue their barbarities, wipe them out."[149] Included among those making such requests was the widely respected pioneer and trailblazer, John Bozeman. Bozeman advised Meagher that there were families of homesteaders leaving the Gallatin Valley in response to concerns of the perceived threat of Indian attacks. Bozeman, or perhaps actually someone on his behalf, would write, "We have reliable reports here that we are in imminent danger of hostile Indians . . . ."[150] As added justification to take Bozeman's report seriously, an army command led by Captain William Fetterman had been annihilated in late December along the Bozeman Trail.

As previously cited, Sidney Edgerton's earlier attempt to form a militia had failed, so, without a standing militia force, Meagher made his initial approach for help to Ulysses S. Grant (then responsible for all U.S. military forces) on April 9. In his message to General Grant, Meagher repeated the petitions made by the territory legislators for federal troops and also requested Grant's permission to take the interim step of raising a militia. Meagher further proposed that the expenses of such a militia—their service and supplies—should be reimbursed by the federal government. Grant did not make a decision on Meagher's request, other than to forward it to Secretary of War (and cousin of Lyman Munson) Edwin Stanton. Grant scribbled a personal note to Stanton on Meagher's message which read, "If there is the danger which Governor Maher [sic] apprehends, and there wood [sic] seem to be, judging from all the information reaching us, the Citizens of Montana ought to have some organization to defend themselves until the troops of the United States can give them the required protection. I think however the Governor should know what self defence [sic] requires these citizens to do, and if the services rendered by them warrant it, they should, afterward look to Congress for compensation."[151] While Meagher's request was being casually passed around Washington, the situation gained an even greater sense of urgency back in Montana with some startling news from the Gallatin Valley—John Bozeman had been killed!

There are elements of the Bozeman murder story that would later taint it with rumors of scandal, but the general facts, at least as were known at the time, galvanized the territory's citizens. Bozeman, reportedly with some reluctance, had agreed to serve as guide for Thomas Cover. Cover intended to visit the military forts along the Bozeman Trail (C. F. Smith, Kearny, and Reno) in an effort to obtain contracts to provide them with supplies. After a day and a half of travel, Bozeman and Cover arrived at a point along the Yellowstone River (approximately fourteen miles east of present-day Livingston) where they made a mid-day camp on April 18. While the men were encamped, they were surprised by the appearance of a small party of Indian braves. A confrontation subsequently erupted and Bozeman was killed, but Cover managed to escape. Cover wrote to Meagher on April 22, giving his account of the incident and further stating: "From what I can glean in the way of information I am satisfied that there is a large party of

Blackfeet on the Yellowstone, whose sole object is plunder and scalps."[152] Cover had been one of the men in the original party that had made the discovery of gold in the Alder Gulch and had become a prosperous businessman and mill owner in Gallatin County, so, whether or not it was deserved, his name gave veracity to this report and compounded growing fears among the white settlers.

News of the murder must have come as a sad validation to Meagher of Bozeman's recent warning of possible Indian attacks. Still lacking any response from General Grant, and with denials of requests for support from the commanders at forts C.F. Smith, Phil Kearny, and Camp Cooke in hand, Meagher decided to push ahead and issued a proclamation on April 24 that called for the establishment of a territorial militia. The proclamation called for 600 volunteers (200 from Madison County, 300 from Edgerton, and 100 from Deer Lodge) to serve a three-month enlistment and directed that volunteers should report to one of the newly appointed militia officers: J. X. Beidler, John Featherston, or Granville Stuart.[153] While this request did attract some men who were willing to serve, most were quickly discouraged—and many disbanded—upon learning that any reimbursement was tenuous. Similarly, local merchants were reluctant to provide any supplies without any guarantee of payment.

Additional support for Meagher's efforts to obtain help would come from an unlikely source at this point. "Justice Hosmer, who lost no love on Meagher, was one of his main supporters in the action."[154] Judge Hosmer sent an urgently worded message directly to President Johnson asking the president lend his support to Meagher's request. Unfortunately, the reality of politics would again come into play. Johnson had a very cool relationship with his military commander and passed Hosmer's request to General Grant without providing any directive. Grant, in turn, responded to Judge Hosmer with much the same message as he had attached in his note to Secretary Stanton saying, in effect, you can form a militia if you wish, but don't expect Congress to pay for it.

In the meantime, Meagher received a report from one of his

militia officers, Colonel Thomas Thoroughman, that the Indians were actively preparing for hostile action, although the militia had not actually engaged any enemy force. Fears of Indian attacks were so compelling that the garrison at Fort C.F. Smith (south of the present-day city of Billings) was near starvation because no suppliers would dare travel. The crisis at Ft. Smith was finally relieved when the militia provided an escort from Bozeman of food and supplies and reported that the only Indians observed were "a couple of Crow Indian families living near the fort."[155]

Meagher's barrage of telegrams to Washington finally prompted Secretary Stanton to contact Lieutenant-General William T. Sherman. Sherman had received the enormous, and impossible, command of the Military Division of the Mississippi. From its headquarters in St. Louis, Sherman's command included all the area westward from the Mississippi River (except Louisiana and Texas) to a line along the western boundaries of what would become the states of Montana, Utah, and New Mexico. After making a quick, understandably superficial, tour of his command area soon after his appointment, Sherman had stated, "It is these awful distances that make our problem out here so difficult."[156] It also appears that Sherman was quick to recognize the vulnerability and logistical challenge of Montana's position. On April 19, 1866, immediately prior to the departure of Inspector General D. B. Sacket's own official tour of the area, Sherman advised, "I want to send Cavalry up into that remote region, but it would be absurd to attempt it till we know forage can be had at some price below its weight in gold."[157] Sacket would confirm the need for a military presence after his visit to the Montana Territory, writing to Sherman that there was a genuine danger of Indian attacks to the new settlers.

This vast geographic area and the attitudes and prejudices of the new arrivals presented a daunting situation. The entire area enveloped by the Division of the Mississippi was being flooded with waves of immigrants and those seeking a new start from the ashes of the Civil War. Few of these new settlers had any awareness of existing Indian treaties, and if they did, they showed no respect for such. One of the keys to the economic development of this vast region was the establishment of additional rail lines. Sherman accepted this as a priority, perhaps for reasons both personal and professional, recognizing the critical importance of the rails to military maneuvers, and would write that once the rail lines were sufficiently extended " . . . we can act so energetically that both Sioux and Cheyennes must die or submit to our dictation."[158]

In Stanton's message to Sherman, he expressed official Washington's concern with regard to territorial militias but reminded the general that it was within his (Sherman's) authority to initiate the formation of a militia force and arrange for its necessary supplies if deemed appropriate.[159] Sherman, who had also been receiving regular messages similar to Meagher's from every other territorial governor in his command area, replied to Stanton in the tone of a frustrated military professional: "You are perfectly right that discretion to call out the militia in Montana, or any of our Territories, cannot safely be lodged with their Governors, for, to be candid, each has an interest antagonistic to that of the United States."[160] Moreover, he expressed the opinion that "Meagher, in Montana, is a stampeder," and that the governors of the other western territories were similarly inclined to be alarmists.[161] Exhibiting what was still a naive understanding of the West, Sherman further suggested to Stanton that the answer to resolving the dilemma of these conflicts was simply a matter of establishing a better sense of order. "Instead of extending thin settlements, and putting their horses and stock in tempting proximity to the Indians, they should make their settlements in groups and colonies capable of self-defence [sic]."[162] To what extent the previous animosities between Sherman and Meagher may have played into these circumstances is impossible to determine but is a factor to be taken into consideration.

General Sherman acknowledged that the territories should have established volunteer militias and that they should be entitled to federal reimbursement for authorized service beyond thirty days, but he indicated to Secretary Stanton that he did not wish to use his authority to create such militia at this time. In what appears to have been an effort to "keep his cards close to his vest," Sherman intended to send General Alfred Terry (operating in Dakota Territory) into the Montana Territory with a brigade of troops should conditions reach some undefined flashpoint.[163] In the meantime, Sherman also had the opportunity to have a personal meeting with Governor Smith, who was returning to Virginia City from Washington, and as a result, agreed to send a shipment of 2,500 firearms to Montana in order that its citizens could defend themselves.[164]

It was also as a result of his meeting with Governor Smith that Sherman was motivated to make an attempt to gather some first-hand, independent information regarding the situation in the Montana Territory. On May 6, Sherman directed General Augur (at Fort Omaha) to send an officer to Montana on a fact-finding mission with regard to the Indian threat and to begin extending his military operations westward.[165] Sherman's growing uncertainty was also reflected in the message he sent the same day to J. M. Castner, the mayor of Virginia City, "If the inhabitants of Gallatin valley are in such imminent danger from Indians you may organize your people and go to their defense under the general direction of your Governor."[166]

The next day, May 7, Sherman communicated directly to Meagher with a message that would later become a point of bitter controversy hinging upon one word. Sherman would claim he authorized a militia of 800 volunteers to be in service until such time as regular troops reached the Yellowstone if Indians "*entered*" the Gallatin Valley. As Sherman's telegraph message was reported in the *Montana Post*, it authorized such a force if the Gallatin Valley was "*threatened*."[167] Robert Athearn's implication that Meagher may have altered Sherman's message prior to its release to the *Post* is not only unsubstantiated, but also would have been a moot point. Either version could be interpreted as a "fait accompli"; clearly some Indians had already entered the Gallatin Valley and, unmistakably, the white settlers believed themselves threatened. More significantly, Sherman's message still did not authorize any financial support for the militia force, which had the effect, intentional or otherwise, of negating its formation.

In the meantime, General Augur had selected Major William H. Lewis for the assignment of reconnaissance, and Lewis arrived in Virginia City on May 19. Major Lewis made an assessment of circumstances and sent a report to Sherman in which he expressed the opinion that there was, indeed, some threat of Indian attacks. In response, Sherman telegraphed that Lewis had the authority to muster in a battalion of 800 men for two months, to be paid by the United States.[168] To Meagher, this notice must have seemed (and may well have been) the answer to his prayers, as well as those of area merchants, who were now more than willing to provide for the needs of the new militia—at premium prices. But within a few days Sherman did an about-face and ordered Major Lewis to proceed to Salt Lake City, "apparently without countermanding the permission he had given for the mustering of the troops and, worse, for their provision by the merchants."[169] This oversight, if it was an oversight, with regard to providing supplies would lead to gross abuse by those seeking to feed at the government's trough.

Wilbur Sanders had returned to Virginia City (Governor Smith had delayed his return by stopping in Kentucky and St. Louis) and in a public meeting on the evening of May 21, Sanders made a public speech in which he attempted to explain the annulment of the Second and Third Sessions and vindicated his role in the political machinations. Standing before the assembled crowd at Content's Corner, which would have required some courage, or audacity, Sanders said that he was motivated to lobby Congress because "I saw the poor orphan [Montana] in Washington." In what may be regarded as putting a "positive spin" on his efforts, Sanders proudly stated that through his efforts, "It was possible to procure the passage of laws which should be a reproof to the apostles of disorder."[170]

CHAPTER 31

*"[Meagher] was . . . sincere in his interest in Montana
and doubtless his ill starred last venture was motivated
by the real belief that the populace was threatened."*

Burlingame & Toole

While charges and counter-charges of partisan politics were thick in the mountain air, Meagher was keeping his distance from the political frays and enthusiastically working to recruit troops, and generously awarding officer commissions, in the new militia. Acknowledging the burden of his commitments—or finding a convenient excuse—he declined an invitation to address the Fenian convention in San Francisco. "I fear greatly that I cannot be with you. Governor Smith won't be here till the middle of July, and it is uncertain when Secretary Tuffts [sic] will arrive."[171]

By mid-June, there were perhaps 250 militia volunteers and nearly twenty-five percent of them held officer appointments as a result of Meagher's largesse. Among the most notable, and paradoxical, appointments was those of Henry Blake and Thomas Thoroughman. Blake, editor of the *Montana Post*, and Meagher's former would-be dueling opponent, was appointed as Colonel and adjutant general of the militia. Thoroughman, who "procured his military experience through service for the Southern Confederacy," was appointed by Meagher as the militia's brigadier general.[172] Additionally, two militia posts were established (Camp Ida Thoroughman and Camp Elizabeth Meagher) to guard the eastern entrances to the Gallatin Valley and offer protection along the Bozeman Trail.

Despite the ardent recruitment efforts of Meagher, it appears the territory militia remained a small, generally disorganized, force.

Discipline was lax, or nonexistent, as men frequently drifted away as a result of boredom, or when rumors of a new gold strike would reach their camps. There were no engagements with the Indians, and the whole of their activity was basically limited to providing patrols of the more commonly used roads and some desultory drills. While Meagher recognized the many shortcomings of his militia (at one point referring to his " . . . not an invincible, but invisible force."[173]), he clearly enjoyed serving in the role of commander-in-chief and the fraternity of being on a military campaign, and genuine in his belief that the mission was protecting Montana's citizens. It was also during this expedition that Meagher resumed his journalistic efforts and prepared the first installment of an intended series of articles, "Rides Through Montana," for *Harper's New Monthly Magazine*. Written under the pen name "Colonel Cornelius O'Keefe, Late of the Irish Brigade," it appears his motivation was to extol the beauty of the territory and to rekindle his name in the popular press.[174] Of course, the possible financial remuneration may have also been an important factor by this point. At the very least, his writing, and time around the campfires, must have provided grateful relief from what had been months of haggling with political opponents, military commanders, and government officials.

Unquestionably, there were some at the time—and several in later years—who were critical of the militia effort, its financial costs (justifiably so), and Meagher's possible hidden agenda. Author Paul Sharp would write, "Acting Governor Thomas F. Meagher aggravated Indian problems during his brief administration by playing upon public fears to rehabilitate his waning political fortunes."[175] Robert Athearn makes what seems an outlandish claim regarding the motivation for action against the Indians: "Driving off the Indians would serve the dual purpose of opening up new prospecting areas and committing the currently popular act of 'killin' Injuns.'"[176] While the militia operations could certainly have been more efficiently managed, charges that the mobilization was unnecessary or politically motivated seem unwarranted. Although it appears from the vantage point of more than 150 years there was no genuine threat of significant hostile action, one should consider the context of the time in question. These were people who were often living miles apart from their nearest neighbor, or in small, undefended settlements, and with the memory of the Fetterman Massacre and murder of the heroic John Bozeman prevalent in their minds. Rumors and inflammatory articles in the territory's newspapers had compounded these concerns even prior to Meagher's arrival.

As to Meagher's intentions, it should be remembered that his initial—and sustained—effort was to obtain the service of regular army troops for the protection of the territory, and that he regarded the militia to be an interim solution to an immediate problem. It is also arguable that had General Sherman apprised Meagher of the directive to General Augur to begin operations westward, and of the possible reserve use of General Terry's troops, that the sense of urgency in establishing a militia force may have been greatly diminished. The only clear evidence we have of Meagher's intentions regarding his political aspirations is that he had already resigned his appointment as Secretary and his requested (though unanswered) appointment to serve as superintendent of Indian affairs for the territory; if such position were created. Whether Meagher reasoned that leading a martial force against the Indians would enhance the probability of the new position, and his consequent appointment, is pure conjecture.

Meagher had been notified that General Sherman was sending the supply of munitions promised to Governor Smith via riverboat and, estimating their probable arrival time at Camp Cooke (located at the junction of the Judith River with the Missouri River), he began the long ride to meet the shipment. While en route, Meagher became very ill—reportedly suffering from a case of dysentery— and had a layover of approximately six days in Sun River until he felt well enough to again ride.[177] Accompanied by a small militia escort, Meagher and his party finally arrived at Fort Benton on July 1, expecting, and no doubt hopeful, that the arms shipment had already been transferred to that location from Camp Cooke. Beyond this point, Thomas Francis Meagher's remaining hours of life become as dark and unsettled as the Missouri River.

PART V

*The Controversial Death
of a Controversial Man*

CHAPTER 32

"We started [the voyage] *at daylight. Our first exploit*
was to run into the steamship 'G.A. Thompson,'
smashing their cookhouse into small pieces
and seriously disarranging their breakfast...."
Diary of John Knox Miller, June 8, 1867

"There were no guards around the deck.
They had been broken in a previous accident."
Martin Maginnis

"O! happy deaths—deaths without the darkness
and impurities of the grave... the mountains are not so grand,
nor the rivers so abundant in their blessings,
nor the stars so fraught with the lustre of the Angels!"
Thomas Francis Meagher

As Thomas Francis Meagher arrived at Fort Benton on July 1,
1867, he probably found the settlement largely unchanged from
his visit in October of 1865 when he had participated in the
Blackfeet Treaty session. The outpost of Fort Benton had originally
been established in 1846 by the American Fur Company and took
its name to honor Senator Thomas Hart Benton of Missouri, a
vigorous proponent of the development of the western regions.
Fort Benton was the furthest inland point where the Missouri River
was navigable to steamships, and by 1865 " . . . a busy freight line
was in operation from Benton to Virginia City by way of
Helena . . . ."[1] It had, therefore, become an important juncture of
commercial trade and traffic into the Montana Territory, as well as

Canada via the Whoop-up and Fort Walsh trails. Called "The Chicago of the Plains," the settlement " . . . was a busy and prosperous village, containing a floating and promiscuously mixed population of about four or five hundred souls."[2]

Meagher and his escort party rode into Fort Benton in the late morning of what promised to be another hot, dry day. In just over a month he would be celebrating his forty-fourth birthday, and was probably feeling every bit his age and showing the obvious effects of his recent illness. Meagher dismounted and went into I.G. Baker's store, "perspiring and unsteady," to seek some relief from sun and saddle.[3] No doubt compounding Meagher's weariness was the news that the munitions shipment had not been forwarded from Fort Cooke, which would necessitate his traveling an additional one hundred miles or so. Mr. Baker offered Meagher a glass of blackberry wine, which he accepted, and a seat in the shade of his shop to rest.[4] In an article which would appear some years later, Mr. Baker related that Meager " . . . had lunch with me [and] was in excellent spirits, but didn't seem to be in the best of health."[5]

From this point of commonly accepted circumstances diverge two principal versions regarding the course of events in the remaining hours of Meagher's life. One version was related by a riverboat pilot, Johnny Doran, the other by Wilbur F. Sanders. Over time, various authors have used some portion of one or both of these stories when writing of Meagher's death. Inasmuch as there are some rather significant variances between these accounts, what follows is a summary presentation of both men's stories and appropriate background. Unless otherwise cited, the source of the Doran version is from W.F. Lyons's book (*Brigadier-General Thomas Francis Meagher: His Political and Military Career*), and the source of Sanders's account is from a statement he made soon after Meagher's death and which appears in Helen F. Sanders's book (*A History of Montana, Volume I*).

The Johnny Doran version:

In the autumn of 1868, P. J. Condon (a former member of the Irish Brigade) was the supervising engineer on a bridge project at Omaha, Nebraska. While there, Condon chanced to meet a boatman who served aboard the steamship *G.A. Thompson* at the time of Meagher's death in Fort Benton. Condon was so intrigued by the boatman's story that he sought out the pilot of the *G.A. Thompson*, Johnny Doran. Doran recounted the circumstances of Meagher's death, which not only verified the boatman's story, but also provided additional details to which Doran was privileged. Condon proceeded to have each man give a sworn statement detailing their stories and notified W.F. Lyons, another veteran of the Irish Brigade, who was serving as editor of the *New York Herald*. Lyons obtained a copy of Doran's statement, which he subsequently used in his 1869 biography of Meagher.

According to Doran's story, he had originally made the acquaintance of Meagher when serving as pilot of the steamer *Ontario*. Elizabeth Meagher had been a passenger aboard the *Ontario* when she came to join her husband in the Montana Territory. Meagher had introduced himself to the pilot, and the acting governor made a point of expressing his appreciation to Mr. Doran for his watchful consideration of Elizabeth during her journey up the Missouri River.

Doran docked the *G.A. Thompson* at Fort Benton on June 29, 1867. When he heard the news that Meagher had arrived in town on July 1, Doran quickly made his way to Baker's store where he was "greeted most warmly" by Meagher. Meagher was suffering badly from the "summer complaint" (diarrhea) and told Doran that he had been especially ill while at Sun River, requiring an extended stay at that settlement. Doran sat with Meagher in a back room of Baker's store where Meagher rested and chatted with the occasional visitor, "except for some trips into the brush behind the building due to his illness." During the afternoon, Meagher sipped two more glasses of the blackberry wine, and Doran invited him to have dinner and spend the night aboard the *G.A. Thompson* since Meagher did not have any arrangements for accommodations in Fort Benton.

Following dinner aboard the *G.A. Thompson*, Doran accompanied Meagher on a brief walk through the settlement, then both men returned to the boat where they sat on deck. I. G.

Baker would later claim that a drinking bout took place aboard the *Thompson* that evening which he believed included Meagher, although Baker was not aboard the boat and did not personally witness such an event.[6] Doran stated that Meagher spent some time quietly reading and writing letters which included those later received by Richard O'Gorman and Territory Auditor, John Ming (requesting salary payments due for his service as governor be sent to him at Fort Benton).[7] After having passed some time in this quiet manner, Meagher abruptly exclaimed, "Johnny, they threaten my life in that town!" Meagher suddenly appeared to have become "wearied and nervous," and Doran convinced him that he should retire to bed inasmuch as it was already "pitch-dark, the hour being about half-past nine." Doran escorted the shaken Meagher to the stateroom (on the port side—open to the river), helped him to get settled, then went to the boat's lower deck. Doran had only been on the lower deck for a short time before he heard a splash and the cry of "Man overboard!"

Doran rushed to the sound of the alarm, which had been given by the aforementioned boatman who was serving as sentry that night. The sentry reported he had seen someone dressed in bedclothes near the "temporary accommodation place" (where the railing had been previously damaged) and had discreetly turned and walked toward the bow. Moments later, the sentry heard a sharp cry and a splash in the river. Doran immediately knew it had to have been Meagher who had fallen and directed his crew to raise the alarm along the docks. Life buoys were thrown out, and the *G.A. Thompson* crew and others from boats docked nearby began to search for some sign of Meagher in the dark river, which was running high and very fast. The would-be rescuers searched along the riverbank for a short time before it became obvious that any further attempts in the darkness would be pointless.

The Wilbur F. Sanders version:

Mr. Sanders was also in Fort Benton on July 1, 1867. He was waiting to meet his family who had been slowly making their way up the Missouri aboard the *Abeona*.[8] His family, whom Sanders had accompanied for a portion of their long voyage, was in the process of returning from a visit to Ohio. Sanders and Governor Smith had recently returned to the territory from their political adventures in Washington. Sanders recounted that he observed Meagher's arrival at the settlement of Fort Benton "About 12:00 or 1:00 o'clock . . ." and welcomed him in friendship. Sanders indicated that he joined Meagher, and "The afternoon was delightfully spent in social visits through the business portions of the town, and General Meagher seemed at his best in a conversational way, but he resolutely and undeviatingly declined that form of hospitality with which Fort Benton then abounded." At some point during the afternoon, Sanders and Meagher were in Baker's store when Sanders says he was approached by "a ship's pilot or mate" who " . . . doubtingly interrogated me as to whether this was the famous Thomas Francis Meagher." After Sanders convinced the man this was, indeed, Meagher, the man "could not conceal his delight at meeting so distinguished a person."

Sanders writes that it was also while in the store that Meagher received an invitation to dinner that evening at six o'clock with "Major" T. H. Eastman (superintendent of the American Fur Company operation), which he accepted. Apparently Sanders left the gathering at Baker's store some time in the late afternoon and next observed Meagher about dusk. At that point, Meagher was with a few companions in town and, " . . . after listening for a moment, it was apparent he was deranged." Sanders stated that Meagher was "loudly demanding a revolver to defend himself against the citizens of Fort Benton, who in his disturbed mental condition, he declared were hostile to him."

Sanders, with the help of Meagher's companions, assisted the ailing man aboard the *G.A. Thompson*, and into a room "which was on the starboard side of the boat next [to] the bank. As he had removed his outer garments and lain down in his berth, we did not apprehend there would be further trouble, the temporary aberration the result of the hot and exhausting ride of the morning, which sleep would speedily correct." Thus having seen Meagher comfortably settled, Sanders then left the boat and proceeded to the local Indian agent's office, about fifty yards from the river.

Approximately thirty minutes later, Sanders heard a cry that Meagher had drowned and he rushed from the agent's office back to the *G.A. Thompson*. The merchant Baker claimed that he was awakened "about nine o'clock" when " . . . the dock watchman came into my room and said he had just seen a man fall off the boat . . . he seemed to be vomiting and lost his balance."[9]

Once on board, Sanders immediately encountered a crew member. "There was a colored man, one of the men connected with the boat—the barber I believe—who, replying to my interrogation, said a man had let himself down from the upper deck to the lower deck and jumped into the river and gone downstream." Sanders stated that he quickly returned to shore, where he ran along the shoreline sounding an alarm and joining others in the search which was " . . . kept up all night and for two or three days thereafter." Despite their efforts " . . . the mighty river defied all our solicitudes and kept its treasure well." Mrs. Sanders wrote in her diary that, after arriving at Fort Benton the evening of July 4, the family, with Mr. Sanders, left on the stage for Helena at two o'clock on the morning of July 5.

These two versions of Meagher's death draw enticingly close together on some points, only to sharply carom away from each other on other details. Sanders implies that Doran (who, logically, must have been the "ship pilot or mate" he mentions) did not recognize Meagher upon arriving at Baker's store. It is reasonable to expect that Sanders simply misinterpreted what may have been a reasonable inquiry on the part of Doran to confirm what had been second-hand information regarding Meagher's arrival. Likewise, the disparity regarding Meagher's dinner plans may be easily explained with the scenario that Meagher did initially accept Major Eastman's invitation, while Sanders was present, but later changed plans to be with Doran aboard the *Thompson*. Considering Meagher's physical condition, it is very possible the thought of a private evening in close company was more appealing than serving as centerpiece for a larger, more public, gathering.

While Doran mentions Meagher's post-dinner stroll through town, he does not cite any outburst of aberrant behavior during this time, a point he may have selectively omitted. Sanders certainly could have observed Meagher during this time, assuming he was returning from dinner with Eastman. Sanders may have even assisted in returning Meagher to the boat, however, this would obviously contrast with Doran's account. It is interesting to note that Doran and Sanders are also in conflict as to which side of the boat Meagher's room was located; one would assume a ship's captain would be clear on that point. Sanders's account implies he was responsible for not only initiating the attempted rescue of Meagher, but that it was an exhaustive, all-night attempt. Doran's version that he and his crew immediately began a search, but that there was a relatively brief effort made in view of the circumstances, seems more reasonable. Yet, it is certainly possible there were two search groups operating independent of one another.

Finally, and most intriguing, is the tone of warmth and fellowship with which Sanders characterizes his association with Meagher on July 1. Clearly the men had not been close heretofore and, considering Sanders's recent political maneuvers in Washington, the thought of their camaraderie at this point is paradoxical. There were probably no two other men in the territory at this time less likely to be friends with one another. Meagher had once referred to Sanders as, "the most vicious of my enemies, an unrelenting and unscrupulous extremist."[10] Perhaps old wounds healed quickly in the deep, cold waters of the Missouri.

Merchant I. G. Baker provided at least two accounts in later years of the events surrounding Meagher's death. One story was featured in the *Anaconda Standard* on September 9, 1901, and another is recorded in the papers of James Bradley. The details of his two accounts are notably at variance with one another (as well as the Doran and Sanders versions), but a common denominator with his stories is his claim that a drinking party occurred on board the *G.A. Thompson* the evening of July 1. Although not aboard the *Thompson*, and despite the contrary statement of another passenger, Baker related that the group of men involved in the drinking spree included Meagher—who became deeply intoxicated and even threatened to shoot one of the other revelers. Baker would conclude that it was either "in a fit of sleepwalking, or in the state of unsteadiness induced by the evening's dissipation," and facilitated by the absence of guard rails, that must have led to Meagher's fall from the boat.[11] It is difficult to accept Baker's stories as anything more than tabloid hearsay.

As Sanders closed his account of the events, he indicated that " . . . it seemed my duty to tell her [Elizabeth Meagher] the sad story," writing to her in Virginia City. It was otherwise reported, however, that the task of notifying Elizabeth fell to a local Catholic priest and that Elizabeth was actually waiting for her husband in Helena.[12] In either case, Elizabeth immediately came to Fort Benton where she reportedly walked the banks of the Missouri River, and employed others as well, in an extended search for the body of her husband.

Citizens' meetings were called in Virginia City and Helena once news of Meagher's death reached those communities. At the Virginia City meeting, Judge Hosmer would address the large crowd which had gathered and declare, "I am oppressed with a sense of gloom that I find it difficult to overcome."[13] There was a committee appointed to draft proclamations of sympathy to Meagher's wife and father and to have copies of such forwarded to newspapers in New York and Ireland. Mr. Meagher would reply to the secretary of the Virginia City committee with a letter which expressed his appreciation for their sympathy, adding: "It will be my duty to remember, with deep gratitude, the generous and warm welcome which awaited him [Thomas Francis] in the United States."[14]

A meeting of Helena's citizens on July 4 was called to order by Governor Smith, who announced a proclamation with the offer of a $1,000 reward for recovery of Meagher's body for " . . . a proper and christian burial . . . ."[15] The governor spoke of his admiration for Meagher and would eulogize Meagher by stating: "He sacrificed himself for the freedom of Ireland. Banished though he was in body, he left his brightest hopes, his heart, and his prayers with his people, he never lost sight of that high and noble sentiment of his sacrifice."[16] The governor also directed that all territorial and federal offices be draped in mourning for a period of thirty days.

The governor's monetary reward was immediately matched by the citizens' group in Helena, whose chairman was Nathaniel P. Langford, former member of the Executive Council of the Virginia City Vigilantes. Adding to the intrigue of these dramatic events, and further evidence of Meagher's popular support, was the widespread concern as to the exact circumstances of Meagher's disappearance. "At the time of his [Meagher's] death there was sufficient doubt of the Sanders story to inspire a popular subscription of ten thousand dollars to investigate the death."[17] Despite all efforts—and the generous incentives—Meagher's body was never recovered. By the end of September, Elizabeth abandoned the search for her husband's remains and returned to New York City to live again in her father's home.

CHAPTER 33

"To the end, I see the path I have been ordained to walk,
and upon the grave which closes in on that path,
I can read no coward's epitaph."

Thomas Francis Meagher

On August 14, 1867, a requiem mass was held at St. Francis Xavier Church in New York City to honor Thomas Francis Meagher. Later that day, the eulogy was delivered by Richard O'Gorman— friend, fellow party member of Young Ireland, and now a very successful attorney in New York. O'Gorman mentioned that he had received a letter Meagher had written on the day of his death in which he had indicated plans to return for a visit to New York "at the end of the week."[18] Then, after reciting Meagher's speech from the Clonmel prison docket, O'Gorman continued:

"These words he uttered looking death in the eye. Tell me, have you ever known of any man, that in such a trying hour, uttered a more gallant, noble, dignified protest?

Think of this, you, if there be any who deem that we who knew this man loved him above his deserts: you who knew him only by his faults, and who may now be disposed to magnify them and belittle his virtues, fancy yourselves, if you can dare to fancy it, in such a strait, and tell me if you could have raised your souls to so grand an eminence as his who that day set the prisoner above the judge who tried him, and dignified the felon's dock till it became in the eyes of the world, a temple of freedom."[19]

Robert Athearn would write that the memorial ceremony for Thomas Francis Meagher " . . . was a ceremony which in many ways was two years late. When the General had left New York in the summer of 1865, he had, to all intents and purposes, ended his career."[20] This declaration suggests that Meagher, and the Territory of Montana, was inconsequential in the course of events from 1865 to 1867. In either case, this would be an oversight. While one may argue points of judgment or even the legal authority of Meagher's actions, it is certain that he played a critical role during the truculent infancy of Montana. Although far from the spotlights of the theatres of America's eastern cities, and far from the impassioned throngs of Irishmen cheering for their sovereignty, Thomas Francis Meagher fought to bring political order, establish his church, add a bit of elegance, and infuse others with his dream of a glorious future for Montana—a legacy worthy of consideration.

Even following his death, Thomas Francis Meagher continued to provide fuel to barroom and ballroom conversations for several years. Among the controversies surrounding his death were his physical condition. "The extreme bitterness of his enemies had spread the legend of his [Meagher's] insobriety so far and wide in Montana that the story of a drunken demise fell on willing ears."[21]

The intrigue and debate was rekindled in 1913 by a story that appeared in the *Missoula Sentinel* on May 29. The front-page story reported that, in what he presumed to be a deathbed confession, Frank Diamond (alias Pat Miller) shared a tale of how he had been paid $8,000 by Axel Potter, on behalf of influential men, to kill Meagher. Diamond claimed to have crept aboard the *G.A. Thompson* on the night of July 1, fatally shot Meagher and then dumped his body into the Missouri River.[22] Diamond then escaped notice amid the confusion and excitement which followed the "man overboard" alarm. Within a few days of his confession, Diamond recovered from what he had believed was certain death, and he quickly recanted his story, which he said must have been hallucinated while he was suffering from "delerium tremens."[23] "Patrick Conlon, a close personal friend and admirer of General Meagher, scouted the Diamond story and denounced it as false."[24] In the meantime, another man seeking absolution (or a moment of fame?) came forward with what he knew to be the truth of Meagher's death.

In an article which appeared in New York's *The Sun*, David

Billingsley (also known as Dave Mack) indicated that Meagher had, indeed, been assassinated; however, Billingsley (who alleged to be a Vigilante member himself, but vowed he did not take part in this action) claimed that a group of Vigilantes had gone aboard the *G.A. Thompson* and kidnapped the sleeping Meagher. They proceeded to take Meagher to an isolated spot on the outskirts of Fort Benton where he was hung, then buried in an unmarked grave.[25]

The possibility that the Vigilantes may have assassinated Meagher lives on as a popular lore, but is extremely implausible. In the first place, the fervor of the Vigilante movement was greatly diminished throughout the territory by the time of his death. Notices had been posted in the Alder Gulch area in mid-February that advised, "We are all well satisfied that, in times past, you did do some glorious work, but the time has come when law should be enforced."[26] Moreover, the notice warned that should any further extra-legal incident occur that there would be retaliation "five for one." The *Montana Post*, in commenting on the situation, would report: "This notice, and other reliable information, indicates that there exist, in different localities, secret and sworn leagues to resist the Vigilantes."[27] Even the backlash to the hanging of James Daniels, which reportedly included one of the largest funerals in Helena to that time, suggests the time of the Vigilantes was nearly "played-out." One of those credited as briefly reviving a vigilante effort in later years, Granville Stuart, discounted any Vigilante involvement in Meagher's demise: "I was in Virginia City about that time and if there was any quarrel between Meagher and the Vigilantes, I never heard of it. I would naturally have heard of it had there been, for I was close to those men at that time, although not a member of the organization."[28] Another reason to question any lingering animosity is that at least two of the men Meagher had appointed militia officers, John X. Beidler and John Featherston, had been prominent Vigilantes.

The most obvious reason to question Vigilante involvement would seem to be that of motive, what purpose would Meagher's assassination have served? Green Clay Smith had recently returned to assume the governorship, presumably for at least the extent of his term, and a new Territorial Secretary had been appointed, therefore Meagher was no longer a political impediment. Moreover, considering his letters to O'Gorman and Ming, it is not altogether unreasonable to assume that Meagher may have been on the verge of leaving the territory. And while Sanders and Meagher had been strident political opponents, there is nothing to suggest Sanders would have risked his future by taking any role in Meagher's death.

Montana's attorney general immediately ordered an investigation into the stories of Billingsley and Diamond, but nothing was found to support their claims. One piece of information that did result from the investigation was a letter from a man who had been a personal acquaintance of John Leaman (who was deceased), night watchman aboard the *John D. Lee* at Fort Benton on July 1, 1867. Mr. Leaman had told the story that the night of July 1 featured "an exceptionally bright moon" which caused the dock area to be clearly illuminated. "Towards midnight" two men, one he recognized as the boat's pilot, boarded the *G.A. Thompson* and proceeded to rooms on the waterside. It was about ten minutes later when the man who had been in the pilot's company, dressed in underclothes, came out to stern and "leaned over the rail as if to vomit" and then fell into the river.[29] While at odds with the versions of Doran, Sanders and Baker, and another hearsay report, there is a tone of reliability in Leaman's account.

Among the more bizarre claims were those that Meagher's body had actually been recovered. One story appears to have originated during the summer of 1899, when Arthur Miles began displaying what he purported to be a "petrified man," with what appeared to be a bullet hole in its forehead. Miles reportedly purchased this phenomenon from a man who found the body on a Missouri River sandbar, then hauled it to Yellowstone National Park where he met Miles. The Petrified Man was widely exhibited in tent shows for some time before a startling story broke on December 6, 1899, when the *Bozeman Chronicle* published an article claiming that the petrified remains were those of Thomas Francis Meagher![30] A photograph in the *New York World* (December 21, 1899) purports to show the naturally mummified Meagher; but the mystery—or hoax—quickly dissipated. The December 20 issue of the *Bozeman Chronicle* carried an article citing the infamous "Liver Eating" Johnson, who had seen the "mummy," and claimed it bore a strong resemblance to his former partner, "Antelope Charlie," who had been killed by Indians some twenty years earlier. Others were also questioning whether the object had actually been human. In a report of the *Livingston Post* on January 24, 1900, Mr. Miles reported that he himself had some concern whether the mummy was genuine and indicated that he intended to send the controversial object to the Smithsonian Institution for verification. Despite Miles's vow to "spare no pains to find out the truth," the "Meagher mummy" never actually found its way to the Smithsonian and seems to have disappeared without a trace—perhaps back into the Missouri River.[31]

In 1923 Lewis F. Crawford would claim to have known a man (unidentified) who swore that Meagher's body had been found on a sandbar in the Missouri River by Indians, approximately two months after the fateful night at Fort Benton. The Indians brought the body to the nearby Fort Berthold where it was buried. The mysterious witness claimed that the facial features were too decomposed as to make identification, " . . . but the laundry mark on the band of the drawers was still perfectly plain and marked 'T.F.M.'" According to Crawford's informant, a relative of General Meagher's arrived "some months afterwards" to claim the body, and it was taken ("he thinks") to Fort Leavenworth for re-interment.[32]

While the assassination and "recovery" stories, including another that suggests British agents were involved, are wonderful grist for speculation, each is due its own measure of skepticism. What does appear to be a common theme among many of the various stories are the thinly veiled attempts toward self-promotion. Despite all the nefarious intrigue, the most plausible answers as to the events of Meagher's death are, in all probability, the most ingenuous. Somewhere between the versions of Johnny Doran (who may have been inclined to have a "sheltering" recollection), John

Leaman (who had no discernible interest, but was a very limited witness), and that of Wilbur Fisk Sanders (who was almost certainly inclined to enhance his own reputation at every opportunity) lies the tragic truth of Thomas Francis Meagher's tormented final day of life.

For a man whose first view was of the "noble river" Suir, who sailed across wide oceans—first into exile, then to freedom—and whose final remains are at rest in the greatest of America's rivers, perhaps the imagery of Meagher's life journey as a watercourse is especially appropriate. "Across generations and around the globe, humans . . . have seen rivers as both our source and way out of this world. The Osage Indians use the same word, ni, for water, river, sap, breath, life. To the ancient Egyptians and Greeks, the afterworld lay on the far side of a river, a bourn from which no traveler returns."[33]

> *"Ah, would to God his grave had been*
> *On mountain side, in glen or plain,*
> *Beneath the turf kept soft and green*
> *By wind and sunshine, dew and rain.*
> *That men and maids in after years,*
> *Might come where slept the true and brave,*
> *And plant and wet with flooding tears,*
> *The Irish shamrock on his grave."*
>
> T. D. Sullivan

EPILOGUE

FAMILY

*"In the afternoon I called on Mrs. Meagher.
She is one of the cleverest women, and most brilliant
in conversation, that I have ever met. Her husband,
Thomas Francis Meagher, the Irish patriot . . .
was drowned in the Missouri River . . .
she will soon return to New York City, going down the river
by boat from Fort Benton."*

Bishop Daniel S. Tuttle

Following the death of her husband, Elizabeth Townsend Meagher returned to New York City to live quietly with her father. Prior to her departure she took time to remember those who had been important in the life of her husband while in Montana. John Owen recorded in his journal, "Recd a very Kind Note from Mrs. Gen. Thos. F. Meagher with Photographs of herself & husband— Poor Woman she is sorely afflicted. The pictures shall be a treasured Souvenier & Shall occupy a place in My Album with others dear to Me."[1] The only time she returned to Montana appears to have been during the summer of 1887, when she briefly visited Yellowstone National Park and the city of Helena. While in Helena, she was the honored guest at a meeting of the Society of Pioneers, where she presented a portrait of her husband. During her Montana visit she also was lured into purchasing one-third of the Assumption Lode mine for $3,000. As she confessed in a letter to Andrew O'Connell, "I was ashamed to tell you I made a small investment in a gold mine. It is so like gambling."[2] The investment would later prove, like most gambling, to be unsuccessful.

Elizabeth also traveled to Ireland in the summer of 1886.

During a ceremony in Waterford, before a crowd estimated in excess of 100,000 people, she would present to the city several mementos of her husband's; including a sword, an Irish Brigade battle flag, and a portrait of her husband—a duplicate of the one she later presented in Montana.

Following the death of her father, it appears that Elizabeth experienced financial difficulties. In another letter to O'Connell written from Rye, New York, she would confide that "one of my niece's husband made some trouble for us—for my Father's estate" and this trouble was compounded by "the city of N.Y. laid a heavy tax on me."[3] In February of 1887 she would petition for, and be granted, a military widow's pension of $50 per month by Congress. In the statement of support for this action, the Committee Report concludes, "His widow, an estimable lady, . . . is in need, and in this her hour of adversity instinctively turns to the Government in the fond hope and strong faith that by it the past has not been forgotten."[4] Elizabeth would die at her home in Rye, New York, on July 5, 1906, just a few days past the thirty-ninth anniversary of her husband's death. In an article noting her passing, the *Montana Daily Record* would write: "She had not lived in Montana for many years, but her attachment to and interest in the welfare in this state and its people was retained by her while life lasted. Her memory is linked with that of her husband and will ever be held in fond remembrance by all Montanans."[5]

Information regarding Thomas Francis Meagher II and other descendants is very obscure. In 1869, John Mitchel would refer to Meagher's son when he wrote, " . . . there grows up at this moment another young shoot of that old Tipperary stock, a youth now of fifteen years . . . what reflections must have passed through that youthful head . . . did the young heart swell with pride, and hope, and a longing and craving to be riding that moment by his father's side?"[6] Another mention was by Gerald Sullivan, who wrote in 1905, "Meagher's only son is now residing in the Philippines . . . on my way to Manila in 1898, I had the pleasure of meeting him."[7] Reginald Watson writes that Meagher's son died on November 28, 1910, and is buried in Manila at the Del Norte

Cemetery.[7] Watson's claim is supported by the wife of Thomas Francis Meagher, III.

In 1946, Mrs. Thomas Francis Meagher, III wrote: "The General had one son, Thomas Francis Meagher, II buried at Manilla [sic] and one grandson, Thomas Francis Meagher, III, my husband, buried at St. Helena, California. We had 2 children, James Francis and Helen."[8] An unidentified, newspaper clipping of August 13, 1927 would seem to support this information, in that it reports Thomas Francis Meagher III, "grandson of General Thomas Francis Meagher," had been critically injured in Stockton, California. He was further reported to have his wife and two children by his side.[9] At the time of her June 1946 letter, Mrs. Meagher would also write that James had two children (James Timothy and Karron Marie) and Helen a son (John L. Carr).

YOUNG IRELAND
AND IRISH NATIONALISM

*"What to do with the rest of your life when the cause
in which you have invested everything has failed?"*

John Mitchel

In 1853 William Smith O'Brien was permitted to leave his term of exile in Tasmania, and he received a full pardon in 1856. O'Brien initially lived in Belgium upon leaving Tasmania and, following his tour of the United states in 1859-60, returned to Wales by 1864. Although he would write *Principles of Government, Meditations in Exile*, and was a periodic contributor to the *Nation* after his return, he remained apart from any political controversy. O'Brien died on June 16, 1864, at the age of sixty and is buried in Rathronan, County Limerick. Not without some irony, a statue in his honor is located on O'Connell Street in Dublin.[10]

As an American rebel, Mitchel again paid dearly for supporting an unsuccessful rebellion. Two of Mitchel's sons who served with the Confederate Army died in its service. One son (Willie) was among the many sons of the South who did not return from Pickett's Charge at the battle of Gettysburg.[11] Mitchel's surviving son, James, returned north following the war, and James's son (John Purroy Mitchel) became mayor of New York City in 1914.[12]

Mitchel served a brief prison term (imprisoned with Jefferson Davis at Fort Monroe) following the end of the Civil War for his outspoken support of the Confederate cause. It was reportedly the powerful influence of the Fenian Brotherhood which expedited his release.[13] Mitchel gave a brief period of service to the Fenians in France, then returned to New York in 1867. In 1874, despite not having been granted amnesty, Mitchel defiantly returned to Ireland and immersed himself once again in the battle of politics. Mitchel was elected to a seat in Parliament with a platform which included a denunciation of the "Home Rule" concept and proposed amnesty for all Fenians. His election was declared invalid due to the fact he was an undischarged felon, but he won again in a re-vote in March, 1875 and this election was validated.[14] He died, however, at the age of sixty, before he could begin his term of service. John Mitchel is buried at Newry, County Down.

One of the few prominent figures in the Young Ireland movement to escape prosecution was Charles Gavan Duffy. Duffy remained active as editor of the *Nation* and was elected to Parliament in 1852. Duffy, however, grew frustrated that the Catholics and Protestants of Ireland would not unite for the cause of land reform and left Ireland for Australia where, in 1871, he was elected prime minister of Victoria. It would have been interesting to have witnessed the reaction of his fellow colleagues of Young Ireland when Duffy received a knighthood in 1873. Sir Duffy wrote the seminal work regarding the Young Ireland movement, *Four Years of Irish History, 1845-1849,* just eleven years before his death in 1882.

The site of the single engagement of the failed rebellion of Young Ireland—the "Widow McCormack's home"—in Ballingarry is now a national monument.[15]

The Fenian Brotherhood met in New York City on August 13, 1867, the day prior to Meagher's memorial service, and issued a resolution of condolence—with no mention of his membership. The Brotherhood staged another raid into Canada in 1870 and again in 1871. Both attempts, as the initial invasion, failed rather miserably. By 1885 the Fenian organization had ceased to exist as a viable organization in America. In the meantime, another group had taken root which would provide significant financial support to Irish nationalists for several years. "Clan-na-Gael, the American counterpart of the Irish Republican Brotherhood in Ireland . . . from the moment of its founding in 1867 was [for] the complete independence of Ireland from all English authority. Its methods were those of 'physical force' rather than parlimentary obstruction."[16]

In Ireland, the Brotherhood staged an unsuccessful action, known as the Fenian Rising of 1867, against the British forces. The American Fenians had continued to cling to the idea of a direct invasion of Ireland to support their Irish comrades, but this had been rebuked. "O'Mahoney and the Americans wanted to equip and despatch an expedition: James Stephens, who had undertook to organize the movement in Ireland, insisted that American assistance should be confined to money . . . and the consequent quarrel between the Irish and American leaders was fatal to the chance of success."[17] Effectively broken by the failure of 1867, some disparate clusters of Fenians lived on for several years but eventually gave way to new generations of nationalist groups.

Under the leadership of Michael Collins, the Irish Republican Army was finally successful in negotiating a treaty with Britain. The treaty established the twenty-six county Irish Free State and a separate Northern Ireland district, a compromise that resulted in a lingering civil war. As difficult as it may have been for Meagher to accept the thought of a divided Ireland, the vision of Irishmen killing one another on their native soil would surely have caused him greater anguish. The Irish of Montana, however, were able to take a measure of pride in the fact that William W. McDowell, a former lieutenant governor of Montana, was named as the first United States Ambassador to the Irish Free State.

The Robert Emmet Circle of the Fenian Brotherhood, headquartered in Nevada City, Montana, continued to exist until the early 1870's. Other Montana Circles were known to have been established at Helena, Fort Benton, and Diamond City, but most seem to have ceased to be active by 1875.

MONTANA

*"The Territory is, indeed, a most beautiful and glorious one.
I take great pride in it, am heartily fond of it.
The people are brave, energetic, highly intelligent—
in every respect fine masterly specimens
of American nationality . . . ."*

Thomas Francis Meagher

Governor Green Clay Smith quickly attempted to reconcile the chaotic circumstances of the territory following Meagher's death and the nullification act of Congress. On July 14, 1867, Smith issued General Orders #1 in order to form a "more perfect organization and consolidation of the volunteer forces . . . ."[18] This order significantly reduced the number of active militia and "excused" most of the officers from further service. In accordance with the terms of the newly revised Organic Act, Smith also directed that new elections be held for territorial legislators and called for a meeting of the newly elected legislature—which was thoroughly dominated by representatives of the Democratic Party.

What is interestingly referred to as the "Fourth Session," or "Extra Session," of the legislature convened in Virginia City on November 4, 1867. Upon Smith's recommendation, the Legislature would adopt the "California Practice Act" which expedited the process of establishing a set of laws and practices without rewriting all the bills which had been previously implemented by the "illegal" Second and Third Legislative Sessions. One unique bit of business the Fourth Legislature would enact was to change the name of Edgerton County (initially named in honor of Sidney Edgerton) to Lewis & Clark County. The bill to make this change was introduced by J. W. Rhodes—from Edgerton County. Wilbur F.

Sanders responded that this decision was " . . . actuated by the smouldering embers of political hatred . . . ."[19] The vast majority of Montana's citizens, however, seem to have been either supportive, or indifferent, to the change. As W. Y. Pemberton would write, "In a thorough search of the newspapers of that date we find but little comment on this legislation."[20]

Early in 1869, Green Clay Smith left Montana and returned with his wife and two daughters to Kentucky. Smith began service as a Baptist minister to a small congregation soon after his arrival in Kentucky, but he had another brush with politics and national fame in 1876 when he was nominated by the Prohibition Party for the presidential race, which he very convincingly lost. Smith's participation did make a difference, however, inasmuch as this presidential election was contested as a consequence of the vote being splintered and had to be finally resolved by a vote of the U.S. House of Representatives. Green Clay Smith died June 29, 1895, while serving as minister of the Metropolitan Baptist Church in Washington, D.C.[21]

Undoubtedly both professionally and politically frustrated, Judge Lyman E. Munson also retreated from the Montana Territory to his home in New Haven, Connecticut. The Fourth Session of the Territorial Legislature passed a resolution which declared both Munson and Chief Justice Hosmer to be "incompetent" and requested their resignations.[22] Apparently the pressure of the legislature did have a wearing effect, as Helen Sanders would observe that, "While Judge Munson's term of office did not end until April 5th, 1869, he was absent from the territory after the coming of Judge Warren and Judge Knowles [December, 1868], and never returned to the territory."[23] Munson died at the age of eighty-six on February 13, 1908.

The most durable of those pioneers in early Montana would be Wilbur Fisk Sanders, who was among Meagher's first acquaintances upon arriving in the territory and (presumably) a friend to the end. Sanders continued to fight the battles of Montana politics for the Republican party including another lobbying effort to Congress, this time for the removal of Governor Benjamin F. Potts in 1877.[24] Another intrigue in which Sanders became involved was an effort to split the Montana Territory into two territories. This effort, Sanders claimed, was initiated because the existing territory "was too large to afford the convenience of a civilized commonwealth."[25]

Although Sanders was consistently defeated in his bid for election as territorial delegate, he was elected to the territorial legislature in 1872 and his political perseverance was ultimately rewarded in 1890, predictably amidst great controversy. After being admitted to statehood, Montana held its first election for the U.S. Senate which—true to course—ended in dispute. Unable to resolve the deadlock, the state legislature of Montana sent two Republicans (Thomas Power and Sanders) *and* two Democrats (William A. Clark and Martin Maginnis) to Washington, where the impasse was resolved by a vote of the Republican-controlled Senate, which seated both Republicans. Lots were drawn between Power and Sanders in order to stagger the terms of the initial senators, and Sanders " . . . drew the short term which gave him less than three years of service . . . ."[26] Sanders returned to Montana following his brief stint in the Senate, and although he would not be re-elected to public office, he remained an active force in Republican politics and the Montana legal profession (he organized and served as the first president of the Montana Bar Association).

Wilbur Fisk Sanders died on July 7, 1905, and was eulogized at his Helena funeral by Rev. W. H. Sloan: "We bury him today in the valley surrounded by the mountains he loved to look upon, and which are fit symbols of his forceful character and mental vigor."[27] His memory is perpetuated by virtue of the state legislature naming a Montana county in his honor a few months prior to his death. A statue was also erected in Helena that commemorates Sanders, with the inscription at its base "Men Do Your Duty," the command used to proceed with a Vigilante execution. Sanders's uncle, and Montana's first governor, Sidney Edgerton, who had been stripped of "his county" as a result of the backlash for his nephew's political wrangling, died in Akron, Ohio, on July 19, 1900. Somewhat remarkably, Edgerton had joined the Democratic Party a few years prior to his death.[28]

The man arguably most responsible for the creation of the Montana Territory, James M. Ashley, finally arrived upon the scene in May of 1869 as a result of Green Clay Smith's resignation. As if his role in establishing the Montana Territory wasn't enough, Ashley had secured his spot in American history trivia as the man who filed the resolution of impeachment against Andrew Johnson. In what was no doubt a very questionable appointment by the newly elected President U.S. Grant, Ashley—an avowed enemy of Democrats everywhere—was named as governor of the Montana Territory (which was solidly in the control of the Democratic Party). An editorial in the *Weekly Independent* of Helena apparently reflected the consensus of the Territory's residents by declaring, "The broken down political hack, James M. Ashley, has been appointed Governor of Montana. How long are the people [of Montana] to be scorned and insulted . . . ?"[29]

Ashley served a remarkably brief and turbulent term as territorial governor due to an astonishing deficiency of political tact. Although Virginia City was no longer the Territory's population center, it nevertheless remained the territorial capital, and the Madison County legislative contingent remained a potent political force. Ashley snubbed Virginia City, however, and proceeded to make his residence in Helena, which he predicted was soon to be selected as the territory's next new capital.[30] Ashley's battles with the territorial legislators was brought to an abrupt close in December, when he was dismissed by President Grant. It doesn't appear to have been his lack of effectiveness as governor which disturbed Grant so much as a speech, in which Ashley referred to the Republican Party as "dumb in the presence of a dummy."[31] As Edgerton, Ashley also affiliated with the Democratic party upon his return to Ohio.

Among the most poignant footnotes in the early history of those men and women who established the Montana Territory would be William Fairweather, the man credited with the initial discovery of gold in the Alder Gulch. Fairweather was a man unable, or unwilling, to accept a life of sedate comfort and wealth. He left Virginia City, selling all his mining claims, and returned to the life of a prospector upon learning of the gold strikes in Alaska.[32] Fate did not allow Fairweather a second fortune, however, and he returned to Virginia City. He died, alcoholic and penniless, on August 25, 1875, at the age of thirty-nine and was buried in the Virginia City cemetery—less than a mile from what had been one of the richest gold strikes in North American history.

Politics would continue to be something akin to a contact sport in Montana for several decades. Ashley's prediction that the city of Helena would soon become the territorial capital proved to be a bit premature. In a referendum election in September 1867, Virginia City won the vote between it and Helena to remain the capital. The issue was again put to a public vote by the legislature in January 1869; however, the ballots were mysteriously destroyed by fire. Again, in August 1874, the legislators (no doubt genuinely inconvenienced by what were becoming second-rate facilities) put forward another vote to move the capital. In what must be regarded as a textbook case of political machination, the votes of Gallatin County (which voted overwhelmingly to retain Virginia City as capital) were rejected by the legislature as "flawed." Moreover, the voting results of Meagher County were "thought to be incorrect."[29] When the new returns were received from Meagher County, Territorial Secretary James Callaway reported they were sufficiently in support of Helena so that the legislature enthusiastically declared that city the new territorial capital and quickly abandoned Virginia City.

Benjamin Potts would follow Ashley in the procession of men from Ohio to serve as governor of the Montana Territory. Territorial Delegate Martin Maginnis admonished Potts to keep in mind that "Montana is Democratic, and no governor, clique, faction or 'sorehead' can make it otherwise."[33] Although he had a unsteady start, Potts quickly—and successfully—learned to lead by compromise and through wisely formed alliances. Even though Potts was an unqualified Republican, his most difficult faction to contend with was the die-hard Radical Republicans. Potts was regularly vilified by Robert Fisk, editor of the *Helena Daily Herald*. For his part, Potts, in a letter to President Rutherford Hayes, would refer to Wilbur Fisk Sanders as "the most unscrupulous man that ever disgraced the legal profession."[34] Potts would even go so far as to write to one of the leading Democrats of the territory, Samuel Hauser, that "No satellite of W. F. Sanders shall hold office in Montana if I can prevent it."[35] Potts served for three terms, until 1882, before finally returning to "the States."

Despite the misgiving of some prominent Republicans and Democrats, another Territorial Convention was called to convene in January of 1884 for the sole purpose of developing a constitution. After a month of wrangling, the Constitutional Convention produced a document, which was overwhelmingly ratified by the territory's citizens in November of the same year. The copy of this constitution successfully made its way east to Washington—where it died in the murky waters of political swampland. As a result of bitter partisan fighting, the United States Senate would not approve its passage, and Montana's territorial status lingered on. "Nor did the policy of the federal government in legislating for the territory provide much relief. If change came about, it was usually after years of supplication."[36]

Montana finally became the beneficiary of political wrangling in February 1889 when the lame-duck Congress passed the Omnibus Bill. This bill opened a window of opportunity for Montana, and another Constitutional Convention was quickly convened in July. Under the chairmanship of William Clark, the constitution which resulted from this convention was approved by popular vote in October, and Montana was accepted as the forty-first state on November 8, 1889, slightly less than thirty-four years after Acting Governor Meagher had first called for a Territorial Convention with the dream of statehood.

By the late 1800's the Great Northern Railroad had pushed into Montana, its route passing far south of the once vital port and trailhead of Fort Benton. The availability of the railway's much faster and more reliable service was the death knell for the Missouri River steamboats and the "Chicago of the West." Commercial steamboat traffic from Fort Benton ended by 1890, and the last steamboat to serve the old river town was an excursion boat (the

O.K.), which made one short trip from the town in the summer of 1907.[37]

Although Meagher had claimed it was his intention to populate Montana with good Irish stock, no man would be more successful in single-handedly achieving that goal than Marcus Daly. Daly, an Irishman, first came to Montana in 1876 as superintendent of a silver mine, but quickly established his own company that began to mine copper in the town of Butte. Daly built an economic empire known as the Anaconda Company that made no secret of its preference for hiring those of Irish heritage. By 1900, twenty-five percent of Silver Bow County's (Butte) population had been born in Ireland or were first generation Irish-Americans.[38] Butte quickly became a bastion for the Democratic party (often referred to as "Daylcrats") and Irish associations (including the Robert Emmet Literary Association, a "camp" of the Clan-na-Gael, and the Ancient Order of Hiberians). Together with Marcus Daly's support and the Anaconda Company's interests, these organizations formed a blanket which would comfort friends and smother enemies. For all the influence the Irish may have had with regard to local and, to a somewhat lesser extent, state politics, their ability to affect national policy—at least in one important regard—was not as significant. America's official relationship with Great Britain continued to warm and, particularly with America's entry into World War I, many Irish-Americans found their loyalties strained by their deep-rooted hatred of England.

Perhaps it was inevitable that there would be yet another fight for the capital of Montana, and that Marcus Daly would be in the center of the ring. In 1894, Daly championed an effort to name his company town of Anaconda as the "permanent" site for the territory's capital. His principal opponent in this effort was his bitter professional competitor, and fellow "Copper King," William Clark. Clark would be successful in retaining Helena as the capital, but many claim that it was Daly who had the last laugh.

It was also in Helena in September, 1931, that a utility crew uncovered human remains in a rough pine casket. The hillside site of the discovery was a few hundred yards from the location of where Helena's infamous "hangman's tree" once stood. Following an examination by the city coroner, David Hilger, a librarian of the state historical society, declared the remains to be those of James Daniels.

INDIAN CONFLICT

*"Hear me, my chiefs, I am tired; my heart is sick and sad.
From where the sun now stands I will fight no more forever."*

Chief Joseph of the Nez Perce

If there was anyone who believed that conflict between the Indians and white settlers of Montana had ended, or that Meagher's warning about the tenuous peace of the treaties was bluster, they were sadly mistaken. On August 1, 1867, a spirited battle (known as the "Hayfield Fight") occurred near Fort C. F. Smith between a small party of soldiers and a large combined force of Sioux, Cheyenne, and Arapaho warriors.[39] Although Governor Smith formally concluded the militia campaign on October 1 at the request of General Alfred Terry, deep-seeded trouble still remained.

Frustrated by a continuing series of Indian raids led by the Oglala Sioux warrior Red Cloud, and unwilling to engage in an all-out war, General Grant would authorize a treaty in March of 1868 that directed all the military posts along the Bozeman Trail be closed. This had the effect of, essentially, ending the use of the trail as an immigration route; but did not end the continuing waves of white settlers and certainly did not end treaty violations by the whites—or salve the increasing anger of Indians in Montana. By mid-1869 the Blackfeet, through sporadic raids, were resisting the incursions of whites into their homeland, swelling the crescendo of white settler's pleas that the military intervene. Directed to take decisive action, Major Eugene Baker began a campaign that culminated in the atrocity known as the "Baker Massacre." On January 23, 1870, along the Marias River near Bozeman, Major Baker rode out of Fort Ellis with four companies of cavalry and two infantry companies and initiated a pre-dawn attack against a village of peaceful Blackfeet. When the guns finally stopped firing, 173 Indians, including fifty-three women and children, lay dead.[40]

While on a government-sponsored tour of the eastern United States in July of 1870, Red Cloud would address a packed audience at the Cooper Institute in New York and plead for justice. Red Cloud had earlier visited Washington and had been taken to task for not observing all the articles of the 1868 treaty. Red Cloud, however, claimed he was never aware that some of the articles in question were even included in the treaty.[41] Concessions were made by the government, but soon ignored.

Although several have challenged Meagher's intent and administration of the Indian conflict, Governor Potts waged a more sustained effort against the Indians. Potts requested government troops to resolve another threat to the Gallatin Valley settlers in 1871, and again in 1872 in order that the development of railroad service would not be impeded. In 1872 Potts was successful in arranging for 1,000 rifles and 200,000 rounds of ammunition from the federal government for the area's settlers.[42] The conflict was further aggravated in 1874 by the development of the Yellowstone Road and the Yellowstone Expedition—both of which Potts endorsed. Potts would repeatedly urge the federal government for strong military action, suggest a reduction in the size of reservation lands, and seek permission to form a new territory militia.[43] His requests would be generally ignored—until 1876.

Continued conflict, spurred by the incursions of white settlers and gold seekers, would lead to one of the most famous of all American battles on June 25, 1876. Southeast of the present-day Billings, Montana, near a stream known as the Little Big Horn, troops under the command of George Armstrong Custer would be nearly annihilated by a force of combined Indian tribes. The public outrage at this catastrophe caused William Tecumseh Sherman to redouble his efforts toward the subjugation of the Western tribes. The closing chapter in Montana's Indian wars ended on October 5, 1877 (southeast of present-day Havre, Montana), when approximately 400 members of the Nez Perce tribe finally surrendered after being pursued for nearly 1,300 miles by U.S. Army troops.[44]

THOMAS FRANCIS MEAGHER

"There are few men in our day . . .
whose lives were more varied by remarkable incidents,
more checkered, more twisted and tortured by the whirlpools
of fate than was that of Meagher . . . ."

W.F. Lyons

Understandably, different writers have variously interpreted the words and actions of Thomas Francis Meagher. Through a combination of the incredible course of events during his lifetime and the force of his powerful words and personal energy, Meagher placed himself in the forefront of controversies which shaped the course of nations. One suspects there have since been generations who adore—or despise—the name of Thomas Francis Meagher based upon nothing more than their family's political affiliation or cultural heritage. It seems a cruel irony that Meagher, a man who had stood in defiance to the British government on behalf of the Irish, would be vilified for his efforts in his life's final chapter. Thomas Keneally has observed, "It seemed crucial to some members of the Montana establishment, then and later, that from early 1866 Meagher be written off as the crassest of political opportunists, at dalliance with Secessionists, a reckless violator of the Organic Act, a tyrannical opponent of the public will, and a man in all of who decisions strong liquor took too substantial a part."[45] Perhaps author and educator Merrill Burlingame offered one of the most appropriately dispassionate reviews when he wrote, "His [Meagher's] personal ambition no doubt led him into taking positions where chance played an important part, and his impetuous nature clouded his judgment at times. There can be no doubt, however, that he had a deep interest in Montana, wished

245

fundamentally to do his work well, and that out of his work, warmth of feeling, and vigor of personality, he gained the affection of the people of Montana as no other early leader was able to do."[46]

Through the efforts of the Butte-based Meagher Memorial Association, Charles J. Mulligan was employed to craft a sculpture of Meagher. Supported by the influence, and financial resources, of Marcus Daly, the Memorial Association was able to secure a prominent space on the grounds of the Montana State Capitol in Helena as the site for the sculpture. There were many who believed this was not only an opportunity for Daly to honor a fellow Irishman, but to provide his enemies in Helena a constant source of discomfort. In the public announcements inviting donations for the monument, it was specifically mentioned that all donors, with one exception, were welcome. The exception, Wilbur Fisk Sanders.[47]

Amidst a gala celebration on July 4, 1905, three days prior to the death of Wilbur Fisk Sanders, Miss Anastasia O'Meara (daughter of Clan-na-Gael leader, J. J. O'Meara) was given the honor of unveiling the large bronze statue to the huge crowd which had assembled.[48] The statue depicts a larger than life-size Meagher in military uniform astride a spirited horse with—very symbolically—a sword in his upraised hand, and posed as if about to engage in combat. The inscriptions on the statue's base include these words from Richard O'Gorman's eulogy: "In Ireland, in America, he invited no man to danger he was not ready to share. He gave all, lost all, for the land of his adoption, was her true and loyal soldier."[49] No doubt Meagher would have approved of this memorial, and it's likely that his only regret, as his spirit may have witnessed the ceremony, is that he couldn't have once again appeared upon the stage for another hour to address the multitude. Considering all the speculation surrounding Meagher's life, and death—and the often chaotic chain of events which occurred following his death—it is interesting to consider what would have been the theme of such a final oration.

It is also tantalizing to speculate on what may have been the next chapter in the story of Thomas Francis Meagher's life had he survived the accident at Fort Benton. Inasmuch as he was without a position in Montana it is very reasonable to assume that his return to New York was, indeed, imminent. Even had he remained in the territory following Green Clay Smith's resignation, there is certainly no reason to believe that President Grant would have appointed Meagher to the position of Governor . . . or any other post. It also appears that Meagher was struggling with regard to his financial position. In late September of 1866 Meagher had solicited a loan from Cornelius ("Baron") O'Keeffe of $1,000, and the letter he wrote to Territorial Auditor, John Ming, on the final day of his life suggests Meagher's financial picture had not improved.[50] It is certainly possible that Meagher would have returned to the lecture circuit in an attempt to earn a living, but it is almost certain he would not have eagerly done so—at least not in the United States.

There is apparently some recent evidence which suggests that Meagher had contacted his father in late 1866 regarding arrangements for meeting—with Thomas, II—in Paris.[51] It would be very reasonable to assume that such a rendezvous may have been connected with a speaking tour of European cities. Assuming he would focus his presentations on his adventures in the "wild west" of America and his exploits during the Civil War, Meagher may have not only found financial success on the European lecture circuit, but may have facilitated a pardon from the British government for his return to Ireland. Although it's unlikely that he could have subsequently remained apart from Ireland's political struggle given such a scenario, it seems reasonable that Meagher would have pursued the cause of Irish nationalism as a Member of Parliament rather than as a rebel dissident.

Regardless of the course he may have chosen to follow, one can easily imagine Meagher would have spent the remaining years of his life speaking his mind boldly—and always eloquently—seeking new adventures, and often at the center of controversy. Even now, more than one hundred thirty-five years since his death, Thomas Francis Meagher is able to draw strong feelings from those who talk of the history of Irish nationalism, or of the legendary units and leaders of the American Civil War, or of those men who shaped the foundation of the bold new land that became Montana.

> " . . . he retired from the scene of his first conquest
> with a throbbing heart, and every vein a stream of fire,
> confident that the funeral-car was won, that his statue
> would be reared in public places when he was gone,
> and that he would be one of the imperishable memories
> of the Republic."
>
> Thomas F. Meagher

PART I. NOTES

"Life As A Rebel—Life As An Exile"

Chapter 1 Cavanagh, *Memoirs*, 13.

1. Meagher manuscripts, Montana Historical Society.
2. Cavanagh, 13.
3. Ibid., 14. Harry Meagher would serve in the Papal Brigade and his sister join a religious order.
4. Ibid., 21.
5. Ibid., 26.
6. Ibid., 23.
7. Ibid., 28. Later reporters of Meagher's speeches commonly express surprise at the lack of a "brogue" in his accent.
8. Ibid., 32. Another incident of Meagher's independent nature during his time at Stonyhurst was his refusal to play with the school band during an anniversary ceremony in tribute to the British victory at Waterloo.
9. Ibid., 35.
10. Laxton, 20-21.
11. P. Johnson, 73.
12. *The Nation*, May 20, 1843.
13. Donnelly, 188.
14. Cavanagh, 40.

Chapter 2 Duffy, *Four Years*, 9.

15. Keneally, 91.
16. Kee, 201.

17. Charles Gaven Duffy provides great detail regarding the operations of the *Nation* in his book, *Four Years of Irish History 1845-1849*. John Mitchel served as an Assistant Editor to Duffy following the death of Thomas Davis.

18. Keneally, 113.

19. Kee, 188-189.

20. Duffy, 141.

21. Ibid., 10.

22. Ibid., 610.

23. Irish Monthly (1886), 220. Apparently Mitchel and Meagher had been previously introduced, but it was Meagher who initiated this extended meeting.

24. Cavanagh, 50.

25. Kee, 249.

26. *The Nation*, May 14, 1846.

27. Donnelly, 192.

28. Athearn, *Thomas Francis Meagher*, 4.

29. Duffy, 234.

30. Cavanagh, 65.

31. Ibid., 66.

32. Ibid.

33. Ibid., 75. O'Connell's younger son, Maurice, would later confirm to Duffy the sincerity of the elder statesman's desire to reuinte the factions.

34. Ibid., 77. Also see "Young Ireland Rising" in the July 30, 1998 issue of *An Phoblacht* written by Aengus Snodaigh regarding the formation of Young Ireland Clubs throughout Ireland, England and Scotland.

35. Ibid., 165.

36. Bowers, 369-370.

37. Duffy, 47. Duffy provides specific details regarding the agricultural production and export of such goods.

38. Lyons, 27. Meagher would later meet the ship's captain aboard the transport *Ariel*.

39. www.local.ie. Authorship not determined.

40. P. Johnson, 91.

41. Laxton, 186.

42. Ibid, 74.

43. Ibid, 70.

44. Ibid. A group known as "Ribbonmen" are mentioned for their role in anti-landlord activities.

45. Mitchel.

46. The United Irish organization was active in the late 1700's. Robert's brother, Thomas, escaped to the United States. The United Irish surrendered to Lord Cornwallis in 1798.

47. Cavanagh, 99.

48. Ibid., 86.

Chapter 3 Duffy, *Four Years*, 560. It is certainly arguable this wasn't the *only* mistake the Council of Young Ireland made with regard to the uprising, but it was a very critical factor. O'Brien's great hope to the end, was that the upper-class Irish would embrace the cause and provide much needed financial support and political clout for a successful rebellion.

49. Athearn, *Thomas Francis Meagher*, 39.

50. Cavanagh, 107.

51. Duffy, 563. Other sources do not mention this aspect of the Confederation's agenda, but it is reasonable to accept that there were a significant base of "Wild Geese" (as the Irish immigrants of 1691 were known) descendents in France to have cultivated this scenario.

52. Cavanagh, 150.

53. Ibid., 127.

54. Bulletin of the Department of External Affairs (Ireland), No. 761:20, VI, 1967, page 6. Other authors also support Meagher's role in the creation of the flag, but disagree on whether it was initially displayed in Waterford or in the village of The Commons.

55. www.local.ie. Author uncertain.
56. Walton.
57. By this time Mitchel was not on good terms with many within the Council of the Irish Confederation and had actually been invited to the meeting by members of the Limerick Club Council.
58. Bowers, 349.
59. Cavanagh, 175.
60. Duffy, 596.
61. Ibid, 597.
62. Keneally, 148.
63. *Irish Tribune*, July 1, 1848.
64. Cavanagh, 206. The Council was reduced to approximately one-half its original membership size. Duffy, in *Four Years*, mentions that William Smith O'Brien was absent from this meeting, but was nevertheless elected to the new Council.
65. Ibid., 212. Duffy wrote that the Council approved either Meagher *or* Father Kenyon were to serve as representative and that another (unnamed) delegate was also elected to serve a similar mission to France. Duffy quotes Meagher as accepting his appointment with the condition that 'he should be at liberty to return to Ireland before the harvest was ripe." (Duffy, 609-610) Clearly Meagher expected to serve, inasmuch as he wrote to O'Brien that "I am off for New York, God willing, on Saturday," a note which was intercepted by British authorities and used against Meagher at his trial (Duffy, 610).
66. Duffy, 610. Munster is a district of southern Ireland counties.
67. Ibid, 625.
68. Keneally, 153. Printed copies of Meagher's statement were distributed to the crowd.
69. Duffy, 638-639.
70. *The Nation,* February 15, 1851. Meagher was the houseguest of Patrick Smyth at the time of the announcement.
71. Among the towns visited were Callan, Cashel, Killenaule—where another brief conference was held—Mullinahone and Ballingarry. Meagher, Dillon and Leyne had been sent to

Templederry, but turned back after a meeting with Father Kenyon dissuaded them.

72. Duffy, 652.
73. Cavanagh, 253-289.
74. Ibid., 276. Every day's delay was certainly eroding already poor prospects for success.
75. Ibid., 285.
76. Ibid., 289.
77. Athearn, *Thomas Francis Meagher*, 9.
78. *An Phoblacht/Republican News*, July 30, 1998.
79. Cavanaugh, 264.
80. Thomas Francis Meagher letter to C. Duffy, February 1850, Duffy papers, Royal Irish Academy.
81. O'Brien reportedly ordered the rebel to not fire at the house once he learned that the MacCormack children were inside.

Chapter 4 Duffy, *Four Years*, 760-761.

82. Ibid., 698.
83. *New York Weekly Tribune*, September 9, 1848.
84. Duffy, 697.
85. Cavanagh, 40.
86. *London Times*, October 25, 1848.
87. Lyons, 60-62.
88. Ibid., 63. The poem is titled "Prison Thoughts" and dated October 1848.
89. Duffy, 269. W. O'Brien letter to C. Duffy; Duffy Papers, Royal Irish Academy.

Chapter 5 VonStieglitz, *History of Ross*, 20.

90. Cavanagh, 299.
91. Cullen, 63.
92. Ibid, 64.
93. Athearn, *Thomas Francis Meagher*, 17.

94. Archives Office of Tasmania, "Convict Profile of Thomas Francis Meagher."

95. Letter of T.F. Meagher to C. Duffy, Duffy Papers, Royal Irish Academy.

96. VonStieglitz, 19-20.

97. Ibid., 15-16.

98. Ibid., 20.

99. Letter of T.F. Meagher to C. Duffy, Duffy Papers, Royal Irish Academy.

100. Athearn, *Thomas Francis Meagher*, 20.

101. Duffy Papers, Royal Irish Academy.

102. Letters of Thomas Francis Meagher 1847-1857, National Library, Dublin, Ireland.

103. Cavanagh, 303.

104. Mitchel, *Jail Journal*, 227.

105. VonStieglitz, 20.

106. Lyons, 70.

107. Cullen, 46-47. Quote of John Mitchel describing a visit he made to the Meagher home at Lake Sorell with John Martin.

108. Meagher manuscripts, Montana Historical Society.

109. Cavanagh, 305.

110. Ibid., 307.

111. Lyons, 71.

112. Cavanagh, 308.

113. Congressional Globe, 11, 32nd Congress, First Session, Vol. 21, part I. The resolution was read twice on the Senate floor, considered and amendments were proposed by Senators Shields and Seward. The resolution generally called upon England to free the exiled members of Young Ireland for the United States to offer sanctuary.

PART II. NOTES

"Life of Celebrity—From Immigrant to American"

Chapter 6 *Boston Pilot,* May 15, 1852. Editorial reaction to the news of Meagher's imminent arrival in America.

1. Emmons, *The Butte Irish*, 39.
2. Cavanagh, *Memoirs*, 315.
3. *New York Herald,* May 29, 1852.
4. *New York Herald,* July 2, 1852.
5. Athearn, *Thomas Francis Meagher*, 31.
6. Cavanagh, *Memoirs*, 328-329.
7. Athearn, *Thomas Francis Meagher*, 39.
8. pg 333, Cavanagh; op cit.
9. Watson, *Life and Times*, 52.
10. Cavanagh, *Memoirs*, 336.
11. *New York Daily Tribune,* October 7, 1861.
12. *New York Herald,* December 12, 1853.
13. www.odur.let.rug.nl. Inaugural address of Franklin Pierce, March 4, 1853.
14. Athearn, *Thomas Francis Meagher*, 40.
15. T.F. Meagher letter to W. O'Brien, August 8, 1856. William Smith O'Brien papers, National Library, Dublin.
16. H.W. Allen letter to G. Mannering, April 8, 1853.
17. Cavanagh, *Memoirs*, 339.
18. www.thewildgeese.com
19. *Irish American,* November 11, 1853.
20. Lyons, *Brigadier-General Meagher*, 263-264.

21. Cavanagh, *Memoirs*, 343. T.F. Meagher letter to James Houghton, March 24, 1856.
22. Watson, *Life and Times*, 65.
23. *Kilkenney Journal*, May 10, 1854
24. Ibid.
25. Mitchel, *Jail Journal*, 376.

Chapter 7 Athearn, *Thomas Francis Meagher*, 170.

26. Meagher responded to the editor of the *New York Herald* regarding an article recounting Meagher's escape from Tasmania which had appeared in the March 28, 1854 edition by writing, "This statement is entirely incorrect. The Irish Directory did not pay the expenses of my escape from Australia. That liability I charged to my own account."
27. *Irish American*, July 22, 1854.
28. Ibid., November 11, 1854
29. T.F. Meagher letter to W.E. Robinson. Division of Manuscripts, New York Historical Society.
30. Athearn, *Thomas Francis Meagher*, 50. Elizabeth's paternal grandfather founded the Sterling Iron Works.
31. Corby, *Chaplain Life*, 118.
32. T. F. Meagher letter to Elizabeth Townsend, undated; Meagher manuscripts, Montana Historical Society.
33. *New York Daily Times*, November 16, 1855.
34. Athearn, *Thomas Francis Meagher*, 50.
35. Laxton, *Famine Ships*, 32.
36. *The Irish News*, October 18, 1856.
37. Ibid, October 8, 1857.

Chapter 8 www.dioltas/raidoath

38. Cavanagh, *Memoirs*, 344-345.
39. www.local.ie
40. Ibid.

41. Keneally, *The Great Shame*, 298. Walker was forced to escape Nicaragua as a result of military action and returned to the United States.

42. T.F. Meagher letter to James Buchanan, January 20, 1857; Meagher manuscripts, Montana Historical Society. The letter also included a request that "Col. Doheny" be appointed as an attorney general of "one of the Territories."

43. Athearn, *Thomas Francis Meagher*, 67-69.

44. *Irish News,* May 13, 1858.

45. A series of articles which appeared December 1859, January 1860, and February 1860.

46. Cavanagh, *Memoirs*, 361. Also see Keneally, *The Great Shame*, 307.

47. Meagher letter to W. O'Brien, August 15, 1859. W.S. O'Brien papers.

48. *The Irish American,* September 11, 1858.

49. Keneally, 308. Letter of William Smith O'Brien to his wife, March 10, 1859; O'Brien papers, National Library, Dublin.

50. Cavanagh, 48.

51. *New Haven Leader,* June 11, 1905.

52. Harper's New Monthly Magazine, January 1861.

53. Athearn, *Thomas Francis Meagher*, 86-87.

54. T.F. Meagher letter to John Fogle, October 13, 1859. Leggat Collection.

55. Lyons, *Brigadier-General Meagher*, 42-43.

PART III. NOTES

"Life Of A Soldier—The Civil War"

Chapter 9 DeMille, James, "Song of the Irish Legion," 1861.

1. *The Spectator*, May 14, 1861.
2. *Harper's Weekly*, October 20, 1860.
3. Conyngham, *The Irish Brigade*, 19-20.
4. Ibid., 369
5. Jones, *Irish Brigade*, 75.
6. Offical Reports series 2, 2, 371-373.
7. Jones, *Irish Brigade*, 86.
8. Conyngham, *The Irish Brigade*, 37. The battle at Fontenoy (in Belgium) occurred in 1745 where a unit of ex-patriot Irish soldiers, fighting for France, defeated the British.
9. Bilby, "Remember Frontenoy."
10. *New York Daily Tribune*, July 26, 1861.
11. Conyngham, *The Irish Brigade*, 41-42.
12. Ibid., 43.
13. T.F. Meagher letter to J. Fogle, September 27, 1861. Leggat Collection.
14. Jones, *Irish Brigade*, 95.
15. Keneally, *Great Shame*, 338.
16. Jones, 98.
17. Lyons, *Brigadier-General Meagher*, 86-87.
18. Cavanaugh, *Memoirs*, 420.

Chapter 10 Conyngham, *The Irish Brigade*, 50. The unit took its name to honor the brigade of Irish ex-patriots who fought with the French Army against the British at the battle of Fontenoy.

19. Ibid., 54.
20. Lyons, *Brigadier-General Meagher*, 104-105.
21. Official Reports series 4, 13, 4-6.
22. Ibid.
23. Bilby, 33.
24. Conyngham, *The Irish Brigade*, 56.
25. Ibid., 67.

Chapter 11 Wright, *The Irish Brigade*, 48. Alternative interpretations include "they do not *shrink* from the clash of arms" and "they do not retreat from the clash of *spears.*"

26. Corby, *Chaplain Life*, 28.
27. Ibid., 75.
28. Cavanagh, *Memoirs*, 431.
29. *Irish American*, January 11, 1862.
30. Conyngham, *The Irish Brigade*, 69. John W. Forney was Secretary of the Senate and a personal friend of Lincoln. Forney had previously held the post as Clerk of the House of Representatives and, concurrent with his Senate post, was editor of the *Washington Chronicle*.
31. "A Petition on Behalf of Colonel Thomas Francis Meagher." Merrill G. Burlingame Collection, 1880-1990.
32. Conyngham, *The Irish Brigade*, 145-148.

Chapter 12 Gaelic battlecry believed to have been first used by the Irish Legion of France.

33. Official Reports series 1, 11, 775-779.

34. Foote, *Sumter to Perryville*, 448.
35. Conyngham, *The Irish Brigade*, 154.
36. Cavanagh, *Memoirs*, 417.
37. Conyngham, *The Irish Brigade*, 158.
38. Sears, *Landscape*, pg 243.
39. Conyngham, *The Irish Brigade*, 186.
40. civilwarhome.com. Meagher's report of July 6, 1862.
41. Conyngham, *The Irish Brigade*, 213.
42. Foote, *Sumter to Perryville*, 513.
43. Bradford, *Battles and Leaders*, pg 173.
44. Conyngham, *The Irish Brigade*, 247.
45. Official Reports series 1, 11, 325.
46. Conyngham, 241.
47. Ibid., 246-247.
48. T.F. Meagher letter to A. Lincoln, July 30, 1962, Burlingame Collection. Letter is marked "Personal & Confidential" by Meagher.
49. Ibid.

Chapter 13 Bradford, *Battles and Leaders*, pg 251.

50. Sears, *Landscape*, 242-243.
51. Corby, *Chaplain Life*, 371.
52. Official Reports series 19, 27 & 28, 293-295.
53. Sears, *Landscape*, 243.
54. Official Reports series 19, 27 &28, 293-295.
55. General George B. McClellan's Official Report, July 19, 1862.
56. Conyngham, 306.
57. Jones, *Irish Brigade*, 30.
58. Bradford, *Battles and Leaders*, 269.
59. Mulholland, *116th Regiment*, 13.
60. Ibid.
61. Sears, *Landscape*, 342. McClellan would write "I have this moment returned to my tent after witnessing, with a full heart, a most painful yet noble scene."
62. *New York Daily Tribune*, November 28, 1862.

Chapter 14 Mulholland, *116th Regiment*, 44.

63. Keneally, 527.
64. Welsh, *Green & Blue*, 37. Letter of December 8, 1862.
65. Mulholland, 71.
66. McCarter, *My Life*, 15-16.
67. Ibid.
68. Corby, *Chaplain Life*, 131.
69. Official Reports series 1, 21, 240-246.
70. Ibid.
71. Callahan, "Red & Green."
72. Bradford, *Battles and Leaders*, 310.
73. Conyngham, *The Irish Brigade*, 343.
74. McCarter, 184.
75. Welsh, 43. Letter of December 25, 1862.
76. McCarter, 182-183. McCarter was wounded in his lower leg, left shoulder, left ankle, right arm, and left wrist. He also wrote that one of the minie balls lodged into his blankets with such force it felt as if it had embedded in his skull.
77. Official Reports series, Meagher's report of December 20, 1862.
78. Ibid.
79. Keneally, 375.
80. Inman, *Soldier of the South*, 30-31. December 14, 1862 letter of George Pickett to his wife, 12/14/62.
81. *London Times*, December 15, 1862.
82. Meagher's official report of December 20, 1862.
83. Keneally, 375.
84. Lyons, *Brigadier-General Meagher*, 165. Surgeon's Report of Dr. F. Reynolds, Acting Chief Medical Officer of Hancock's Division, Fredericksburg, Virginia; December 15, 1862.
85. Cavanagh, *Memoirs*, 474.
86. Ibid., Appendix 33. Letter of T.F. Meagher to H. F. Spaulding, December 5, 1863.
87. McCarter, 216.
88. Cavanagh, 475-476.

89. Athearn, *Thomas Francis Meagher*, 122.

90. Conyngham, *The Irish Brigade*, 365.

91. Department of War, Adjutant-General's Office. T.F. Meagher letter dated February 3, 1864.

92. Cavanagh, *Memoirs*, Appendix, 25-26.

93. Ibid., 370.

94. Welsh, 64-67. Letter of February 3, 1863.

95. Sears, *Chancellorsville*, 78.

Chapter 15 Foote, *Fredricksburg to Meridian*, 133.

96. Ibid., 143.

97. Conyngham, *The Irish Brigade*, 404.

98. Department of War, Adjutant-General's Office. T.F. Meagher letter dated May 8, 1863.

99. Cavanagh, *Memoirs*, 485-486.

Chapter 16 Conyngham, *The Irish Brigade*, 380-381. The song was "written by a poetical rival" of Dr. Lawrence Reynolds, who served as poet laureate of the Irish Brigade, and it was initially performed by Captain Blake at the St. Patrick's Day celebration on March 17, 1863.

100. Cavanagh, 361.

101. D'Arcy, *Fenian Movement*, 32.

102. Cavanagh, 362.

103. T.F. Meagher telegraph to A. Lincoln (June 16, 1863), Burlingame Papers.

104. Cavanagh, 489.

105. Keneally, 377.

106. *Irish American*, October 15, 1864.

107. Athearn, *Thomas Francis Meagher*, 133.

108. Department of War, telegrams of U.S. Grant, National Archives. September 11, 1864 telegram of U.S. Grant to H. Halleck.
109. *Irish American,* November 12, 1864.
110. Athearn, *Thomas Francis Meagher,* 136-137.
111. Ibid., 138.
112. War of the Rebellion, Series I, Vol. 47, Part II, 318.
113. Athearn, *Thomas Francis Meagher,* 138.
114. Cavanagh, *Memoirs,* 492.

Chapter 17 Text of the pass issued to Thomas Francis Meagher as a member of the honor guard for the body of Abraham Lincoln. Library of Congress, Manuscript Division.

115. *The Galaxy,* Vol. 12, no. 4, 526.
116. *The Journal of the American Irish Historical Society,* Vol. 30 (1932), 85-86.
117. Athearn, *Thomas Francis Meagher,* 142.

PART IV. NOTES

Life in the Montana Territory: "The Acting One"

Chapter 18 Ambrose, *Undaunted Courage*, 254. This occurred at the end of July 1805.

1. Athearn, *Thomas Francis Meagher*, 144.
2. *St. Paul Press*, August 3, 1865.
3. *St. Paul Pioneer*, July 25, 1865.
4. *St. Paul Press*, August 3, 1865.
5. Meagher, "Rides Through Montana," Harper's, October 1867.
6. *Salt Lake City Daily Telegraph*, September 23, 1865.

Chapter 19 Motto of Montana. The motto originally adopted was "Eldorado," but was changed by a resolution introduced by Territorial Council member Anson Potter of Madison County.

7. Grant, *Guide*, 14.
8. Defenbach, *Idaho*, 370.
9. McClure, "Wilbur Fisk Sanders," Contributions, 27.
10. Stuart, *Forty Years*, 237.
11. *Precious Metals*, 36. Letter of Emily Meredith to her father, April 30, 1863.
12. Diary of J. H. Morley, entry of May 18, 1863. Montana Historical Society.
13. McClure, "Wilbur Fisk Sanders," Contributions, 27.

Chapter 20 Birnery, *Vigilantes*, 211-212. Oath of the Vigilantes signed at a meeting held in Virginia City, Montana on December 23, 1863. Original document with the Montana Historical Society.

14. Ives was convicted of murdering Nicholas T'Vault, although it may have actually been Alex Carter—as Ives' implicated with his last words—who committed the murder.
15. Raymer, *Montana the Land*, 220.
16. Fletcher.
17. Birney, *Vigilantes*, 216.
18. Dimsdale, *Vigilantes*, 280.
19. Ibid, 220-221.
20. Ibid, 221.
21. Raymer, *Montana the Land*, 210, 592. Upon the creation of a lodge in Helena, the lodges of Nevada City and Virginia City combined to form Montana Lodge #1.
22. Burlingame, "Montana's Righteous Hangmen," 36-49.
23. Gould's, *Freemasonry*, 396.
24. Sanders, "Organization of Vigilance Committee." W.F. Sanders Papers, MC 53, Box 5; Montana Historical Society.
25. Dimsdale, *Vigilantes*, 110 and McClure, "Wilbur Fisk Sanders," Contributions, 28.
26. Raymer, *Montana the Land*, 225.
27. Munson, "Pioneer Life in Montana," Contributions, 209.
28. James Fergus papers; K. Ross Toole archives, Mansfield Library, University of Montana. Fergus later served as Recorder and Commissioner for Lewis & Clark County and was elected to the state legislature.
29. Langford, *Days & Ways*, 338.

Chapter 21 Ashley, "Govenor Ashley's Biography and Messages," Contributions, 188. S. Edgerton in letter to W.F. Sanders, March 21, 1886.

30. Malone & Roeder, *Two Centuries*, 72.
31. Spence, *Politics*, 18.
32. Ibid. Coburn would accept a position as Associate Justice for the territory in 1884.
33. Sanders, *A History*, 331. At the time of the U.S. Census in 1870, the white population of the Territory was cited at 18,306—including 1,584 who were "natives of Confederate states."
34. Burlingame and Toole, A *History of Montana*, 222.
35. Ibid. Refers to the forces of Sterling Price.
36. Thane, "Acting One," 47.
37. Spence, 21.
38. Joaquin Miller, *Illustrated History*, "History of the Democratic Party in Montana," Samuel Word, 592-617. Fort Union was located at the junction of the Yellowstone and Missouri Rivers in the Dakota Territory; present-day North Dakota.
39. Burlingame & Toole, 222.
40. Spence, 25.
41. Athearn, "Civil War and Montana Gold," Contributions, 65.
42. Burlingame and Toole, *History of Montana*, 223.
43. Rogers would later move to Deer Lodge where he became editor of the *Independent*.
44. Sanders, *A History*, 329-330.
45. Paladin, "Henry Blake," Montana Magazine of Western History.
46. Neally letter to H. Hosmer, May 7, 1865. Hosmer papers at Yale University.
47. *Montana Post*, February 9, 1866.
48. Ibid., September 30, 1865.
49. Ibid.

50. Ibid. Although Sidney Edgerton has annunced his intention to leave the territory, this comment is surprising.
51. Ibid., September 25, 1865.
52. Ibid., September 30, 1865.

Chapter 22 Letter of Ellen Fletcher, July 26, 1866. Fletcher papers, Montana Historical Society.

53. Grant, *Guide*, 53.
54. Raymer, *Montana the Land*, 251.
55. Barsness, *Gold Camp*, 68-69.
56. Ibid, 71-72.
57. Cushman, *Gold Frontier*, 96-97.
58. Pace, *Golden Gulch*, 44.
59. Burlingame, *Montana Frontier*, 165.
60. Athearn, *Thomas Francis Meagher*, 147.
61. *Montana Post*, January 21, 1864.
62. Spence, *Politics*, 33.
63. Lacy, *Montana Militia*, 7.
64. Hosmer letter to S. Hauser, June 24, 1865. Hauser papers, Montana Historical Society.
65. Meagher, "A Journey to Benton," Montana Western History, 47.
66. Ibid. Letter of T.F. Meagher to Fr. deSmet dated December 15, 1865.
67. Hamilton, *Wilderness to Statehood*, 182.
68. Ibid.
69. Munson, "Pioneer Life in Montana," Contributions, 220.
70. Council Journal of the Second Session. Thomas Francis Meagher's address to the Second Territorial Legislature of Montana.
71. Bradley papers; Book II. Montana Historical Society.
72. Hamilton, *Wilderness to Statehood*, 182.
73. *Dillon Examiner*, April 14, 1919. Article based upon Lyman Munson's account.
74. Hamilton, *Wilderness to Statehood*, 183.

75. Thomas Francis Meagher letter to Major General Frank Wheaton, October 26, 1865. Territorial Papers of Montana.
76. Thomas F. Meagher to William Seward, December 11, 1865. Territorial Papers.
77. Records of the Department of the Missouri. Thomas F. Meagher to William T. Sherman, December 16, 1865.

Chapter 23 *Precious Metals*, 137. Letter of Robert E. Fisk to his fiance', Elizabeth Chester, dated December 7, 1866. Robert was a brother of expedition guide James Fisk.

78. Thomas Francis Meagher letter of November 17, 1865. TFM papers, Montana Historical Society.
79. Burlingame and Toole, *History of Montana*, 226. The authors suggest Meagher's motivation was his hope for election to a seat in the U.S. Senate.
80. Thomas F. Meagher to William Seward, December 11, 1865. Territorial Papers.
81. *Montana Post,* December 23, 1865.
82. Letter of John H. Shober, December 16, 1865. Meagher papers, Montana Historical Society.
83. Thane, "Thomas Francis Meagher: The Acting One," 24.
84. Thomas F. Meagher to President Andrew Johnson, January 20, 1866. Johnson Papers, Division of Manuscripts, Library of Congress.
85. *Montana Radiator,* January 27, 1866.
86. *Montana Post,* January 20, 1866.
87. W. J. Boyer papers, page 8; Montana Historical Society (SC #1545).

Chapter 24 Langford, *Vigilante Days*, 388.

88. Ibid., 387.
89. Thomas Francis Meagher pardon of James B. Daniels, dated February 22, 1866. Alexander Leggat Collection.

90. Munson, "Pioneer Life in Montana," 211.
91. Langford, *Vigilante Days*, 387-388.
92. *Butte Daily Post*, September 25, 1931.
93. Johnson, *Bloody Bozeman*, 172.
94. Langford, 388.
95. H. Sanders, 588-589.
96. Langford, xiii.
97. Hamilton, *Wilderness to Statehood*, 506.
98. H. Sanders, 567.
99. Haines, *Yellowstone Story*, 89-90.
100. Land purchase recorded in Book I, page 212, of Madison County Deeds, Grants and Transfers. Meagher paid $200 for "320 acres of land on Madison Valley." T.F. Meagher letter to Rev. George Pepper, January 20, 1866. Meagher papers at William Andrew Clark Memorial Library, University of California at Los Angeles.

Chapter 25 Thomas F. Meagher to William Seward, February 20, 1866. Territorial Papers.

101. Ibid.
102. William Chumasero to Lyman Trumbell. Territorial Papers.
103. Maginnis, "Thomas Francis Meagher," Contributions, 104-105

Chapter 26 *Montana Post*, March 1, 1866. Appeared as an "open letter" from Munson to Meagher.

104. Council Journal of the Second Session.
105. Ibid.
106. Ibid.
107. *Montana Post*, August 18, 1866.
108. Council Journal, Second Session. Congress would pass the Act on July 26, 1866. The Act provided that mineral rights of the territory were of the public domain and were free and open to exploration and occupation.
109. Ibid.

110. Ibid.
111. William T. Hamilton letter to Meagher, February 27, 1866. Meagher papers, Montana Historical Society. Hamilton cited the reason for delay in reporting to the legislature was due to the fact "the county clerk has been killed by Indians."
112. Council Journal, Second Session.
113. H. D. Upham letter to Meagher, March 15, 1866. Meagher papers, M.H.S. Upham was serving as the "Acting Agent for the Blackfeet."
114. W.T. Sherman to Meagher, February 17, 1866. Meagher papers, M.H.S. Sherman indicates in letter he had also received a similar request from Edgerton.
115. Thane, "Thomas Francis Meagher: The Acting One," 31.
116. Meagher papers, M.H.S.
117. Meagher letter to R. B. Parrott, March 19, 1866. Meagher papers, M.H.S.
118. Council Journal of the Second Session.
119. Ibid.
120. *Anaconda Standard,* March 17, 1914.
121. Sanders, *A History,* 354.
122. Spence, 99. While there were presses available in the territory, it may have actually been less expensive to have the work printed in "the States" and shipped back.

Chapter 27 www.dioltas/raidoath. Fenian soldier's song.

123. Neidhardt, *Fenianism,* 29.
124. *Montana Post,* December 16, 1865.
125. dioltas/raidoath
126. *Montana Post,* October 7, 1865
127. Ibid. January 6, 1866.
128. Thomas Francis Meagher to Andrew Johnson. Johnson Papers.
129. Bruce, *Lectures,* 55.
130. *Rocky Mountain Gazette,* August 25, 1866.
131. Athearn, *Thomas Francis Meagher,* 155.

Chapter 28 Callaway, "Governor Green Clay Smith," Contributions, 117.

132. Davidson, "Green Clay Smith, the Preacher," *Contributions*, 186.
133. Ibid.
134. Spence, 43.
135. Callaway, Governor Green Clay Smith," 108.
136. Ibid., 114.
137. Thane, "Thomas Francis Meagher: The Acting One," 69.
138. Bruce, *Lectures*, 84.
139. *Montana Post,* October 6, 1866.
140. Paladin, 48.
141. *Montana Post*, October 20, 1866.
142. Miller, *The Road,* 103.
143. H. Sanders, 335.

Chapter 29 Burlingame and Toole, *History of Montana*, 228.

144. Letter of W.F. Sanders to J.E. Callaway; May 16, 1904. Leggat Collection.
145. United States Statutes, 39th Congress Second Session, Section 6, Chapter 150, 426.
146. Maginnis, "Thomas Francis Meagher," 106.
147. Spence, 48.
148. Owen, entry of March 24, 1867. Owen Papers, M.H.S. James Tufts was appointed to the position of Territorial Secretary March 28, 1867.

Chapter 30 *American Quotations*, 595. F. Scott Fitzgerald letter to Andrew Turnbull, 1904.

149. *Montana Post*, January 26, 1867.
150. Johnson, *Bloody Bozeman*, 292.

151. Letter of U.S. Grant to Stanton. Johnson Papers.
152. *Montana Post,* May 4, 1867.
153. Bruce, *Lectures,* 62.
154. Thane, "The Acting One," 76.
155. *Montana Post,* May 25, 1867.
156. Athearn, *Sherman,* 66.
157. Athearn, "General Sherman and the Montana Frontier," Montana History, 57.
158. W.T. Sherman to Grenville M. Dodge, February 20, 1867. Grenville M. Dodge Papers.
159. Office of the Secretary of War. E. Stanton to W. Sherman, May 3, 1867.
160. Ibid. Sherman to Stanton, May 4, 1867.
161. Ibid.
162. Ibid.
163. Athearn, *Sherman,* 139.
164. Office of the Secretary of War. Sherman to Stanton, May 4, 1867.
165. Department of War, Division of the Missouri. Sherman to Augur, May 6, 1867.
166. *Montana Post,* May 11, 1867.
167. *Montana Post,* May 18, 1867.
168. Department of War, Division of the Missouri.
169. Thane, "The Acting One," 80.
170. *Montana Post,* May 22, 1867.

Chapter 31 Burlingame and Toole, *History of Montana,* 230.

171. Cavanagh, 494. Meagher letter to John Hamill, June 7, 1867.
172. Paladin, 43.
173. Bruce, *Lectures,* 56.
174. *Harper's New Monthly Magazine,* October 1867.
175. Sharp, *Whoop-Up Country,* 145.
176. Athearn, *Sherman,* 134.
177. *The Sun,* June 2, 1913.

PART V. NOTES

"The Controversial Death of A Controversial Man"

Chapter 32 Miller, *The Road*, 124.

Maginnis, "Thomas Francis Meagher," Contributions, 107.

Bruce, *Lectures*, 9. Meagher's lecture to the Young Men's Literary Association of Virginia City, January 15, 1865, entitled *"The Penalties of Public Life—Its Duties and Rewards."*

1. Callaway, "Gov. Green Clay Smith," Contributions, 110.
2. Ibid. John Knox Miller in his diary (op cit) would refer to Fort Benton as " . . . a collection of adobe huts and large wooden storehouses."
3. Athearn, *Thomas Francis Meagher*, 170.
4. Ibid., 165.
5. *Anaconda Standard*, September 9, 1901. Quote of Isaac Gilbert Baker.
6. Bradley manuscript, "Account of the Drowning of Thomas Francis Meagher," Contributions 131.
7. Thomas Francis Meagher letter to John Ming, July 1, 1867. Meagher papers, Montana Historical Society. Meagher's letter urged Ming to forward salary benefits to Ft. Benton as soon as possible inasmuch as he was "utterly—utterly—out of funds."

8. Johnson, "Slow Boat to Benton," Montana Western History, 2. Story is based upon the diary of Harriet Sanders, wife of Wilbur Fisk Sanders. Mr. Sanders had accompanied his family on their return as far as Omaha, but the gone overland to Virginia City. He met them again on June 16th and accompanied them as far as Fort Cooke, where he, again, disembarked an traveled overland to await the family at Fort Benton.

9. *Anaconda Standard,* September 9, 1901. The Bradley Papers version records *10:00* p.m.

10. T.F. Meagher to W. Seward, February 20, 1866. Territorial Papers of Montana, Vol. 2, National Archives.

11. Bradley Papers, Montana Historical Society.

12. *Montana Daily Record,* July 6, 1906.

13. Bruce, *Lectures,* 78.

14. Ibid., 80. Letter was posted from Bray, Ireland where Mr. Meagher indicated he "was staying at the present."

15. Ibid., 84. The announcement was dated July 5, 1867 and called for "the recovery . . . and safe delivery at Fort Benton, St. Louis, or either of the Military Forts on the Missouri where it can be procured by friends."

16. Ibid.

17. Raymer, *Montanta the Land,* 264.

Chapter 33 Meagher's response to the sentencing of John Mitchel. Quote inscribed upon the monument to Meagher on the grounds of the Montana capitol building in Helena.

18. Bruce, *Lectures,* 86.

19. Appendix, Memoirs of General Thomas Francis Meagher, Michael Cavanagh.

20. Athearn, *Thomas Francis Meagher,* 166.

21. Ibid.

22. *Missoula Sentinel,* May 29, 1913. There was apparently some suspicion afterwards that the story may have been promoted as an attempt to boost sales of the struggling paper.

23. *Daily Missoulian*, May 30, 1913.
24. Sanders, *A History*, 337.
25. *The Sun*, June 2, 1913. Billingsley was 86 years old at the time of his "confession."
26. Raymer, *Montana*, 236-237.
27. Ibid.
28. Sanders, *A History*, 337.
29. Dennis Nolan letter to D. H. Kelly, June 4, 1913. Montana Attorney General records, Montana Historical Society.
30. "The Wonderful Petrified Man," Montana Western History.
31. Ibid.
32. L.F. Crawford letter to E. McDonald, May 15, 1923. Meagher file, Montana Historical Society.
33. Least-Heat Moon, *Riverhorse*, 117.

Finis: One stanza of a poem by T.D. Sullivan, written in 1873.

EPILOGUE NOTES

Family: *Reminiscences of a Missionary Bishop*, Daniel S. Tuttle. Entry dated

"Virginia City, Montana, July 27, 1867.

1. *Journals of Major John Owen*, entry for August 8, 1867.
2. Elizabeth Meagher letter to A. O'Connell, September 2, 1887. Catherine Young papers, Montana Historical Society.
3. Ibid. Letter of November 21, 1902.
4. Senate Resolution 1731, House Resolution 8463, February 22, 1887. The resolution called for a pension of $50 per month, which appears to have been a standard payment.
5. *Montana Daily Record*, July 6, 1906.
6. Lyons, *Brigader-General Meahger*, 39.
7. *Montana Daily Record*, July 5, 1905. Included in an article regarding the dedication of Meagher's statue which was to be dedicated that day.
8. Mrs. Thomas Francis Meagher, III letter to Robert Athearn, June 30, 1946. Meagher papers, Montana Historical Society.
7. Watson, *Life & Times*, 91.
9. Meagher file, Montana Historical Society Library.

Young Ireland: Mitchel, *Jail Journal.*

10. clarelibrary.ie
11. thewildgeese.com
12. ireland.com. John Purroy was elected mayor as an anti-Tammany Hall candidate, and was a popular reformer in New

York City politics. He was killed in a military training plane crash on July 6, 1918.

13. Jones, *Irish Brigade*, 252. Following his release, Mitchel reportedly went to France on behalf of the Fenians, but became disenchanted with their cause. His wife and daughters had gone to France at the outbreak of the Civil War, which may have been a more likely motivation for his trip.

14. Keneally, 527.

15. ie.com

16. Emmons, *Butte Irish*, 104.

17. Henry, *Sinn Fein*, 34.

Montana: Thomas Francis Meagher to William Seward, February 20, 1866. Merrill Burlingame Collection, Montana State University.

18. Callaway, pg 136, "Governor Green Clay Smith," Contributions, 136.

19. Pemberton, "Changing the Name of Edgerton County," Contributions, 324.

20. Ibid.

21. Davidson, "Green Clay Smith, the Preacher," Contributions, 185.

22. Hamilton, *Wilderness to Statehood*, 326.

23. Sanders, *A History*, 594.

24. Malone and Roeder, *Two Centuries*, 83.

25. May 24, 1889 speech of Wilbur Fisk Sanders. Burlingame Collection.

26. McClure, "Wilbur Fisk Sanders,"Contributions, 29. The other Montana Republican who was seated as Senator by the vote of Congress was T.C. Power.

27. *Butte Miner*, July 11, 1905.

28. Spence, *Politics*, 34.

29. Malone and Roeder, *Two Centuries*. 82.

30. Ashley, "Governor Ashley's Biography & Messages," Contributions, 191.

31. Malone & Roeder, *Two Centuries*, 82.
32. Purple, *Perilous Passage*, 177.
33. *Daily Rocky Mountain Gazette*, July 21, 1870. Spence, 72.
34. B. Potts letter to Hayes, December 28, 1878. D.S. Wade file, Department of Justice; National Archives.
35. Potts to S. Hauser, November 24, 1878. Hauser papers, Montana Historical Society.
36. Spence, 231.
37. Henry, *Our Land*, 217.
38. Emmons, 13.

Indian Conflict: Hampton, *Children of Grace*, 307. From November 17, 1877 issue of *Harper's Weekly*.

39. Army Historical Series, *Winning the West*, 307.
40. Malone & Roeder, *Two Centuries*, 90. The chief of the band was reportedly wearing the peace medal he had been presented as a treaty signatory.
41. Josephy, *Nations*, 392-395.
42. United States Statutes at Large, Vol. 17, May 21, 1872.
43. Spence, 112-113.
44. Hampton, *Children of Grace*, 307.

Meagher: Lyons, *Brigadier-General Meagher*, 209.

45. Keneally, 430.
46. Burlingame, *Montana Frontier*, 165.
47. Emmons, 119.
48. Maginnis, "Thomas Francis Meagher," Contributions, 139.
49. Bruce, *Lectures*, 88. The eulogy was delivered August 14, 1867 at the Cooper Institute in New York City, where Meagher had heard the lecture which created his interest in going to Montana.
50. Oberley, Edith, "The Baron C. C. O'Keeffe," Montana Magazine of Western History, Vol. 23, #3. Letter of Meagher

to O'Keeffe, September 26, 1866. Meagher requested the $1,000 "loan" from his fellow Irishman in order to pay debts he had incurred, and thus return to Virginia City without a cloud of financial distress, "It is my ambition—it is indeed, and in truth my heart's desire—to be the representative and champion of the Irish Race in the wild great mountains . . . ." O'Keeffe appears to have made the loan, and Meagher may have expressed his gratitude by securing an appointment for the "Baron" as Missoula County Commissioner.

51. Hearne, John, lecture for the Montana Historical Society, May 13, 2003.

Finis: Bruce, *Lectures*, 13. Thomas F. Meagher's lecture to the Young Men's Literary Association of Virginia City, January 15, 1865. This rather somber address, entitled "The Penalties of Public Life—Its Duties and Rewards," was an obvious personal reflection.

BIBLIOGRAPHY/RESOURCES

Books/Theses

Ambrose, Stephen. *Undaunted Courage*. New York: Simon & Schuster, 1996.

Athearn, Robert. G. *Thomas Francis Meagher: An Irish Revolutionary in America*. Boulder: University of Colorado Press, 1949.

———. *William Tecumseh Sherman & the Settlement of The West*. Norman: University of Oklahoma Press, 1956.

Barsness, Larry. *Gold Camp: Alder Gulch and Virginia City, Montana*. New York: Hastings House, 1972.

Bell, W. S. *Old Fort Benton*. Helena, 1909.

Bilby, Joseph G. *Remember Fontenoy! The 69th New York and the Irish Brigade in the Civil War*. Hightstown: Longstreet House, 1995.

Birney, Hoffman. *Vigilantes*. Philadelphia: Penn Publishing Company, 1929.

Bowers, Claude G. *The Irish Orators*. Indianapolis: The Bobbs-Merrill Co., 1916.

Boyce, D. George. *Nationalism in Ireland*. Baltimore: Johns Hopkins University Press, 1992.

Bradford, Ned, editor. *Battles and Leaders of the Civil War*. New York: Appleton, Century, Crofts, Inc., 1956.

Brown, Mark H. *The Plainsmen of the Yellowstone*. New York: G.P. Putnam's Sons, 1961.

Bruce, John P. *Lectures of Gov. Thomas Francis Meagher in Montana*. Virginia City: Bruce & Wright Press, 1867.

Burlingame, Merrill G. *The Montana Frontier*. Helena: State Publishing Company, 1942.

Burlingame, Merrill G., and K. Ross Toole. *A History of Montana, Vol. I*. New York: Lewis Historical Publishing Company, 1957

Callaway, Llewellyn L. *Montana's Righteous Hangmen*, edited by Lew L. Callaway, Jr. Norman: University of Oklahoma Press, 1982.

Carruth, Gorton, and Eugene Ehrlich. *The Harper Book of American Quotations*. New York: Harper & Row, 1988.

Cavanagh, Michael. *Memoirs of Gen. Thomas F. Meagher*. Worchester: The Messenger Press, 1892.

Chittenden, Hiram Martin. *History of Early Steamboat Navigation on the Missouri River, Vol II*. New York: Francis P. Harper Press, 1903.

————. *The Yellowstone National Park*. Edited by Richard A. Bartlett. Norman: University of Oklahoma Press, 1964.

Coleman, Julie L. *Golden Opportunities, A Biographical History of Montana's Jewish Communities*. Helena: Sky House Publishers, 1994.

Conyngham, David Porter. *The Irish Brigade and its Campaigns*. Edited by Lawrence Frederick Kohl. New York: Fordham University Press, 1994.

Corby, William. *Memoirs of Chaplain Life, Three Years with the Irish Brigade in the Army of the Potomac*. Edited by Lawrence Frederick Kohl. New York: Fordham University Press, 1992.

Cullen, John H. *Young Ireland In Exile*. Dublin, 1928.

Cushman, Dan. *Montana—The Gold Frontier*. Great Falls: Stay Away Joe Publications, 1973.

D'Arcy, William. *The Fenian Movement in the United States: 1858-1866*. Washington: Catholic University Press, 1947.

Defenbach, Byron. *Idaho The Place and Its People, Vol. I*. New York: The American Historical Society, Inc., 1933.

Dimsdale, Thomas. *Vigilantes of Montana*. Helena: McKee Publishing Company, 1865.

Donald, David Herbert. *Lincoln*. London: Jonathan Cape, 1995.

Donnelly, James S. Jr. *The Great Irish Potato Famine*. Gloucestershire: Sutton Publishing Limited, 2001.

Donovan, Frank. *River Boats of America*. New York: Thomas Y. Crowell Company, 1966.

Duffy, Charles Gavan. *Four Years of Irish History 1845-1849*. Dublin, 1882.

Dunbar, Seymour and Paul C. Phillips. *Journals and Letters of Major John Owen, Volumes 1 and 2*. New York: Edward Eberstadt, 1927.

Ellingsen, John, John Deltass, Tony Dalich, and Ken Sievert. *If These Walls Could Talk, A History of the Buildings of Virginia City, Montana*. Virginia City, 1977.

Emmons, David M. *The Butte Irish*. Urbana: University of Illinois Press, 1989.

Foote, Shelby. *The Civil War, A Narrative, Fort Sumter to Perryville*. New York: Random House, 1958.

_____. *The Civil War, A Narrative, Fredericksburg to Meridian*. New York: Random House, 1963.

Foster, R. F. *Modern Ireland: 1600-1972*. New York: Penguin, 1989.

Furgurson, Ernest B. *Chancellorsville, 1863 The Souls of the Brave*. New York: Alfred A. Knopf, 1992.

Gates, T. B. *The Civil War Diaries of Col. Theodore B. Gates, 20th New York State Milita*, Seward R. Osborne, editor. Hightstown: Longstreet House, 1991.

Grant, Marilyn. *A Guide to Historic Virginia City*. Helena: Montana Historical Society Press, 1998.

Hackett, Francis. *Ireland: A Study in Nationalism*. New York: B.W. Huebsch, 1919.

Haines, Aubrey L. *The Yellowstone Story, A History of Our First National Park, Vol. I*. Boulder: University Press of Colorado, 1996.

Hamilton, James McClellan. *History of Montana, From Wilderness to Statehood*. Portland: Binsford & Mort, 1957.

Hampton, Bruce. *Children of Grace, The Nez Perce War of 1877*. New York: Henry Holt & Company, 1994.

Hebard, Grace Raymond. *The Bozeman Trail, Vol. I*. Cleveland: Arthur H. Clark Company, 1922.

Henry, Ralph C. *Our Land Montana*. Helena: State Publishing Company, 1969.

Henry, Robert Mitchell. *The Evolution of the Sinn Fein*. New York: B. W. Huebsch, Inc., 1920.

Howard, Joseph K. *Montana: High, Wide and Handsome.* New Haven: Yale University Press, 1959.

Inman, Arthur C. *Soldier of the South: General Pickett's War Letters To His Wife.* New York: Houghton Mifflin, Company, 1928.

Jackson, W. Turrentine. *Wagon Roads West.* Berkley: University of California Press, 1952.

Johnson, Dorothy M. *The Bloody Bozeman: The Perilous Trail to Montana's Gold.* New York: McGraw-Hill, 1971.

Johnson, Paul. *Ireland: Land of Troubles.* London: EyreMethuen Ltd., 1980.

Jones, Paul. *The Irish Brigade.* New York: Robert B. Luce, Inc., 1969.

Josephy, Alvin M., Jr. *500 Nations.* New York: Alfred A. Knopf, 1994.

Kee, Robert. *The Green Flag.* New York: Delacorte Press, 1972.

Keneally, Thomas. *The Great Shame.* New York: Nan A. Talese, 1999.

Kohl, Lawrence F. and Margaret C. Rich. *Irish Green and Union Blue, The Civil War Letters of Peter Welsh.* New York: Fordham University Press, 1986.

Lacey, Richard H. *The Montana Militia.* Dillon: Dillon-Tribune Examiner Press, 1976.

Laxton, Edward. *The Famine Ships.* New York: Henry Holt and Co., 1996.

Lang, William L. and Rex Myers. *Montana Our Land & People.* Colorado: Pruett Publishing Company, 1979.

Langford, Nathaniel Pitt. *Vigilante Days and Ways.* Chicago: A.C. McClurg & Company, 1912.

Least Heat-Moon, William. *Riverhorse.* New York: Houghton Mifflin, 1999.

Leeson, M.A. *History of Montana 1739-1885.* Chicago: Warner, Beers & Company, 1885.

Lepley, John G. *Birthplace of Montana, A History of Fort Benton.* Missoula: Pictorial Histories Publishing Company, 1999.

Lyons, W.F. *Brigadier-General Thomas Francis Meagher: His Political and Military Career.* New York, 1869.

Malone, Michael P. and Richard B. Roeder. *Montana, A History of Two Centuries.* Seattle and London: University of Washington Press, 1976.

Mather, R. E. and F. E. Boswell. *Hanging the Sheriff, A Biography of Henry Plummer.* Missoula: Historic Montana Publishing, 1998.

_____. *Vigilante Victims, Montana's 1864 Hanging Spree.* San Jose: History West Publishing Company, 1991.

McCarter, William. *My Life in the Irish Brigade: The Civil War Memoirs of Private, William McCarter,* edited by Kevin E. O'Brien. Campbell: Savas Publishing Company, 1996.

Miller, James Knox Polk. *The Road to Virginia City, The Diary of James Knox Polk Miller.* Edited by Andrew F. Rolle). Norman: University of Oklahoma Press, 1960.

Miller, Joaquin. *An Illustrated History of the State of Montana.* Chicago: The Lewis Publishing Company, 1894.

Miller, Kerby. *Emigrants and Exiles: Ireland and the Irish Exodus to North America.* New York: Oxford Press, 1985.

Mitchel, John. *Jail Journal.* London, 1913. The Montana Historical Society. *Not in Precious Metals Alone, A Manuscript History of Montana.* Helena: Montana Historical Society Press, 1976.

Mulholland, St.Clair A. *The Story of the 116th Regiment,* edited by Lawrence Frederick Kohl. New York: Fordham University Press, 1996.

Neidhardt, W.S. *Fenianism in North America.* University Park: Pennsylvania State University Press, 1975.

Osborne, Seward R. *The Civil War Diaries of Col. Theodore B. Gates, 20th New York State Militia.* Hightstown: Longstreet House, 1991.

Owen, John. *Journals and Letters of Major John Owen 1850-1871,* edited by Seymour Dunbar. New York: Edward Eberstadt, 1927.

Pace, Dick. *Golden Gulch, The Story of Montana's Fabulous Alder Gulch.* Butte: Jursnick Printing Company, 1962.

Purple, Edwin. *Perilous Passage.* Edited by Kenneth N. Owens. Helena: Montana Historical Society Press, 1995.

Raymer, Robert G. *Montana The Land and the People, Vol. 1.* Chicago: Lewis Publishing Company, 1930.

Reinhart, Herman Francis. *The Golden Frontier,* edited by Doyce B. Nunis, Jr. Austin: University of Texas Press, 1962.

Sanders, Helen F. *A History of Montana, Vol. 1.* Chicago: Lewis Publishing Company, 1913.

Sanders, Helen Fitzgerald and William H. Bertsche, Jr. editors. *X Biedler: Vigilante.* Norman: University of Oklahoma Press, 1957.

Sanders II, W.F., and Robert T. Taylor. *Biscuits and Badmen: The Sanders Story in Their Own Words.* Butte: Editorial Review Press, 1983.

Seagrave, Pia Seija. *The History of the Irish Brigade, A Collection of Historical Essays.* Fredericksburg: Sergeant Kirkland's Museum and Historical Society, 1997.

Sears, Stephen W. *Landscape Turned Red The Battle of Antietam.* New York: Book-of- the-Month Club, 1994.

_____. *Chancellorsville.* New York: Houghton Mifflin Company, 1996.

Sharp, Paul F. *Whoop-Up Country, The Canadian-American West 1865-1885.* Norman: University of Oklahoma Press, 1955.

Sievert, Ken, and Ellen Sievert. *Virginia City and Alder Gulch.* Helena: American & World Geographic Publishing, 1993.

Smith, Phyllis. *Bozeman and the Gallatin Valley, A History.* Helena: TwoDot Press, 1996.

Spence, Clark C. *Territorial Politics and Government in Montana 1864-89.* Urbana: University of Illinois Press, 1975.

_____. *Montana A History.* New York: W. W. Norton & Company, Inc., 1978.

Stout, Tom. *Montana, Its Story & Biography.* New York: American Historical Society, 1921.

Stuart, Granville. *Forty Years on the Frontier, Vol. 1.* Edited by Paul C. Phillips. Cleveland: Arthur H. Clark Company, 1925.

Thane, Jr., James L. "Thomas Francis Meagher: The Acting One." Missoula, 1967.

_____. *A Governor's Wife on the Mining Frontier.* Salt Lake City: Tanner Trust Fund, University of Utah Library, 1976.

Toole, K. Ross. *Montana, An Uncommon Land.* Norman: University of Oklahoma Press, 1959.

Towle, Virginia Rowe. *Vigilante Woman.* New York: A.S. Barnes & Co., Inc., 1966.

Tuttle, Daniel S. *Reminiscences of a Missionary Bishop.* Helena: The Helena Letter Shop, 1977.

Utley, Robert M. *The Indian Frontier of the American West 1846-1890.* Albuquerque: University of New Mexico Press, 1984.

Von Stieglitz, K.R. *A Short History of Ross, With Some Tales of the Pioneers.* Tasmania: Telegraph Printery, 1949.

Watson, Reginald A. *The Life and Times of Thomas Francis Meagher.* Tasmania: Anglo-Keltic Society, 1989.

Wert, Jeffry D. *General James Longstreet.* New York: Simon & Schuster, 1993.

Wolle, Muriel S. *Montana Pay Dirt.* Athens: Ohio University Press, 1963.

Wright, Steven J. *The Irish Brigade.* Springfield: Steven Wright Publishing, 1992.

Newspapers and Periodicals

An Phoblacht/Republican News
Anaconda Standard
Boston Pilot
Bozeman Chronicle
Butte Daily Post
Clongowes Wood News
Dillon Examiner
Irish American
Irish Monthly
Irish News
Irish Tribune
Kilkenney Journal
Livingston Post
London Morning Chronicle
London Times

Montana Daily Record
Montana Post
Montana Radiator
New Haven Leader
New York Daily Tribune
New York Herald New York Weekly Tribune
St. Paul Pioneer
St. Paul Press Salt Lake City Daily Telegraph
The Butte Miner
The Daily Orleanian
The Irish Times
The Mercury
The New York Sun
The Spectator
The United States Democratic Review
The New York World
Tombstone Epitaph

Allen, Frederick. "Montana's Vigilantes and the Origins of 3-7-77," Montana The Magazine of Western History, 51 (Spring 2001).

Ashley, Charles. "Governor Ashley's Biography & Messages," Contributions to the Montana Historical Society, 6 (1907).

Athearn, Robert. "Early Territorial Montana: A Problem in Colonial Administration," The Montana Magazine of History, 1 (July 1951).

Athearn, Robert. "General Sherman and the Montana Frontier," The Montana Magazine of History 3 (January 1953).

Athearn, Robert, "The Civil War and Montana Gold," Montana Magazine of Western History 12 (April 1962).

Burlingame, Merrill G., "Montana's Righteous Hangmen: A Reconsideration," Montana the Magazine of Western History, 28 (October, 1978).

Bradley Manuscript, Book II. "Account of the Drowning of Thomas Francis Meagher," Contributions to the Montana Historical Society, 8 (1917).

Callaghan, James. "Red on Green," Civil War Times Illustrated, 6 (December, 1998).

Callaway, James E. "Governor Green Clay Smith, 1866-1868," Contributions to the Montana Historical Society, 5 (1904).

Davidson, Rev. A.C. "Green Clay Smith, the Preacher," Contributions to the Montana Historical Society, 5 (1904).

Davison, Stanley R. and Dale Tash, "Confederate Backwash in Montana Territory," Montana Magazine of Western History, 17 (October, 1967).

Edwards, Rev. George. "Presbyterian Church History," Contributions to the Montana Historical Society, 6 (1907).

Fletcher, Bob. "Montana Medley: Virginia City," Montana Magazine of Western History, 3 (Summer, 1953).

Glynn, Gary. "Meagher of the Sword," America's Civil War Magazine (September 1995).

Hunt, Lewis W. "The 1913 Murder Confession Hoax," Montana Magazine of Western History, 12 (January, 1962).

Jackson, W. Turrentine. "Montana Politics During the Meagher Regime, 1865-1867," The Pacific Historical Review, 12 (June, 1943).

_____. "The Fisk Expeditions to the Montana Gold Fields," The Pacific Northwest Quarterly, 32 (July, 1942)

_____. "The Appointment and Removal of Sidney Edgerton, First Governor of Montana Territory," Pacific Northwest Quarterly 34 (January, 1943).

Johnson, Dorothy M. "Slow Boat To Benton," Montana Magazine of Western History, 11 (January, 1961).

Leslie, Preston H. "Biographical Sketch of Green Clay Smith," Contributions to the Montana Historical Society, 5 (1904).

Maginnis, Major Martin. "Thomas Francis Meagher," Contributions to the Montana Historical Society, 6 (1907).

McClure, Col. A.C. "Wilbur Fisk Sanders," Contributions to the Montana Historical Society, 8 (1917).

McCormack Jr., John F. "Never Were Men So Brave," Civil War Times (December 1998).

McCraig, Donald. "The Bozeman Trail," Smithsonian Magazine (October 2000).

Meagher, Thomas Francis. "A Journey to Benton," Montana Magazine of Western History 1 (October, 1951).

————. "A New Route Through Chiriqui," Harper's New Monthly Magazine (January 1861).

————. "Holidays in Costa Rica," Harper's New Monthly Magazine (December 1859, January 1860, February 1860).

————. "Rides Through Montana," Harper's New Monthly Magazine (October 1867).

Munson, Major Edward L. "Lyman Ezra Munson," Contributions to the Montana Historical Society, 7 (1910).

Munson, Lyman E. "Pioneer Life in Montana," Contributions to the Montana Historical Society, 5 (1904).

Oberley, Edith Toole, "The Baron C. C. O'Keeffe: The Legend and the Legacy," Montana Magazine of Western History, Vol. 23, #3 (Summer 1973).

Paladin, Vivian, "Henry N. Blake: Proper Bostonian, Purposeful Pioneer," Montana Magazine of Western History 14.

Pemberton, W. Y. "Changing the Name of Edgerton County," Contributions to the Montana Historical Society, 8 (1917).

Pepper, George W. "Personal Recollections of General Thomas Francis Meagher," Donahoe's Magazine (May 1899).

Plassman, Martha E. "A Biographical Sketch of the Hon. Sidney Edgerton," Contributions to the Montana Historical Society, 8 (1917).

Smith, Green Clay. "Second Message of Governor Green Clay Smith," Contributions to the Montana Historical Society, 5 (1904).

Stuart, Mrs. Granville. "When Virginia City Was The Capital Of Montana Territory," The Montana Magazine of History, 3 (January 1953).

"Steamboat Arrivals at Fort Benton, Montana and Vicinity," Contributions to the Montana Historical Society, 1 (1876).

Thane Jr., James L. "The Myth of Confederate Sentiment in Montana," Montana Magazine of Western History 17 (April 1967).

Walter, Dave. "Weaving the Current, Montana's Watershed Events of Two Centuries, Part I: 1800-1883," Montana Magazine 159 (January/February 2000).

Walton, Julian C. "Thomas Francis Meagher," a lecture on the presentation of Meagherabilia to the Treasures of Waterford Museum, December 7, 2001.

Welles, Gideon. "Lincoln & Johnson, Their Plan of Reconstruction and the Resumption of National Authority," The Galaxy, 13 (April 1872).

"The Wonderful Petrified Man," Montana Magazine of Western History, 12 (January 1962).

West, Elliott. "Thomas Francis Meagher's Bar Bill," Montana Magazine of Western History, 35 (Winter 1985).

Libraries and Special Collections:

Alexander Leggat Collection (Montana State University, Bozeman, Montana)

W. S. Boyer Papers. (Montana Historical Society, Helena)

Bozeman Public Library (Bozeman, Montana)

James H. Bradley Papers, 1872-1895. (Montana Historical Society, Helena)

Merrill G. Burlingame Collection, 1880-1990 (Montana State University; Bozeman, Montana)

Butte-Silver Bow Public Archives (Butte, Montana)

Butte-Silver Bow Public Library (Butte, Montana)

William Andrews Clark Memorial Library (University of California-Los Angeles)

Dillon Public Library (Dillon, Montana)

Gallatin County Historical Society and Museum (Bozeman, Montana)

Great Falls Public Library (Great Falls, Montana)

Grenville Dodge Papers, Iowa State Department of Archives

Havre Public Library (Havre, Montana)

Samual Hauser Papers (Montana Historical Society; Helena, Montana)

Hezekiah Hosmer Papers (Yale University; New Haven, Conneticut)

Idaho State Historical Society Library and Archives (Boise, Idaho)

Madison County Public Library (Ennis, Montana)

GARY R. FORNEY

Martinsburg Public Library (Martinsburg, West Virginia)

McFarland Curatorial Center (Virginia City, Montana)

George Tyler Moore Center for the Study of the Civil War (Shepherdstown, West Virginia)

Montana Heritage Commission (Virginia City, Montana)

Montana Historical Society Library (Helena, Montana)

Diary of J. H. Morley, 1862-1865 (Montana Historical Society; Helena, Montana)

Northern Montana College (Havre, Montana)

Letters and Journals of John Owen (Montana Historical Society; Helena, Montana)

Wilber Fisk Sanders Papers (Montana Historical Society; Helena, Montana)

Ruth Scarborough Library (Shepherd College, Shepherdstown, West Virginia)

Seattle Public Library (Seattle, Washington)

Thomas-Hickman County Library (Virginia City, Montana)

Thomas Francis Meagher Papers (Montana Historical Society; Helena, Montana)

Thomas Francis Meagher Letters, 1847-1857. (National Library; Dublin, Ireland)

K. Ross Toole Archives, Mansfield Library (University of Montana; Missoula, Montana)

Twin Bridges Library (Twin Bridges, Montana)

Western Montana College Library (Dillon, Montana)

Wilson W. Clark Memorial Library (University of Portland, Oregon)

Catherine C. Young Collection (Montana Historical Society; Helena, Montana)

Additional Resources

Andrew Johnson Papers. Library of Congress.

Archives Office of Tasmania (Convict Profile of Thomas Francis Meagher).

Attorney-General of Montana Records (Montana Society Archives, Helena).

Bulletin of the Department of External Affairs (Dublin, Ireland), No. 761:20, 6-1967.

Council Journal of the First Legislative Assembly of the Territory of Montana (December 12, 1864-February 9, 1865).

House Journal of the First Session of the Legislative Assembly of the Territory of Montana (December 12, 1864-February 9, 1865).

Council Journal of the Second Session of the Legislative Assembly of the Territory of Montana (March 5-April 14,1866).

House Journal, Second Session, Montana Legislature (March 5-April 13, 1866).

Council Journal of the Third Session of the Montana Territory of the Legislative Assembly (November 5, 1866-December 15, 1866).

House Journal of the Third Session of the Legislative Assembly of the Territory of Montana (November 5-December 15, 1866).

Department of State, Territorial Papers of Montana, Vol. 1. National Archives.

Department of War, Adjutant-General's Office. National Archives.

Department of War, Official Records of the Department of the Missouri Special File: Letters recieved 1866-1869. National Archives.

Department of War, Office of the Secretary of War. National Archives.

Montana Inventory of County Archives-Madison County (May 1940).

United States Army. "Winning the West: The Army in the Indian Wars, 1865-1890." Army Historical Series, Office of the Chief of Military History.

United States Bureau of the Census; Ninth Census of the United States.

United States Statutes, 39th Congress Second Session, Section 6, Chapter 150.

War of the Rebellion, Official Reports of the Union and Confederate Armies; Series 1, vols. 2, 11, 19, 21, 25; Series 3, vols. 1, 3, 5; series 9, vol. 3. Harrisburg: The National Historical Society, 1971.

Internet Sites

aihs.org
cdl.library.cornell.edu
civilwarhome.com
clarelibrary.ie
dioltas/raid.oath
fotw.digibel.be/flags/ie
gi.grolier.com
his.state.mt.us
info@laceyandlacey.com
ireland.com
ireland.org
local.ie
odur.let.rug.nl
senate.gov/learning/stat
sinnfein.ie
smithsonianmag.si.edu
thewildgeese.com
ucc.ie/celt/online
virginiacity.com

Associations

The Irish Brigade Association; Throggs Neck, NY
TAK Society; Lindisfarne, Tasmania
Veterans Corps, 69th Regiment; Jackson Heights, NY

INDEX

Jackson, Thomas ("Stonewall"), 102, 104, 124-25
Johnson, Andrew, 130, 135, 140, 166, 172, 174, 187, 189, 191-92, 200
Johnson, "Liver Eating," 224
Johnston, Joseph, 103
Junction City (MT), 153

Kansas Grand Lodge (Masonic Order), 153
Kavanaugh, John, 110
"Katie Darling," 100
Kelly, James, 106
Kenyon, Fr. John, 40
Key, Francis Scott, 83
Key, Phillip Barton, 83
Keyes, Erasmus, 101
Kildare (Ireland), 18
Kilkenny (Ireland), 42
King, Preston, 98
Know Nothing Party, 76, 92, 95
Knowles, Judge, 236
Kuppens, Fr. Francis, 177

Lake Sorell (Van Dieman's Land), 56, 58
Lalor, James F., 34, 76, 82
Langford, Nathaniel Pitt, 155, 158, 174-75, 219
Lawrence, Robert, 161
Leaman, John, 223-24
Lee, John D., 223
Lee, Robert E., 102-04, 110, 114, 123
Leggat, Alexander, 176
Leonard, John Patrick, 37
Lewis, William H., 204
Leviathon Hall, 164
Leyne, M. R., 47

Lincoln, Abraham, 87, 95, 98-99, 105, 120, 128-30, 134, 149, 158, 180, 192
Livingston Post, 224
Longstreet, James, 110
London Times, 91, 118
Lott, John S., 153
Lyons, W. F., 49, 58, 84, 212-13

MacCormack, "The Widow," 45, 233
Maginiss, Martin, 237, 239
Maguire, H. N., 186
Malvern Hill, 103
Manila (Philippines), 230-31
Martin, John, 157
Marye's Heights, 115-16, 118
Masonic Order, 153-54, 164
Mathews, S. B., 183
Mayhew, A. E., 181
Meagher, Catherine, 58, 66-67, 69-70, 72-73, 75, 81
Meagher Club-Boston, 63
Meagher Club-New York, 63
Meagher County (MT), 184, 239
Meagher, Elizabeth, 76, 92, 96, 140, 165, 177, 213, 218-19, 229-30
Meagher, Guard (Philadelphia), 63
Meagher, Harry, 18
Meagher, Helen, 231
Meagher, Henry, 18
Meagher, Henry Fitzgerald, 67
Meagher, James Timothy, 231
Meagher, Karron Marie, 231
Meagher Memorial Association, 246
Meagher, Patrick, 18-19
Meagher Rifles, 63
Meagher's Quay, 18
Meagher, Thomas Francis, 17-18, 218

Printed in the United Kingdom
by Lightning Source UK Ltd.
110698UKS00001B/56